THEATER
IN THE
AMERICAS

A Series from
Southern
Illinois
University
Press
SCOTT
MAGELSSEN
Series Editor

AMERICAN SCENIC DESIGN AND FREELANCE PROFESSIONALISM

David Bisaha

Southern Illinois University Press
Carbondale

Southern Illinois University Press
www.siupress.com

25 24 23 22   4 3 2 1

Cover illustration: R. Bergman Studio, Thirty-Ninth Street. *Photo
courtesy of Eugene C. Fitsch.*

Library of Congress Cataloging-in-Publication Data
Names: Bisaha, David, 1985- author.
Title: American scenic design and freelance professionalism /
    David Bisaha.
Description: Carbondale : Southern Illinois University Press,
    [2022] | Includes bibliographical references and index. |
    Identifiers: LCCN 2022003907 (print) |
    LCCN 2022003908 (ebook) | ISBN 9780809338740 (paperback)
    |ISBN 9780809338757 (ebook)
Subjects: LCSH: Theaters—Stage-setting and scenery—
    United States—History. | Set designers—Professional
    relationships—United States. | Discrimination in employment—
    United States. | Self-employed—United States—History.
Classification: LCC PN2091.S8 B475 2022 (print) |
    LCC PN2091.S8 (ebook)

Printed on recycled paper ♻

SĨU
Southern Illinois University System

CONTENTS

LIST OF FIGURES

PREFACE

I began working on this book as an explanation of scenic designers' creative processes. I noted broad similarities in the way designers conceptualized their work ("the design process") and observed that they passed that model down through formal and informal mentorship. As my research progressed, I became interested in the ways in which designing was institutionalized, less as an individual creative process and more as a shared occupational identity. The terms *professional* and *professionalism* repeatedly emerged in my research, and professionalization became the concept around which this book is organized. But, as I researched the history of designers' development, I noted who was excluded from professionalism and why. Black artists were categorically excluded from professional status for most of the twentieth century. White women, white queer persons, and non-Black people of color were given the benefits of professionalism on a conditional basis. They were limited to certain fields or certain levels of professional work, or they were required to hide aspects of themselves to gain access to employment.

Scholars of US theatre history have pointed to examples of racist ideology portrayed onstage and have rightly critiqued them. When discussing canonical artists, stories, and conventions, theatre and performance scholars must acknowledge that they are upholding Eurocentrism and that doing so contributes to the continued dominance of white voices in the American theatre. At the same time, it is important to acknowledge the ways in which the economic and educational systems of American theatre have enacted racist and sexist policy, and still do. In many cases, discrimination hides behind rhetoric of quality, technique, relatability, or standards. These, too, are beginning to receive scholarly attention but not nearly as much.

American Scenic Design and Freelance Professionalism chronicles the emergence of a new cadre of scenic design professionals and also explains its exclusionary and discriminatory effects. This book emphasizes the effects of racism, sexism, and homophobia by giving excluded designers necessary attention in their own sections. In many cases, due to discrimination, the archive is much smaller for excluded designers. Their lives took differing paths, which this book conceptualizes as counterpoints to the predominantly white, male, and elite story of scenic design professionalization. This counterpoint approach acknowledges that Aline Bernstein, Emeline Roche, Perry Watkins, and James Reynolds did not create the system within which they worked. They did not have the power to decide the terms of professionalization when it was being organized by their straight white male colleagues. Their actions were in response to a system that was not built for them, one that was hostile to their work and aspects of their humanity. This book details how such systems of status and exclusion were built, yet it also attends to counterpointing examples to show that exclusionary systems can be broken into, broken down, and broken apart.

In order to change, American theatre must acknowledge that the banner of professionalization has been raised to protect the well-off and to justify exclusion. Examples throughout this book show that the creation of a new labor category benefits those who establish it, but it also empowers them to set the terms of professional membership. Studying the problems of exclusion means looking closely at what professionals gain by claiming the term and what educational institutions gain by teaching students "professional" standards. It requires questioning the givens of the field of scenic design to make it more equitable. Its terms of entry—union dues, apprenticeships, expensive education, a commitment to self-promotion and service—are exclusionary, and some must be completely reformed.

I hope that this history of scenic design's development in twentieth-century America will empower readers to imagine new expressions of and pathways to professional work in theatrical design.

ACKNOWLEDGMENTS

American Scenic Design and Freelance Professionalism was supported by Harpur College, Binghamton University, SUNY. The college provided funding for research, in the form of the Dean's Research Semester, and for publication, through the Harpur College Subvention Award. This project was further supported by a fellowship with the Institute for Advanced Study in the Humanities, by the support of the Department of Theatre at Binghamton University, and by the Brooks McNamara Publishing Subvention from the American Society for Theatre Research.

I would like to thank Kristine Priddy, of Southern Illinois University Press, and Scott Magelssen, series editor, for their thoughtful and enthusiastic responses to this book and for their work in shepherding it through production. Many thanks to Robert Brown for copyediting the final manuscript, the indexer, and the Southern Illinois University Press team. Thank you as well to the anonymous reader for generous criticism that helped me embrace the project's full potential.

To my teachers, mentors, and senior colleagues, thank you for your challenges, patience, and guidance. This book exists because of the teaching and professional service you gave in abundance. I'm extremely grateful to Bruce McConachie, Lisa Jackson-Schebetta, Michelle Granshaw, Laurie Wolf, and Michael Mehler, all of whom helped me think through this project as it transformed in its early phases. Thank you as well to those who engaged with this work at conferences and in earlier publications, especially Arnold Aronson, Heather Nathans, Amy Hughes, Jocelyn Buckner, Rhonda Blair, Christin Essin, Beth Osborne, Derek Miller, Kim Marra, and Jeanmarie Higgins.

Portions of chapter 1 appeared in Theatre Survey ("Defending the Standard Contract: Unmeasured Work, Class, and Design Professionalism in United Scenic Artists Local 829," Theatre Survey 61, no. 2 (May 2020): 231–51). Thank you to editors Nic Ridout and Marlis Schweitzer for your guidance and your encouragement of my project.

My colleagues in the Binghamton University Theatre Department embraced me and my research, despite my idiosyncrasies as a theatre design historian. Thank you especially to Barb Wolfe, Andrew Walkling, Laura Fine Hawkes, Marisa Wade, Sandy Vest, Kari Bayait, Helen Perrault, Theresa Price, and Pam Cahill. I'd like to extend my gratitude to colleagues Pam Smart, Dan Davis, and John Kuhn for their conversations, support, and advice. To my writing group, thank you for your ears and your creation of a shared, productive environment: Diana Gildea, Giovanna Montenegro, Kushariyaningsih Boediono, and Robyn Cope.

Thank you to colleagues who responded to drafts of this work in process, particularly Ariel Nereson, Meredith Conti, David Peterson, and Claire Syler. To those friends and fellow writers who helped me over the many bumps in the road, I'm so grateful: Christiana Molldrem Harkulich, Deirdre O'Rourke Peterson, Kristi Good, Inga Meier, Vivian Appler, Shelby Brewster, Dahlia Al-Habieli, and Bryan Vandevender.

The questions, enthusiasm, and responses of undergraduate and graduate students at Binghamton University helped shape this book. Special thanks to Emily Goodell, Chelsea French, Kasha Pazdar, Rachel Bass, Clarence Hause, and the members of my 2019 design theory seminar (Jenna Brady, Gabby Button, Brenda Darcy, Greg DeCola, Holden Gunster, Kassie Kelso, and Kaleigh Kuehl).

To librarians and research library staff, I'm deeply grateful for your labor, collaborative spirit, and thoughtful suggestions, especially as I sought access to fragile, unwieldy drawings and obscure corners of your collections. Thank you to the staff at the New York Public Library's Library for the Performing Arts, the Harry Ransom Center, the Tamiment Library and Robert F. Wagner Labor Archives, and the Special Collections of Columbia, Yale, Harvard, Wesleyan, and New York Universities. For special assistance, thank you to Eric Colleary, Michael Gilmore, Nancy Friedland, Jenny B. Lee, John Calhoun, and Annemarie van Roessel.

I'm grateful to the administrative staff of United Scenic Artists Local 829, IATSE, for sharing your history and archives with me. In particular, thank you to Beverly Miller, Lawrence Robinson, Cecilia Friederichs, Carl Mulert, and Edward Pierce. Thank you as well to Anthony Fitsch for sharing beautiful backstage drawings and paintings by his father, Eugene C. Fitsch.

Finally, and most of all, thank you to my family for their love and unfailing belief that this work was important and possible. You know what writing and research are like, and you know how best to help when things are "in process." My deepest gratitude to Henry Ward, to my parents, John and Kate, and to Michael, Julia, and Elizabeth. Your love means everything to me.

AMERICAN
SCENIC DESIGN
AND FREELANCE
PROFESSIONALISM

INTRODUCTION: DESIGN LABOR AND FREELANCE PROFESSIONALISM

1 407 Broadway: A modernist column of brick and windows stands on the corner of Thirty-Ninth Street and Broadway, just south of the Times Square–Forty-Second Street subway entrance. This forty-three-story skyscraper now takes up half the block between Broadway and Seventh Avenue. It contains over a million square feet of office space, but before the skyscraper was constructed in 1950, this block hosted the most famous scenic shop of early twentieth-century New York City. There, Robert W. Bergman, scene painter and manager of Bergman Studio, operated his shop in what was then an aging structure. Berg's, as it was known to the painters and designers who frequented it, launched theatrical modernism in the United States.

Bergman's shop was the preferred location for scenic designers associated with the New Stagecraft movement. This movement introduced abstraction and modernist experimentation to the American theatre. Rather than faithfully construct a replica of the world on stage, New Stagecraft designers found inspiration in the European modernists: designers such as Edward Gordon Craig and Adolphe Appia, and director-producers Max Reinhardt and Sergei Diaghilev. New Stagecraft artists turned theatrical presentation into a visual celebration of imagination, expressionism, and complexity.[1] Bergman was the first paint shop manager to align himself with New Stagecraft. For much of the early history of modernist theatrical practice, from about 1918 until midcentury, Bergman's would have been a designer's first choice for challenging painting work. Over time it became an epicenter of scenic design, pulling painters, artists, managers, supervisors, and assistants through its shabby doorway.

As Norman Bel Geddes, scenic and industrial designer, remembered it: "The street entrance let on into total darkness. The stranger, proceeding straight ahead, ran smack into a blank wall. Then he usually stood still and shouted. . . . Pop Hindle, who handles incoming and outgoing scenery, usually heard the forlorn wails of the lost and came to the rescue. The stranger would be led to the right, up a narrow and dangerously steep staircase to the offices above."[2] The second floor, a small office run by

i.1. Photograph of Robert Bergman's Shop, Thirty-Ninth Street,
1933. *Box 52, folder 10, Donald Oenslager Papers and Designs, Billy Rose
Theatre Division, The New York Public Library for the Performing Arts.*

William Pennington, Bergman's business partner, gave way to the third-floor paint shop above it. The narrow paint-floor area, a room three stories in height, had brick walls and harsh overhead lighting. The shop bustled with painters, working by the walls and on the floor, detailing canvases stretched over frames and applying the famous "Bergman bath"—a wash of thinned paint and, occasionally, metallic powder—to scenic pieces laid out flat.[3] Bergman himself alternated between painting on the floor and directing his workers from scaffolding. Finally, nearly twenty feet above the painters, a ten-by-fifteen-foot drafting room concealed a cozy nest occupied by Robert Edmond Jones, who labored over his designs, drawing and sketching, as the paint flowed below. This was the geography of Bergman's studio, a world from which, according to Bel Geddes, "for two decades, the most beautiful scenery seen in New York was painted."[4]

Every now and then, designers, producers, and assistants would climb to Jones's perch to consult on a contract, or else they would make a social call when they were checking on their designs, hanging wet on the frames below. The offices of Bergman Studio—Pennington's underneath the paint floor and Jones's above—were gathering places for designers, who would otherwise have been isolated by their individual production work. Remembrances of Bergman's conjure a parade of designers coming through the door. Bel Geddes recalled that "Bergman's became to the designers and painters of New York what the Algonquin was to the writers, except that at Berg's no one was on exhibition, and no food was served."[5] In another memoir, designer and painter Claude Bragdon caricatured the "short-necked" Bel Geddes, the "lustrous dark eyes" of Lee Simonson, a "tightly buttoned" Jo Mielziner, a "tall, fresh-faced" Donald Oenslager, and added the now-forgotten designer James Reynolds to the mix. Bergman's was "their favourite hangout. . . . This was a place where scenery was painted, but it was also a Republic of the Arts, a club, a salon, a spot of colour in the general drabness."[6] John Ezell, a designer and teacher of the following generation, recalled the bath and the drinking together: "the water and color were sometimes ankle deep and the floor was impassable until the scenery had dried—or the whiskey ran out—whichever came first."[7]

Such fond memories of Bergman's studio capture a golden period of American scenic design, but it is one that was also marked by exclusionary practices. Unfettered by fame, economics, or union politics, the theatre artists at Bergman's shared old boys' club camaraderie. Collectively, they built the contours of American scenic design practice, as paint and

i.2. R. Bergman Studio, Thirty-Ninth Street, by Eugene
C. Fitsch, undated. *Image courtesy of Anthony Fitsch.*

whiskey swirled down the drains. In this building, designers could assert themselves as members of a new movement, discuss one another's work, and form necessary career networks. Bel Geddes recalled that "there were several efforts to form a Stage Designers Club, but none ever achieved the status of Bergman's."[8] Even union membership could not replace the collegiality of Bergman's studio, a "warm and reassuring" place where "grizzled, gray-haired men ladling out color or delicately fitting a joint betray a quiet and contained contentment with their occupation that seems far removed from the nervous, irritable, unstable world of casting offices, rehearsals and dressing rooms."[9] Yet those remembered were exclusively white and predominantly male.[10] Designers memorialized their work and social networks at Bergman's, yet they often failed to name the waged, highly skilled scenic artists working on the paint room's floor. In the memories of Bergman Studio, men populate the "warm and reassuring space." Designers are named while scene painters labor in anonymity. Women artists and assistants do not show up at all.

Bergman Studio serves as an architectural metaphor for the scenic design career hierarchy described in this book. Consider the main elements of the space: the street level is occupied by storage and management; the paint floor, small in area but busy, sits above the street, insulated from city noise. Within the paint room's expanse, the primary orientation is vertical. On the walls, drops hang on paint frames while laborers work with brushes and sponges on rods, extending their reach. Exposed scaffolding rises along one wall, from which painters rig framed canvases, and Bergman himself supervises the shop. Finally, near the ceiling of this large room, Robert Edmond Jones's office completes the picture. A small, covered area, Jones's room is nearest to the heavens, an appropriate position for a designer who, later in life, reminded artists that "each play is a living dream" and that designing "stage scenery is not the problem of an architect or a painter or a sculptor or even a musician, but a poet."[11] Dreams rose above, practicalities remained below, and Bergman stood in the middle.

Norris Houghton, stage manager turned design journalist, found that the Bergman studio captured an intense, creative quietude already slipping from the world when he wrote in 1946: "There, far into the night, while the mascot cat dozed and Bobby Jones pored over his drawing board in the upper room overlooking the paint floor, the red-headed Berg and his colleagues painted and experimented."[12] In this picture there is a literal separation between the designer and the tinkering, innovating Bergman and his staff. Jones was off in his own world, removed from the painting yet maintaining easy access to the action. He remained at a distance from the painting work that he might have executed alongside his colleagues just a decade or two earlier. What happened to cause this distance?

The separation of Jones's office from the paint floor reflects the ongoing separation of scenic design from scenic painting. From approximately 1915 to 1940, scenic designers established themselves as a new type of creative artist. Although they never totally left the craft basis of their occupation behind, designers such as Jones fashioned themselves as artists who drew, specified, and selected more than they painted. As they did so, designers attained more of the lofty status suggested by Jones's creative perch. Design was conducted prior to the painter's work and at a higher level, both in terms of its abstraction and metaphorically with respect to its class status. It was during this period that designers became household names and, in some cases, authorities on the theatre and arts in general. As the aesthetic component of a design became separated from the execution of it, designers became more individually responsible for its content, more valuable to producers, and more likely to claim professional class status. This heightened status was not available to scene painters, even those painters who did design work (although it was not called such) in "model rooms" attached to scenic studios.[13] Moreover, making such a claim to professional class status exacerbated racism and sexism within the field, preventing women and non-white designers from standing as peers. The designers who steered the field toward professionalism ensured that their design work was grounded in the model of the freelance artist. Such a model would endure beyond the careers of its pioneers. Notwithstanding minor changes derived from the development of telecommunications and digital design technology, their model of professional freelance artistry endures today.

This book argues that the emergence of scenic design professionalism is best understood by attending to labor done outside theatrical productions: extra-theatrical labor. The designs Jones and others contributed to the revolution of New Stagecraft are of course notable, but designs alone were not responsible for the scenic designer's new status. Rather, designers undertook consistent professionalization work outside the theatre—in unions, schools, the press, granting foundations, and federal initiatives. A revolution in aesthetic style kick-started New Stagecraft, but the revolution sustained itself through the changes these designers made in their professional lives. New regulations and institutions allowed freelance designing to persevere through difficult times, especially the Great

Depression, World War II, and the glut of design labor that would follow as university design programs began producing large numbers of graduates. By banding together in key moments and allying themselves with additional sources of power in others, designers took hold of their own profession over the span of a generation.

This book calls for theatre design studies to move beyond histories of notable productions. Such production- and designer-based approaches have been the norm in US design history. For instance, Orville K. Larson's 1989 *Scene Design in the American Theatre, 1915–1960*, which is still the definitive chronicle of the period, boldly states that "the history of scene design is the history of successful theatrical productions."[14] I disagree. The birth of the professional designer is not only the result of commercially successful productions but also the changes manifested by doing the craft, discussing it, and institutionalizing it. Other scholarship has extended the field by focusing on specific designers' contributions, in many cases addressing designers' onstage and extra-theatrical work equally. Ralph Pendleton's study of Robert Edmond Jones, Mary Henderson's extensive biography of Jo Mielziner, Arnold Aronson's recovery of the work of Joseph Urban, and Anne Fletcher's synthesis of Mordecai Gorelik's design, politics, and academic career each illustrate the ability of one well-positioned individual to contribute to structural change. Many of these contributions, too, were documented in the portfolio-memoirs that designers themselves penned near the end of their careers.[15] Yet professionalization was not any one individual's project but rather was the sum of many individuals' actions as they furthered their careers. A history of field-level trends must span decades and many designers' careers, and so this book's wide-angle approach considers a variety of case studies.

This work joins other cultural-history-based approaches to theatre design, including the work of Christin Essin, Marlis Schweitzer, Christopher Innes, and Timothy White. Each of these writers considers links between production and modernist trends in American culture writ large. This book's engagement with professional practice complements Essin's production-based material history of modern design, Schweitzer's discussion of fashion and commerce, Innes's connection of theatrical design to other modernist design cultures, and White's urban history of Broadway labor.[16] Their scholarship greatly inspired this study, which shares some key examples with them. To their conclusions this book adds emphasis on the economics and sociology of design labor. By turning toward the extra-theatrical, toward labor contracts, university curricula, and the popular press, this book draws attention to the way that seemingly unremarkable details can come to define an artistic field.

Lastly, this book is inspired by works that link politics, economics, and the culture industries. Such connections necessarily raise historiographic concerns. For one, changes in aesthetics are not always easily compared to changes in cultural power, politics, and group formation outside the arts. Perhaps for this reason, Michael Denning's notable work *The Cultural Front* approaches the politics of art during the years of the Popular Front in the United States (roughly the 1930s until the early 1940s) by identifying two vectors of change. Denning distinguishes "two notions of the politics of art: 'cultural politics,' the politics of allegiances and affiliations, and 'aesthetic ideologies,' the politics of form," with the latter referring to those politics that may be encoded in the structure or style of an artwork.[17] This book's arguments tend toward the first of Denning's distinctions, the "cultural politics" of design labor. The "aesthetic ideologies" of scenic modernism have been well explored in New Stagecraft studies; the "cultural politics" of those who built freelance professionalism have been less well charted.

This work plants the development of the profession in the foreground and questions of modernist style in the background. It attends to the "politics of the cultural field itself, the history of institutions and apparatuses in which artists and intellectuals work. For the kinds of political stances artists and intellectuals take depend on their understanding of the ground on which they work."[18] *American Scenic Design and Freelance Professionalism* is a history of designers' institutions and political stances. In the interwar period, designers effectively consolidated their field under a professional model, yet they did so by engaging in exclusionary practices. One hundred years later, we must attend to those cultural politics and examine the ways in which classism, sexism, racism, and exclusion were inherent in the development of the profession.

Defining Freelance Professionalism

Through their work within institutions, designers established a freelance labor model in scenic design. In a freelance labor model, the designer is self-employed as opposed to being a permanent full-time employee of a single producer or corporation. As a freelancer, the scenic designer functions as the head of a small business. The designer accepts multiple jobs, often overlapping in their duration, from an array of producers or institutions. The designer signs contracts, hires assistants and associates, manages a studio space (which may be in the designer's personal residence), and purchases design tools and materials. The historical transition from the designer as salaried worker to a freelance artist happened quickly, within decades, and it caught on because it framed design as a valuable service. Adopting a freelance model allowed designers to move away from weekly or daily wages and toward contract fee payments; this shift aligned designers with other influential creative workers, such as directors and writers. It also allowed them to claim that the design idea itself—detached from its execution—had inherent value. Through freelance artistry, designers gained independence from exploitative business practices and successfully argued that their designs were worthy of copyright protection.

Freelance artistry was not all liberation, however. Designers consolidated work among themselves, protecting their own interests while making it difficult for later generations to rise. Unions and schools rewarded new designers' meritorious accomplishments in many cases, yet the scenic design profession tended most often to promote the well trained, well connected, well resourced, and personally entrepreneurial. Put in other terms, the shift of scenic design labor from a type of specialized artistic wage labor to a creative freelance professional pursuit brought designers autonomy, authority, and heightened class status, though it came at the expense of younger designers and other theatrical wage laborers.

The linguistic history of the term *freelancer* also provides important nuance. The term was used in the thirties, but its current meaning of contracted work or a nonstandard job was then just emerging. A now rare but then more common usage denoted a politician with no fixed method, party, or viewpoint. The meaning of *freelance* then broadened to cover other types of workers with indeterminate, unpredictable methods, and this sense often was conveyed by a two-word variant, *free lance*.[19] So, at the time of early professionalization in scenic design, *free lance* connoted independence from one established employer or mode of working. It described film actors, writers, and others whose independence made their contributions notable. For instance, industrial designers claimed the freelance title to note the inherent flexibility of their trade and their independence from the companies that employed them.[20] In midcentury, scenic designers operated in what would today be recognizable as a freelance situation, yet the use of the specific phrase *freelance scene designer* only emerged in the New York City press around the seventies. For designers in the thirties and forties, it was more common to discuss "the profession," to confer about the techniques of scene design, or to describe their work within a context of peers who used similar techniques.[21] Therefore, my discussion of freelance professionalism imports a modern sense of the term to describe an emerging socioeconomic formation, beginning in the twenties. This shift is best explained by turning to the sociology of professionalism.

This book's argument centers the concept of professionalization and the related concepts of "the professions" and of professionalism by drawing from studies of work and labor in sociology and particularly from the notion of professions as defined by American academics.[22] In this literature, *profession* refers to one of many relatively high-status occupations that serve public needs (such as health care, legal representation, building design, religious ministry, education) and require specialized bodies of knowledge to carry out. Historically, the clergy, medicine, and law are the most iconic examples of professions. The first sociologists to study professions identified their common traits: foremost were "expertise, collective organization and collegial control, ethical standards, and work in a 'public service.'"[23] No standard definition of a profession exists, but the more that an occupation stakes claims to specialized knowledge, programs of postsecondary education, independent practice of expertise, and ethical standards, the more likely it is to be called a profession.[24] Today, architects, pharmacists, psychologists, accountants, engineers, librarians, nurses, social workers, and academics have all established themselves alongside doctors and lawyers and clerics as practitioners of professional occupations.

Professionals are members of one of these occupational groups, and the concept came to constitute a quasi-class identity in the twentieth century. Such an idea of class is often mobilized in claims to status, in concepts such as Richard Florida's "creative class" or Barbara and John Ehrenreich's "professional-managerial class."[25] From the late nineteenth century in the United States through the first half of the twentieth century, a managerial class emerged in capitalistic society, as the Ehrenreichs show, and the work of that class combined with concepts of creativity or Peter Drucker's "knowledge work," as Florida argues. These sociological changes occurred at the same time as scenic design's occupational reassessment. Scenic designers sensed the opportunity professionalization offered, and so they transformed their occupational identity to align with these larger trends, hoping to attain their own middle-class prosperity.

Curiously, the performing arts and sports have a meaning of *professional* that differs from what sociologists have ascribed to medicine and law. The term principally distinguishes paid workers from amateurs. In theatre the term *professional* has traditionally indicated paid work by actors; work done by actors who are usually paid, even if they are volunteering their labor; or commercial or high-status nonprofit work—as opposed to amateur or educational theatre. Performers and athletes commonly refer to membership in a union or employment by an arts/sports organization (theatre, sports team, orchestra, school) as the mark of professionalism. Using the term to distinguish those who "make a living" at something from those who dabble in it is not my usage here. In this book *professional* does not simply refer to a paid theatre worker but rather to a member of an occupational group that has consolidated itself as a closed community of peers.

Professionalization is the process by which occupational groups emerge as professions or, according to theorists Magali Sarfatti Larson and Andrew Abbott, make claims to a monopoly over certain types of work. Professionalization, in Larson's view, is a "project" through which occupations gain market control and establish institutions to maintain that control. In Abbott's view, professionalization is the process by which occupations defend claims to a jurisdiction against other groups that may want to take responsibility for the same tasks.[26] The existence of professionalization as a process was hypothesized as early as 1964 by Harold Wilensky, who observed that most professions went through a similar process of development with recognizable stages.[27] Later sociologists mostly acknowledge that no single process exists, and professions have taken different approaches toward the same goal: control over their work. Among the steps professionalization may take are winning state recognition of an occupation, forming professional associations, and establishing schooling, norms, and ethical codes. Scenic design took many of these steps in the twenties. An archetypal professionalization process is useful for examining extra-theatrical work by designers, but it is important to avoid the implication that designers intentionally followed this pattern. No formal model of professionalization existed in the interwar period in sociology or among theatre artists. Rather, professionalization emerged as designers attempted to better their careers. Most chose to associate themselves with occupational bodies that would afford labor and intellectual property protections. Professionalization, therefore, was more of a side effect than a stated goal for many designers.

Professionalism, then, refers to the set of cultural values that support a profession's place in society. Professionalism upholds an "occupational or normative value, as something worth preserving and promoting in work and by and for workers."[28] Standards of practice, ethical codes, even codes of dress all support the values of professionalism. To be seen as professionals, a group has to look the part in dress, behavior, and organization. Frequently this has meant borrowing from already established professional groups. Groups that could successfully make such claims were often rewarded with increased income, occupational autonomy, or social capital. Slippage among various definitions of *professionalism* and its casual application in theatre studies illustrate the continued strategic value that the language of professionalization has.[29] In theatre today, professionalism most often refers to standards of decorum for actors, designers, and others in the making of art. It is frequently a value noted as much by its absence as in its existence.[30] The aspirational usage of *professionalism* is an example of the power of professionalism discourse to construct self and class identity. This usage is particularly prevalent in education and theatre training programs.

In theatre studies, the concept of professionalism has been most explored in relation to actors' organization. Actors wanted the status and control over their own work that professionalization could have provided, but they were unable to achieve it. They could not, for instance, wrest control from producers, nor could they lay claim to an abstract knowledge base firmly enough to center it in universities or licensing systems. Speaking of actors' early views on professionalism, Benjamin McArthur notes that the "criteria of professionalism . . . contradicted the nature of their art"; actors' "successful appropriation of the designation 'professional' would not be matched by equal success in making their occupation conform to its meaning."[31] Some actors sought more militant action through unionization. Sean P. Holmes, centering the debate in the creation of the Actors' Equity Association (AEA), argues that "what ultimately emerges out of the early meetings of the AEA was an uneasy compromise between professional pretension and trade-union practice."[32] In light of this division between unionism and professionalism, colored by class politics, theatre workers began to redefine the term *professional* to mean something apart from its narrow reference to the professions. This conflict is discussed in more detail in chapter 1, as unionism and professionalism were key ideas for scenic designers seeking to organize as well.

There is evidence that twentieth-century scenic designers actually saw themselves as professional in the sociological sense. Both the designers and their union brothers in scenic painting used the term *professional* to refer to the designer's work, both positively and negatively, and often with specific class implications. As early as 1922, professionalism was contrasted with trade labor in union documentation; in attempting to organize the motion picture industry, a report of the "trades and professions occupied in the Studios" was requested from the AEA. Soon thereafter, in 1926, working rules for designers in the union singled out "sketches and professional services" with set prices for each in a scenic designer's contract.[33] Among academics, too, the desire for professionalism was seen in the Yale Department of Drama (later School of Drama), which in its first year was billed as a machine for making professionals of the theatre, in the way that law schools conceived of their students.[34] Finally, artists who worked in scenic studios in the mid-twentieth century, and were later interviewed by J. Collom in 1975, occasionally referred to the designing part of the work as a "collar and tie job" or to the designer as "the big man today. The painter is secondary." Others referenced the "inner group of the industry" when referring to designers.[35]

This book turns to sociological explanations of professions because it is primarily interested in institutional and occupational changes. Its group-level analysis strategically constitutes participating designers—of which there were only a few—as a loose association and power bloc, led by and consisting of individuals who were also engaged in a common project. This approach does not claim that any one individual or group intended to make sweeping changes in the occupation but rather that each of them simply attempted to better their own status. Larson notes that professional projects are better understood "ex post facto" and do not represent the intentional action of one or more groups. Rather, they emerge as a collective result of many individuals' self-interested action, which only later can be read as an expression of emergent ideology.[36] Her method also places emphasis on professionalization as a process and has been critiqued by later theorists as overly prescriptive. Acknowledging such critiques, this book takes professionalization as a useful frame for studying extra-theatrical design work and applies it flexibly to account for the ways in which theatre labor markets differed from those of other occupations.[37]

Bringing professionalism discourse to bear on the history of scenic design supplements other theories that have been used to discuss class and culture in theatre studies. Sociologist Max Weber's concept of social closure, on which professionalism theory is largely based, provides an alternative to other theories of social control and class domination that have been applied to the arts. Social closure refers to the process by which social actors restrict access to their own groups, often through an external identity characteristic or qualifying credential. Designers directly intervened in their labor market by strategically wielding union membership and its legal mechanisms. Thus the language of professionalism, jurisdiction, and expertise is a useful adjunct to neo-Marxist and Marx-inspired theories of culture (those, for example, of Raymond Williams, Antonio Gramsci, and Pierre Bourdieu).[38] In the interwar period, designers recognized that their labor was abstract, difficult, and required specialization. As a result they made claims to exclusive jurisdiction and occupational control. They established closure and defended their claims effectively. The theory of social closure better identifies the main ways that designers acquired a foothold in the management of their own labor, whereas Marxist cultural theories explain the ways in which those claims endured.

The professionalization of scenic designers was atypical because they first gained control over their working conditions through association with organized labor. Following the successful organization of actors the decade prior, designers decided to affiliate with the painters of theatrical scenery who were members of United Scenic Artists Local 829, in 1924. This marked the first time that artistic theatre makers paid by contract fees per production (not weekly wages) unionized. Unlike the AEA or the International Alliance of Theatrical Stage Employees (IATSE), scenic designers were at once creative leads on productions, with managerial authority and program credits alongside directors and playwrights, as well as members of a labor organization.[39] Therefore, designers needed to negotiate between the ideal of professional organizations, which they derived from medieval craft guilds and architectural associations, and the proven political strategies of American organized labor. The emergence of new concepts of professionalism in archival documentation of this period suggests that designers claimed professional status as a means of distinguishing their work from other unionized wage work.

Finally, scenic design professionalization did not occur in a vacuum. Other design fields made similar collective moves in the interwar period, and scenic design professionalism falls in the middle, chronologically, of this wave of movements. Scenic design was unique, though; most other occupations sought organization in professional associations, not in unionization. This was especially true of graphic design and architecture, which organized earlier than scenic design, and industrial and interior design, which professionalized somewhat later. In these applied arts fields, the typical professional ideologies of jurisdictional control, individual autonomy, and collegial working relationships among peers led to the creation of firms that emulated non-art professions.[40] Like lawyers and doctors, applied artists such as advertisers, architects, and industrial designers described themselves as experts prepared to solve social problems of a particular type. They organized in peer networks to defend their claims to exclusive jurisdiction. The degree of their state-sanctioned autonomy varied widely, from the more regulated architecture field to the barely organized advertising and interior design fields, and yet all of these groups sought similar closure by insisting on professional association, not unionism. Nonetheless, in the twenties and thirties, no applied arts fields in the United States gained state-sanctioned closure like that seen in medicine and law.[41]

Scenic Design Labor before 1910

Before the emergence of New Stagecraft on US stages in the early 1910s,[42] American scenic design labor had a markedly different form. The scenic artist of the late nineteenth century was not a designer, either in name or in a modern sense of process. *Scene painter* or sometimes *scenic artist* was a more common term for the occupation; his role (and nearly all scenic painters were men) was to create appropriate, pictorially composed, and, at times, thematically linked backdrops for producers.[43] Scenery most commonly adopted a wing-and-drop style, with occasional furniture or built-up relief sections. More elaborate scenic machinery, such as that used in melodramatic spectacles, was left to specialists, while the overarching control of the onstage visual environment was most often given to a lead scenic artist.[44] The lead scenic artist was charged with the design and production of drops, wings, and individual scenic units (stairs, doors, façades, etc.) and the supervision of whatever size shop the company operated. He would make sketches for the major settings of a production, create a series of models to guide their construction, and supervise the painting of the full-scale versions. In most cases the lead artist would himself execute more difficult detail work or forced-perspective painting. Less affluent theatres, on the other hand, frequently reused scenic elements from stock, or else they ordered scenery from a mail-order scenery house. Most of the mail-order sets were schematic, with variations on a typical location—interior, exterior, and exotic locations were advertised in the houses' catalogs. A producer or technical associate who ordered readymade sets would have exercised choice in the matter, but the sets were not "designed" for a particular production in the current sense of the term.

i.3. Portrait, John Young & Bros., scenic artists, ca. 1915. *Byron Company (New York, NY). Museum of the City of New York, 93.1.3.445.*

Because nineteenth-century scenery was mostly concerned with the creation of pictorial illusion, the design of scenery was not seen as an art separate from its execution. Much as an easel painter "designed" and then painted a canvas with oils or watercolors, scene painting also entailed both design and execution.[45] From the proposal of the script through the plans to the final execution in the shop, scenic artists were expected to innovate through the production of elegant pictorial compositions, strikingly accurate renderings of foreign lands, and the creation of multiple points of interest within the painting.[46] This was typically presented in a series of sketches and then in a detailed color model; the model was the primary object of communication, and artisans referenced the model when building and painting the set.

When artists created notable scenic art, they were acclaimed for their technical ability. Articles detailing the "forgotten" or "neglected" work of the scene painter appeared periodically in trade and general-interest publications.[47] During this time scenic artists' knowledge of period styles of dress, architecture, and ornament featured heavily in journalists' descriptions of their expertise. Effective scenic artistry had less to do with creative invention informed by a theme than with the judicious application of correct period style.[48] Artistic contributions were rarely taken to be reflections of the quality of the play, production team, or organization—except, perhaps, the savvy producer. More importantly, few designs radically changed the overall function of the play or the movement of actors. Plays were not written with designed spectacle in mind, with the exception of purposely "spectacular" scenes in large revues and in melodramas. The key difference between turn-of-the-century stagecraft and the model inspired by New Stagecraft techniques was that New Stagecraft designers viewed the production process as an interpretive event, one in which the whole production sought to convey a consistent aesthetic point of view. This view mostly derived from the vision of the director (or the playwright), but it was also supported by those designs created specifically for a production.

Historical forces also modified the market for scenic artistry in the middle and late nineteenth century. Railroads, the centralization of labor in cities, and the dominance of touring performance circuits concentrated scenic artists either in permanent employment with the most successful producers or, alternatively, in the employ of independently operated scenic studios. Earlier in the nineteenth century, scenic artists had often been hired by individual repertory companies whose regular production seasons could support paying a full-time artist. Later, especially outside New York and other major theatrical centers, it became more economical to purchase scenery from afar than it was to build it on-site, and so a staff scenic designer was employable only at large urban theatres.[49] In response to these developments, several larger scenic studios took a factory approach to scenic design, filling orders by mail and telegraph and producing scenic catalogs for their most popular sets.

The economy of transporting standardized sets by rail lowered the barrier of geographic distance and thus concentrated employment for scenic painters.[50] Mail-order enterprises, while profitable, streamlined the design process into a simple procedure of variations on an original design. The resulting scenery became so schematic that one painter suggested it was possible for a scenery shop to receive an order in the morning and have a full drop, of thirty feet square, painted and freighted by nightfall. Author W. J. Lawrence lamented that "the days of glazing and second painting are gone for ever."[51] Employed by these scenery houses, head scenic painters did work in positions of creative authority; for patrons willing to pay for custom work, in-house designers would collaborate with a producer on production-specific designs. In some cases, sketches and models were sent through the mail for revisions.[52] However, this was more the exception than the rule, and mail-order houses did most of their business in generic designs that could be easily reproduced or minimally altered before shipping.

Profit-driven production increased tension among painters in the early twentieth century. E. J. Unitt, longtime scenic artist for the Lyceum Theater, remembered that, in the previous century, "the scene painter was a part of a working staff of the theatre and in daily intercourse with his principals. . . . The method of production is now entirely different. The scene painter is now part of a theatrical staff. He is an employee of a firm. He is required to produce as rapidly as possible the scenery of perhaps twenty plays."[53] In addition to reduced production time in the studio, time spent analyzing the playscript was similarly shortened. "In the rush of affairs now," wrote Homer C. Emens, a scenic artist "may see only one act or perhaps only a scenario."[54] As the time demands on scenic artists grew, scenic studio companies increased in power, and the creative contribution of the scenic artist seemed to be at a low point. At worst, the painter churned out sets to order. Much of the design work consisted of copying and rearranging research material. The time savings afforded by the industrialization of stage art encouraged artists to develop efficient workshops, standardized procedures, and a product orientation.

Around 1900 a growing trend toward efficiency and economy led individual designer-manager pairings to develop their own in-house methods. Such an approach could be a reliable box-office draw. But when designers did gain acclaim for their custom designs, at times even with named billing, it was often in association with powerful producer-managers. David Belasco and Ernest Gros were probably the most influential director-designer duo at the time, but other such pairings included Richard Mansfield and his designer Joseph Physioc, and Augustin Daly and Henry Hoyt.[55] In these pairings, the services of the scenic artist would be called upon once the script was complete and the director had determined the overall look and physical needs of the production. For these designers, successful design depended on the creation of elegant model boxes, which were then scaled up into detailed interior and exterior settings. As early as 1899, Joseph Physioc wrote that "the 'problem' play has done away with the old wing scenes and replaced them with box sets."[56] The three-walled box

i.4. Portrait, Ernest M. Gros, scenic artist, with models and scenery, 1908. *Byron Company (New York, NY). Museum of the City of New York, 93.1.1.8952.*

i.5. Portrait, Joseph Physioc and Co. Paint Shop,
scenic artists, ca. 1900. *Byron Company (New York,
NY). Museum of the City of New York, 93.1.1.9170.*

set necessitated the placement of actual furniture, architectural detail
rendered in three dimensions, and the creation of full rooms rather than
outdoor vistas and painted interiors. Photos of model boxes are some
of the most numerous extant artifacts of Gros's and Physioc's designs.[57]

Whether they were employed by manager-producers like Belasco or
Daly, or employed by scenic studios in New York City or elsewhere, scenic artists conceived of themselves as skilled artisans and craft workers.
Many of them were paid on a wage basis, and in New York, scenic artists first formed a union in 1897 and became an autonomous local of the
Brotherhood of Painters, Decorators, and Paperhangers (BPDPA) in 1918.[58]
Designing labor was part of the job of some members, but knowledge of
scenic design execution—the techniques of preparing, painting, and decorating a set of canvas or wood—was the main source of their occupational
identity. For them, the manual artistry of painting was inseparable from
the mental labor of planning or designing, and artists saw themselves in an
occupation organized as a traditional craft. When the labor of designing

began to separate from design execution during the emergence of the New Stagecraft, the division between the painters and the designers took on elements of the division between waged manual work and salaried knowledge work. Or, put another way, designers attempted to develop a professional identity within the context of an older nonprofessional occupation. The changes initiated by New Stagecraft theory and its designers, mostly occurring after World War I, redefined scenic art by reconfiguring its previously established paradigms of labor, skill, expertise, and authority.

Overview of the Book

This book links scenic designers' work outside productions, that is, their extra-theatrical work, with key changes in national culture and labor discourses, including unionism, higher education, expanding photographic and print media, and growing American global reach. Each chapter investigates one arena in which designers claimed professional status. Conducted in parallel with their work of conceiving sets and supervising construction, designers' extra-theatrical work involved union advocacy, media self-promotion, formal education, and consulting service work.

Chapter 1 argues that unionization was the first and most effective element of design professionalization. Designers' association with United Scenic Artists Local 829 in 1924 established social closure by requiring union membership for Broadway employment. Therefore, the union became the default occupational organization for American theatrical designers. Though their participation in the union was contentious, designers such as Lee Simonson, Jo Mielziner, and Howard Bay advocated for basic standards: namely, a universal design contract, common wage scale, and peer election system. This move consolidated designers' power in the union at a time when the design labor market was growing and work in scenic painting was decreasing. This chapter historicizes the standard contract of the interwar period, tracks its main criteria and developments, and explains the means by which designers transformed union policy to protect professional interests, such as by closing union rolls and instituting union examinations.

Chapter 2 observes that designers began to adopt new self-marketing strategies in the thirties, modeling their strategies on those in architecture and industrial design. The main subjects of this chapter are Norman Bel Geddes and Joseph Urban. Both constructed a media personality that appealed to the general public and to potential clients. Seeing their success, other scenic designers adopted a similar personality-driven approach to scenic design press in the thirties. Although few scenic designers operated offices as large as Urban's or Bel Geddes's, they found that authorizing media coverage of their daily working lives and publishing images of themselves helped to create a version of celebrity, which in turn gave them a platform to advocate for designers' professional goals. Media exposure added value to a designer's personal style and name recognition, making self-promotion an important element of their professional activities.

Professionalization was also made possible through specialized theatre education and testing, in the university and in the union. In both locations, designers specified a set of skills to be mastered and procedures to be followed. Chapter 3 argues that university curricula and union entrance examinations standardized design careers. Primary figures in this chapter are Donald Oenslager, who taught at Yale University beginning in 1925, and Woodman Thompson, who taught at the Carnegie Institute of Technology from 1915 to 1921 and who was also instrumental in designing the union exam. Oenslager's studio-based curriculum at Yale borrowed heavily from Beaux-Arts pedagogy already in practice at the university, while Carnegie Tech's teaching was strongly influenced by the pragmatic, vocational tradition of the technical institute. Finally, the chapter charts the spread of studio and practicum curricula out of Yale and Carnegie Tech to other programs of theatre study in the thirties and forties.

Chapter 4 explains ways in which freelance professionalism developed through consulting and service work. Designers took on leadership through the arts and cultivated portfolios of service that bolstered the new white-collar identity of the scenic designer. Often this involved parlaying their expertise into paid or unpaid consulting jobs. The drive to service peaked during World War II, particularly through the camouflage work of Jo Mielziner and Donald Oenslager and the wartime volunteer leadership of Peggy Clark and Emeline Roche. These women applied design to war needs by teaching classes and supervising the Stage Door Canteen. The chapter then examines the ways in which service functioned differently in the careers of women scenic designers, and it investigates the tactics women used to navigate sexism in their career field. For men, though, consulting continued after World War II through architectural projects, museum exhibition, and cultural ambassadorship sponsored by corporations and the federal government. Here, consulting served the shared good, but it also most benefited those designers who already had networks within which they could sell their services.

A brief conclusion considers the scenic design professionals of mid-century and earlier in relation to the careers of subsequent generations of designers. These younger artists were typically trained in schools, worked for designers as assistants and associates, and made their name in an established profession. They had to fit into the model of professional practice established by their older colleagues, yet they also challenged this model by working in a wider array of locations, styles, and technological contexts.

Design professionalism was the work of many practitioners within a single field. The chapters identify ways in which early moves established models for professional behavior that were then taken up by others. But not all designers of the early and mid-twentieth century followed the same path, nor did they all form similar alliances with institutional power. For many designers, especially those who faced racism and sexism in the industry, strategic responses to power were necessary. These designers took different paths to professional paid work; their approaches intersected less with the male-dominated union, the Ivy League university, or the connected social world of theatrical media. Many excluded designers built their own networks. They worked outside New York City, formed their own organizations and schools, and maintained close social ties in lieu of, or in addition to, the university-union-media axis. The most obvious story of professionalization is one of cultural elitism and occupational closure, but it is not the only story.

To acknowledge these responses to power, there are "counterpoint" narratives in each chapter that draw attention to professionalism's effect on marginalized designers. For instance, the exclusion of African American designer Perry Watkins from union membership (chapter 1) and the reluctance of Robert Edmond Jones to explain his own working process because of his intensely private life, perhaps driven by his sexual orientation (chapter 2), represent responses of othered designers to professionalization projects.[59] Other counterpoints can be found in the work of Woodman Thompson, who tutored scenic design privately rather than in a school (chapter 3); Frank Bevan, who turned away from the commercial theatre to teach design with Oenslager at Yale (chapter 3); and Emeline Roche, who was pushed away from male-dominated scenic design and toward costume design, technical direction, and volunteer service (chapter 4). Chapter 3 also conceptualizes scenic design instruction at the Carnegie Institute of Technology as a counterpoint to instruction at Yale. Some designers considered in the chapters found their careers delayed or diverted by barriers, but most were able to achieve steady work despite racial or

gender bias. These counterpoints are discussed separately from other narratives in order to attend to how professional paths differed for designers
with less privilege. Professionalism attempted to institute a typical path
to career success, but the fact is that a typical path was also a white male
path. Featuring less frequently discussed design careers as counterpoints,
then, allows this work of history to call out exclusion without, it is hoped,
reinscribing it.

In a larger sense, this book is a history of institutional change and
sustenance. It is important to pay attention to the ways in which the givens of our working lives arose out of conflict, as mixtures of hard-won
advances and bittersweet compromises. In the past century, professionalizing designers often supported protectionist strategies to defend their
labor gains. Unions, universities, and federal policies erected ideological
walls, since their main goals were to uphold standards of practice and
foster the welfare of their members, not necessarily to enable future progressive reform. The utopianism of modernism faded into jurisdictional
battles and lawsuits. This book argues, however, that these extra-theatrical
actions came to define the field more than influential designs, by prizing
one model of freelance labor above others. Therefore, each chapter investigates tensions between the high-minded ideals of scenic designers and
the ways in which they managed to gather their profession about them.

1. THE UNIONIZED ARTIST: ORGANIZING THE PROFESSION

Scenic designers found themselves at a crossroads in the early 1920s. Public recognition of scenic design had risen in New York City, mostly due to a wave of new modernist productions. Many of these productions featured abstract and expressionist-inspired settings; this development was generally referred to as the "new movement," later dubbed the New Stagecraft movement. Some designers were also becoming popular names. Producers got wind of this change and began asking for new, complex designs from New Stagecraft designers—but they were not willing to pay the designers more for their suddenly in-demand expertise. The designers began to look for professional relief. Sensing an opportunity, the scene painters' union, United Scenic Artists of America Local 829, attempted to bring designers and "stage architects" into their ranks. To do so, USA 829 would simply need to attract the largest names in the field; the rest would follow, they figured. The designers, though, were conflicted. Could they trust organized labor?

One sought-after artist was Joseph Urban, a Viennese architect and designer whose early acclaimed projects included a number of high-profile designs for the Boston Opera, Metropolitan Opera, and Ziegfeld Follies.[1] In a *New York Times* article published in August 1923, Urban explained his recently changed thinking: "This idea is a new one for me, as I have never had anything to do with unions before."[2] His acceptance of the union would depend on a reorganization of the union into "an artists' guild, with as high esthetic standards as the group of artists collaborating to form the Wiener Werkstetter." Only by establishing "an artists' guild such as existed in the Middle Ages, the only time when a real artcraft flourished and developed," could scenic art organize, he stated. "I would not have all the members of the guild on the same level. . . . At the bottom would be the craftsmen and at top would be the artists. . . . It seems to me that the real artists should be the leaders of such a guild."[3] Urban's demands for radical reorganization of the scenic painters' union would not be fully met, though union president August G. Volz did court Urban with assurances that "the designers may adopt their own rules and legislate for themselves without interference on the part of anybody." Urban's acceptance of the union's overture was heralded as the work of "a Moses who has led the scenic industry into a more beautiful land, and our members join with him in his desire to foster the art which we all love."[4]

This brief conversation reported in the *Times* is noteworthy because it contains the seeds of what would become a long-standing disagreement. As the most prominent and most public New Stagecraft artist to consider union affiliation, Urban led opinion among his peers. Yet, despite Volz's assurances, complete occupational control over scenic design would not materialize immediately. It would take nearly two decades before designers would assume a substantive presence among union leadership. Much of this struggle had to do with the same questions Urban raised: Should the union work as a traditional union or as a guild? Could a medieval model of craftsmen-dominated labor survive in twentieth-century America? Furthermore, the strongly hierarchical organization that Urban imagined—reminiscent of the architectural position of scenic designer Robert Edmond Jones's office above Robert Bergman's paint floor—fueled designers' desire for a commanding influence in the union. The painters disagreed; they saw designing as nothing more than another job, to be paid with wages and judged based on the production's financial success. Designers' alliance with the painters' union, then, was surprising and consequential. Few events accelerated design's move to a freelance professional orientation than the designers' allegiance to USA Local 829, finally formalized in early 1924.

After the designers joined the union, they began to conceptualize their new identity as a professional field, pulling away from union labor tactics in favor of more individualized ones. They wondered whether union organization would be appropriate for what was becoming a more artistic, elite, knowledge-based pursuit. Professionalism can be defined, as Elliott Krause writes, as the combination of "extensive skills with a body of theory, independence from and autonomy and control over the laymen-client, community position and sanction, an occupational group culture, and self-administered codes of ethics with respect to practice in the community."[5] Designers gained many of these characteristics through their association with USA 829, especially control, closure, and an "occupational group culture." But, by working within the union, were they truly professionals?

The organization of scenic designers tested the ability of a union to represent increasingly professional artists. To contemporary eyes, this may seem a natural alliance. Today, differences between professionalism and unionism are often understood in light of the decline in industrial and private-sector unionism and the relative rise in power of public-sector unions.[6] But theorists of professionalism view unionized and professionalized labor as mutually exclusive. For Magali Sarfatti Larson, this is grounded in the inherent individualism of professional organization, contrasted with unionized collectivity.[7] Professionalism depends on its ability "to secure the supports for *individual* dignity and *individual* careers. . . . [I]ndividual differentiation, even though it must be attained within a collectivity and by collective means, is therefore a major promise of the professional project."[8] Professionals' individualism is derived from both their working conditions—individualized practices engaged in client service—and their strategic political alliances that allow professionalism to flourish.

A defining characteristic of professionals is that they use social closure to protect their interests. Max Weber surveyed closure of many types in his posthumous 1921 work, *Economy and Society*, there defining the concept as a monopolistic arrangement that a group assembles around itself on some basis, which might include training, membership in an organization, family membership, ethnic or racial status, or gender.[9] Closure strategies interested late nineteenth-century thinkers of many theoretical and political orientations, including Karl Marx, whose class conflict theory assumes that individual agents will pursue closure based on shared material interests.[10] Actions taken by these groups may resemble those protections that were secured in the United States by unionization efforts: control over payment schedules, working hours, and arbitration.[11] And, although Weber acknowledges that closure may also occur with "freely contracted labor," his approach emphasizes closure by organized groups of workers. Frank Parkin, a sociologist and prominent critic of academic Marxism, adapted Weber's concept of closure by overlaying it with a theory of class relations. For Parkin, closure occurs in two modes, which he terms "exclusionary" and "usurpationary." Each mode is typically used by either the bourgeoisie or the proletariat.[12] Exclusionary closure is practiced by capitalist classes, and it constructs legal monopolies by limiting group membership based on credentials, education, or licensure.[13] Working classes, by contrast, engage in organized class behavior that is usurpationary, meaning that it acts from below and uses tactics such as seizure of resources or withholding of labor.[14] Parkin notes that closure strategies help define class, and social class position in part determines available strategies for closure. In the

matter of designers' craft unionism, a growing preference for exclusionary measures and mostly disdain for usurpationary closure suggest that
designers were appealing to higher class status.

The alliance between professionalism and unionism among entertainment designers is unique among design professions. Many American design professions rejected organized labor, and this is especially true for
design fields that developed after union power declined nationwide in
the mid-twentieth century.[15] Today many designers not in theatre find
that their needs are best met through professional organizations rather
than unions; these organizations can still provide ethical guidance and
accountability while permitting an individualistic approach. Casual reasons proffered for this situation range from practitioners' skepticism over
collective bargaining to the idea that designers, as white-collar knowledge
workers, are somehow above the need to unionize.[16] Material constraints
also discourage unionization; today's designers are often geographically
distributed solo workers and therefore are difficult to organize. Designers are not interchangeable units of a mass labor force hired by a single
employer; thus they are not as easily subject to coercive management.
In general, the professional organization has seemed a better fit for today's atomized knowledge and creative worker.[17] However, this has left
professional organizations without legal justification for enforcing wage
scales, punishing harmful hiring practices, and calling general strikes.
The major exception to this rule is designing in the entertainment industries, including film, television, and theatre. Entertainment designers'
early concentration in two geographic locations (New York City and Los
Angeles) and with two powerful sets of employers (Broadway producers
and Hollywood studios) made unionized professionalism more likely in
the twenties and thirties. Since then, the alliance has endured.

This chapter argues that scenic designers developed their control over
the profession, social closure in other words, by merging with the union
and working within its politics. Scenic designers enforced closure through
union membership, educational credentialing, and informal social relationships. Within the union, designers formed a group of powerful, like-
minded peers, who saw each other regularly in union meetings as well as
in Bergman's shop. This group of peers came to function as a surrogate
professional organization, and their frequent discussion and advocacy
within the union helped establish a working model of design labor. Later
pro-union developments such as the 1935 Wagner Act allowed designers
to sustain the union as a center of power. However, social closure also had

exclusionary effects. Overt racism prevented Black designers from joining USA 829 until the 1950s, with one notable exception. Women worked in the field but were not granted the full privileges of union membership, except on an ad hoc basis. Unionism was the strongest tool for raising the designers' standing and power within the field, but it also institutionalized discriminatory practices.

Initial Union Organization

Before designers joined the union in 1923, there were nonprofessional labor models for scenic design work. Commercial producers either maintained regular, salaried relationships with designers under the producers' more or less exclusive control, or else designers headed their own scenic studios. In the latter case, junior designers worked for these larger firms and were paid salaries by the firms' operators.[18] Both heads of the firms and junior designers worked with equal facility in design and painting work. These firms were large and efficient, and they had established relationships with directors and producers. They were also popular; contracts with firms accounted for a majority of scenic design credits on Broadway before 1920.[19] The practice continued well into the twenties.

However, a different model of design labor was taking hold in the art theatre movement. In partnerships such as Robert Edmond Jones's collaboration with Arthur Hopkins, individual designers were paid on contract to complete settings for productions built outside the commercial pipeline. At first this independence was justified by the experimental aims of art theatre companies and later by appealing to the art theatre as distinct from commercial, predominantly realist production. These designs proved challenging to realize. Jones and other designers encountered resistance from shop managers who did not understand why their designs required ornamental, non-illusionistic forms, unconventional painting techniques, or hung fabrics.[20] Therefore, these sets were either built on-site at the producing theatre or else were sent out to New Stagecraft–friendly shops, which were often staffed by European artists who were more accepting of modern approaches. One such atypical shop was Joseph Urban's studio, which he founded in Boston upon his immigration in 1913. With its cohort of German-trained artists, Urban's studio had the technical skill to execute intricate and unconventional designs by Urban and others, whereas other studios did not. Robert W. Bergman opened his studio in 1918 with funding from Jones and Norman Bel Geddes, both of whom had just received several large painting contracts and were in the market for a friendly studio operator. The Washington Square Players were also interested in Bergman's style, and nearly overnight Bergman Studio became a primary location for New Stagecraft designs.[21]

The independent contractor model of designing was not devoid of drawbacks, however. Without employment by a firm, designers took on the responsibility of paying their own assistants and support staff and also of purchasing drawing and modeling materials. Worse, competition among designers led to an accepted process of working "on spec," in which producers would entertain proposals from multiple designers.[22] Only the designer who received the contract was paid for working on a proposed design. This practice put considerable strain on designers' energy and resources, though it was not out of tune with the exploitative booking and management practices of the older theatrical monopolies such as the Theatrical Syndicate and the Shuberts.[23] Many independent designers gravitated toward supportive relationships with benevolent companies and producers who would hire them repeatedly. Recurrent hiring had some of the benefits of salaried designing, though on a contractual basis.[24]

Scene painters, on the other hand, had been effectively unionized from the end of World War I. Their first union, the United Scenic Artists Association (USAA), was established in 1897. Their numbers grew throughout the latter half of the 1910s. In 1918 the union acquiesced to a somewhat hostile reorganization, in which the American Federation of Labor (AFL) forced USAA, an independent union, to become an "autonomous local" within the Brotherhood of Painters, Decorators, and Paperhangers of America (BPDPA). The AFL assured the union that its jurisdiction would now be legally enforceable over all New York City scenic artists. Meeting minutes from July 1918 indicate that by the time of its reincorporation under the BPDPA as United Scenic Artists Local 829, the union already had an established practice of standardized wages, designations of job hierarchy (apprentice/journeyman), a regular forty-four-hour workweek, and the practice of naming unfair shops and banning union labor there until substandard conditions were rectified. For the majority of scene painters, the reorganization brought some benefits in the labor market of the 1910s, even if it meant sacrificing the union's independence. Organization under the BPDPA ensured them the continuation of steady wages, a reliable arbitration and grievance procedure, and a level of institutional clout necessary to combat anti-labor pressures.

After affiliation, USA 829 began to adopt more aggressive tactics. Samuel Gompers, president of the AFL, encouraged member unions to demand higher wages, to expand union recognition, and to engage in primary and secondary strike action (also called solidarity strikes) if their demands were not met.[25] These tactics, a style of hard-line union bargaining inspired by AFL wins in other industries, created the first cracks in a theatre labor market that had until then been run primarily by producers and managers, not unions.[26] Members of USA 829 were encouraged by the success of other theatrical workers' unions, most notably the recognition of the Actors' Equity Association (AEA) and the eight performances per week agreement approved after the AEA's strike of 1919. The AEA remained powerful and successfully implemented its minimum wage scale five years later. In general, union representation grew throughout the 1920s, and wages increased in several theatre fields, including acting (AEA), technical work (International Alliance of Theatrical Stage Employees, or IATSE), and scene painting and design (USA 829).[27]

Expansion within USA 829 put it on course to intersect with the newly independent designers. Before 1918 the union had already been moving toward a "closed shop" so that it could negotiate more forcefully with studio operators and producers. After 1918, closed-shop policies became the rule; these policies not only required that shops hire union labor, but they also barred union members from working in shops that employed non-union workers. This was their most powerful weapon. The closed-shop goal, when attained, could seriously slow production should union members strike. Though a general strike was never called, in the summer of 1918 USA 829 called several stoppages against individual shops. The union refused to allow its painters to work for what it saw as unacceptably low wages, and shop managers (operators) refused to budge. Five weeks later, the operators relented and accepted new wage scales and working hours.[28] Having begun to exercise its union power, USA 829 sought to expand its jurisdiction between 1918 and 1922.

Given the power of labor in the early twenties, USA 829 was irked that designers were still not unionized. Many did paint sets, but because they did not paint regularly or work for the paint studios, designers for stage and for New York–based film lacked union organization. USA 829's executive board suggested organizing the designers as early as 1921, in an attempt to bar scenic studios from hiring cheaper non-union men in the designing room. Designers were wary of handing their autonomy to a commercially oriented union. However, other unions were also trying to claim jurisdiction over theatrical designers.[29] A 1920 letter from the Allied Designers to USA 829 asking for support of its own collective action mentioned that Allied intended to seek jurisdiction over the creation of scale models, and in 1922 IATSE indicated that if USA 829 did not accept stage architects working in theatre and film into its union, IATSE would organize them. Fearing shops with two-union jurisdiction, USA 829 decided to bring in architects immediately after receiving IATSE's letter.[30] The organization of architects then prompted the need to organize the stage designers. In April 1923 USA 829 adopted a rule that prohibited union painters from using drawings made by non-union members.

The ban on painting from non-union drawings was conceived to rein in designers such as Jones, who had been working under a series of independent contracts. Without the ability to send work to scenic studios, designers were suddenly deprived of production facilities. The union openly acknowledged its intention to "force some of the independent designers who do not conduct studios to either join the union or leave the production field."[31] The bet was a good one, and it brought designers into the union in droves. In early 1923 there were fewer than ten union members who designed—that is, regularly made sketches and working drawings—who were not also studio operators. By the end of the year, most working designers were union members. The scene painters saw the accession of independent designers to the union as one more step toward the complete organization of the theatre workforce. Independent designers, on the other hand, were attracted to the union for the promise of finding better, standardized working conditions. Since the scenic painters already had an established union with a history of successful collective action, alliance with them was the designers' best and fastest option for combating on-spec work.

Some contextual idiosyncrasies worked in the union's favor and helped accelerate 829's strong negotiating position. Oddly, the union's membership included both rank-and-file artists who were employed in the shops, as well as members such as Mabel Buell and Robert Bergman who both ran shops and executed scenic work themselves.[32] This inclusion of workers and shop operators in the union had two effects on union politics. First, it placed the shop owners in a sort of bind, as they had to respect union demands while also competing with other shops whose owners were not union members and therefore could sometimes skirt union regulations.[33] Second, and more practical for the union, the immediate effects of new working rules could be discussed in the meetings with those who actually did some of the hiring. This meant that effects of proposed rule changes on employment were addressed within the union, rather than in formal negotiations. Given this situation, as well as the strong union presence in nearly every reputable scenic shop (though not always among shop owners), USA 829 had effective autonomy to set its own wage scales without negotiation with producers. The union's middle men, the shop operators, relieved much of the pressure between labor and management that led to direct confrontation, as had stalled progress in the negotiation between Actors' Equity and producers.[34] When the union went too far, it was induced to self-correct by its own membership. Such flexibility with working rules, wage scales, and strike action also allowed designing members to acquire a degree of power in the union.

Once in the union, designers wanted to assert their influence quickly. By September 1923, most New Stagecraft designers had joined. Some members delayed their applications because Joseph Urban had not yet applied—perhaps he was waiting to see how many of his conditions would be met—but most were members by the end of the year. A change in union leadership also occurred in late 1923, when Charles Lessing took over from Volz. Lessing was less sympathetic to the designer's needs than Volz had been, and he refused to be bound by Volz's promises to Urban.[35] (Urban joined, eventually, reluctantly.) Such politics within the union ground down hopes for the designers' autonomy, but nonetheless, designers began to advocate for Urban's vision by drafting proposed standard contracts and regulations.

The primary concern was to stop work done "on spec." To do this, designers brought a simple resolution to the union floor: that minimum fees be implemented for drawings and design concepts. Already designers and painters did not see eye to eye. To add to the problem, no New Stagecraft designers sat on the committee that would decide on the payment scale. The drafted proposal suggested minimums of $25 per pencil sketch, $75 per color sketch, and $100 per model. (For comparison, the weekly wage for a journeyman scenic painter at this time was $77 for a forty-four-hour week.)[36] These fees compensated the active time it took to create the sketch or the model, but they did not cover the creative time it might take to conceive, develop, and plan the design. The union approved a less precise agreement in January without a permanent wage scale, simply stating that creative visual work such as sketches or models must be paid and contracted in writing and that the union must be informed when contracts were signed.[37] While this decision did uphold the right of the designer to get paid for making design artifacts, effectively ending work on spec, it prioritized products over time spent.

Later in 1924 the union formed a designers' subcommittee to discuss revisions to the wage scale passed earlier that year. Lee Simonson, New Stagecraft designer and founding director of the Theatre Guild, headed the committee and reported back in September with a new wage scale. Rather than charge per sketch, designers were to be paid a lump sum for each act or set, with an additional fee for "art direction," which included supervision of set installation, set decoration, prop design, and sometimes

1.1. Portrait, Lee Simonson at work on a design. *Photo by Vandamm Studio©. Billy Rose Theatre Division, The New York Public Library for the Performing Arts.*

lighting design. The original proposal was for $500 for a one-act, $750 for a two-act, and $1,250 for a three-act play.[38] This marks the first time that design labor sought general payment schedules using a union standard minimum scale. Under Simonson's schedule, a one-act, one-set design would be paid at six and a half weeks of the union's journeyman rate. This was generous and would have resulted in significantly higher income for designers than for painters. Despite the high wages, the executive board responded favorably to Simonson's proposal and put consideration of the new standard contract before the full membership. Before the proposed minimum schedule was finally adopted in July 1925, negotiations in the union meeting had reduced payments to $250 per act.

Compared to the painters, designers still enjoyed few protections. A revised painters' standard contract was also adopted in 1925; it included payment schedules and also certain conditions designers wanted for themselves, such as payment of one-third of the total fee at contract signing, liability coverage, and mandatory union arbitration of disputes. Designers, by contrast, were left to draft their own agreements, so long as they were in keeping with the payment scale and they notified the union of each individual job. Division grew. Designers wanted larger sums than the minimums and sought compensation for their knowledge and skill as much as for their effort expended in designing. The painters' new contract was proof that change was possible. Meeting among themselves, at Bergman's or in a corner of the union hall, the designers began to formulate proposals that would reinforce the idea they had hoped to protect when they joined the union: scenic design constituted a separate job identity, and it needed more protection.

Freelance Standing Challenged

Tensions between the designers and the painters intensified in 1927, the same year in which the Broadway production boom of the twenties began to contract.[39] Given a limited quantity of available work, the union's painting members introduced a motion to suspend new membership applications. Though its ostensible purpose was "to give our members already in, an opportunity of making a livelihood," testimony by painters at the meeting suggests that the real concern was that some new designer members were not fully qualified as painters. In a meeting soon thereafter, Lee Simonson drew attention to the fact that a designers' committee had begun discussing new proposals. Both the entrance examination and wage scale discriminated against the contract-fee worker, he argued, and designers ought to be able to have their own entrance examination. Swaying the executive board, Simonson was named head of a committee to draft a new examination and contract.[40] Through groups such as Simonson's committee, designers came to have limited autonomy over their own professional rules; approval was subject to voting by the full union, but Simonson embodied a version of union leadership by and for designers. The work of this designers' committee, which was refashioned several times during the interwar years, addressed such labor issues, but it also drew the ire of other union factions.

The designers' committee developed the first full draft of the standard minimum contract in March 1927, along with a designers' membership application and exam.[41] Although the contract did not specify how design ought to be practiced, it formalized a linear model of process through its payment schedule. Designers were to be paid a third of their fee upon signing the contract, a third upon submission of designs, and a final third on opening night. This structure, modeled on a similar provision in the painters' contract, standardized the division of design into phases. After a passing vote on the 1927 contract, designers moved one large step nearer the status of creative professionals who were paid for their planning work as well as the work of drawing, specification, and supervision. Moreover, as a result of the three-part fee structure, designers were prompted to complete more of the design before building began and to view the work of design in the studio as somewhat separate from construction, at least temporally.

The change in rules also provided several other crucial benefits. Under Simonson's leadership, an examining committee would judge applicants' portfolios by new criteria: artistic ability, adherence to technical standards, scale drawing, and shop supervision experience. The new contract also required that out-of-town expenses be reimbursed at standard rates, that designers receive credit-line billing in promotional materials, and that certain intellectual property rules be followed (such as forbidding design alterations after opening and assigning ownership of all drawings to the designer). Designers would now be required to file copies of contracts and drawings with the union office the same day they were created or to arrange for a union representative to view the model in progress. Simonson and his committee acknowledged that federal copyright protection did not fully protect theatrical design ideas, as small changes to designs invalidated US copyright at the time. Therefore, the union established itself as the arbiter of "priority rights" in April 1927, when it accepted the designers' standard minimum contract with few changes.[42] *Billboard* praised this "first important move . . . to stabilize their craft against managerial dominance," citing the three-part fee schedule and intellectual property rights as particularly new and productive advances.[43] These rights allowed designers to negotiate with confidence, and the stabilization of the design profession is due in part to the ways that designers like Simonson advocated for their own freelance working conditions.[44]

Designers' excitement over ratification of the standard contract was soon tempered by the worsening production downturn in 1928 and 1929. In September 1929 one union member even suggested that out-of-work members seek work in designing store window displays, "since our theatrical season did not look so prosperous."[45] The stock market crash later that fall exacerbated matters. It did not immediately curtail theatrical production, but the downward trend continued despite a brief rebound in the spring of 1930.[46] Productions already in progress and relatively high wages insulated the union from the first effects of the crash, yet by the end of 1930, the painters were in the middle of a serious employment shortage. Out-of-work union members searched for explanations. Painter members blamed the designers for their dearth of work, though they also accused the Little Theatre movement and bad overtime policies of worsening the shortage. The designers were accused of shirking payment of 2 percent of their contract fees as union dues, of not designing sets with enough paint work to sustain demand, and in certain cases, of designing productions with no scenery at all.[47]

The union's first policy response to unemployment was to limit the workweek to thirty-two hours and to ban overtime pay. This measure attempted to mitigate the economic hardship by spreading out available work among more workers, but it also exacerbated the differences between wage and contract laborers. At issue was the interchangeability of working scenic painters. Under the no-overtime rule, paint studio operators were forced to hire extra workers when pressed to meet a deadline. In the eyes of the union, all paint labor was more or less equal, and studios should be able to use any worker to finish any other's work.[48] Designers negotiated an exemption from these workweek regulations, since one designer could not be adequately replaced by another, nor could their work be easily measured in hours. This infuriated the painting membership. Worse yet, the reduction to workweek hours was only moderately successful; studio-employed painters lost their overtime wages, while unemployed members got some

work but often not much. Employment was still shrinking. Union meetings in early 1931 often fractured into tense arguments in which painters
were accused of being anti-designer, while the hours-exempt designers
were scapegoated as selfish and greedy. As would occur years later in Actors' Equity, splinter groups within the organization formed in response
to Depression-era stresses, and these groups threatened the balance of
union activism and artistic labor regulation that had been established in
the more prosperous 1920s.[49]

Soon after the thirty-two-hour rule was passed, however, designers
gathered to discuss a response. Secret meetings of a "Stage Designers Club"
came to light in February 1931. Earlier that month, the Paramount studio
on Long Island had been punished by the union with large overtime fines
and the stoppage of design work because the studio had only designated
one thirty-two-hour-maximum-exempt "head man" and barred other "assistant" designers from working more than four days a week.[50] Designers
felt that while the Paramount designers were called "assistants," their work
was effectively designing, so they should also be exempt from the hours
restriction. *Variety* reported the creation of the Stage Designers Club to
protest the Paramount situation and, in the coverage, listed Robert Edmond Jones, Jo Mielziner, and Lee Simonson as attendees. When union
leadership learned of the group, it called all designing members named
before the executive board and accused them of forming a dual organization.[51] Simonson and Jones, chairman and president of the club, respectively, insisted that the club was social in nature and *Variety* had published
speculations. Ever politic, Simonson proposed a resolution in which he and
the Theatre Guild would negotiate with *Variety* to print a retraction. The
designers evaded penalty, yet the retraction was never printed.

This disagreement was only one of many conflicts between the design
subset of the union and the painting members. In January 1931 Norman
Bel Geddes was called before the executive board to explain his interview
in the *Ladies' Home Journal* in which he claimed that "talking pictures will
take the place of the theatre as we know it" and, worse, "manipulation of
lights will entirely eliminate scenery in the theatre."[52] The board found this
statement "detrimental to the craft": by promulgating the idea that light
could be the future of theatre design, Bel Geddes was practically calling
for the end of painted scenery. Bel Geddes claimed that his words were
taken out of context, but he also apologized and agreed to avoid repeating
the same ideas.[53] In 1932 the painters requested that scenic artists' names
be credited in the same manner and type size as the designer in programs

and publicity. Both Robert Bergman and Robert Edmond Jones opposed crediting scenic artists in this obligatory way, as they believed recognition should be merit-based; the measure passed nevertheless, despite designers' protests.[54] Later, union minutes repeatedly show Simonson and vice-president Wood McLean at odds over the two groups' interests.[55] As before, Simonson alleged that new regulations, such as a proposed 1933 repeal of designers' exemption from weekly hour limits, were based on a fundamental misunderstanding of the designer's work. McLean countered that designers were willfully devising sets with less painting work to be done and thereby harming the profession. Collapsing markets demanded radical action, McLean argued, and the union needed to look out for all of its membership, even if it meant cutting into the designers' profits.

McLean's assertion, that designers were designing sets with less painting, was partly true. New Stagecraft had moved fashions away from wing-and-drop scenery and toward more architectural and minimalist designs. For instance, Norman Bel Geddes and Donald Oenslager built abstract, Appia-inspired unit sets and relied more on lighting and costume than on scenery changes; Jo Mielziner and Mordecai Gorelik played with open architectural space and scenic metaphors, and designed fewer detailed realistic settings. In either case, there was much less painting to be done. The painters saw their work as providing a steady commodity (painted sets) to the theatre industry, but this was not at all the designer's perspective. Designers, as professionals, saw their work as serving aesthetics and the needs of producers, not the needs of a painters' labor union. Designers alone could determine the best way of creating a scenic solution for a new play—a classic stance of a knowledge-based professional. Labor simply saw producers trying to save money on painting and designers capitulating. Had scenic carpenters and painters been in the same union, or had designers been allied with producers and management instead of the union, the story might have ended differently. But, because the waged scenic painter and the salaried designer had cast their lots together in USA 829, the conflict between the factions surfaced on the union meeting floor.

What was now openly referred to as a "class distinction" within the union continued through 1932 and came to a head the next year in a report of the "Ways and Means Committee." This report proposed radical revisions to the designers' contract-fee system in the name of fairness. It called for eliminating designers' contract payments entirely and moving to a payment scale for design measured per square foot of designed scenery; the report proposed several per-square-foot rates based on a set's size and complexity.[56] The idea was to regularize the payment of designers with that of scene painters, who would also be paid per square foot of completed work. The resolution further mandated a thirty-hour workweek, union control over contracts through a registration system, and extraordinarily high fines for violating the new rules.[57] The Ways and Means Committee concluded that all members were essentially the same, and by adopting a per-square-foot scale, the union could distribute more work, "abolish unfair competition," and "ABOLISH CLASS DISTINCTIONS [caps in original], making working rules the same for every member however employed."[58] At this time, painters still held a membership majority, but on the question of the square footage proposal, both the designers and the operators were opposed. Together these two blocs almost balanced out the painters' vote, resulting in piecemeal adoption of the per-square-foot contract in the spring of 1933. Designers voiced displeasure with this new system of measurement in special union meetings, and a few refused to pay their 2 percent union membership fee on contracts in protest. Ultimately, the square footage measure was never fully implemented, in part because revisions to the wage scale that summer necessitated forming a new committee. Lee Simonson made sure he was on the new Ways and Means Committee for the revisions, and he talked the new committee down.[59]

In 1934 the union passed other measures designed to level the field with the designers. As a part of the midyear union elections, the union mandated the production of models, citing the need for more standardized documentation on the paint bridge. By requiring that designers produce models, and not merely renderings, the measure protected the work of the assistants and paint men who could be paid for model work. Some designers refused to make models, delaying production schedules to the extent that producers missed opening dates. Sensing a crisis, the newly reelected president of the union, Walter Percival (elected 1933), unilaterally suspended the model rule. This upset everyone, and each side blamed the other for greedy policy during an employment crisis. *Variety* attributed this infighting to the odd union status of the organization, still "the only organization in show business in which employers and employees are at membership parity," and laid blame on a new crop of designers, so-called "small sketch men" who were in the practice of making tiny sketches for the full fee.[60] But, given the going price of $250 for a sketch or model of each act or major set, it was not surprising that many designers, who had to pay for labor and materials out of their fees, preferred to sketch. Ultimately the model mandate was put to a referendum in September

OFFICIAL REFERENDUM BALLOT

AMENDMENTS TO DESIGNING CONTRACT AND
SCENIC ARTISTS' CONSTITUTION.

RESOLVED: That clauses A and B, Article 2, of the United Scenic Artists' official contract known as the designing contract which now reads;

"II. The Designer agrees to design the said production and to render the following services in connection therewith:

(a) To complete either a working model of the settings to scale and the necessary drawings for constructing carpenter, or to complete sketches or sketch models of the settings and necessary working drawings for constructing carpenter.

(b) To supply the contracting painter with color schemes or color sketches sufficient for the contracting painter."

be stricken out and a new clause shall be substituted reading as follows:

A. To furnish approved, completed, fully developed accurately scaled colored models of each setting for the contracting artist and the necessary drawings for the building contractor.

And be it further resolved:

That Sections 54 and 55 of the Constitution of the United Scenic Artists' Local 829 and Section 12 of the Working Rules of the United Scenic Artists' Local 829 entitled sketches, models and designing shall be changed in such a manner that the intent of this resolution shall be carried out and the motion picture condition shall remain unaltered.

And be it further resolved:

That all other parts of the Constitution, by-laws and working rules of the United Scenic Artists' Local 829 which may conflict with the above resolutions shall be revised to conform with the above resolution.

YES ☒ *on account of lawsuit by*

Passed ☐ *designers - President*

issued degree making this illegal

are new as plants remain NO ☐

RESOLVED: That Sections 14 and 15 of the Working Rules of the United Scenic Artists' Local 829 which reads;

14. Prices for Sketches and Professional Services—Any ordered and accepted idea thoroughly worked out for practical use for production, minimum $250 per act. Any ordered and thoroughly worked out not accepted idea for a production, minimum $100.

Any ordered and thoroughly worked and delivered, accepted or not accepted idea for a musical revue, minimum $100.

Personal services calling for supervision of execution of painting, selecting of props and furniture, and arranging of lighting, etc., not less than $250 per production.

Any ordered and accepted, or not accepted idea for vaudeville, fifty dollars minimum.

15. Authorization to Make Sketches or Models—When a member of this organization is authorized to make a sketch or model, it is necessary that the officially adopted authorized contracts of this organization be signed by the producer placing the order. These contracts are obtainable at the office and are made in triplicate. One going to the manager, one retained by the artist and the third mailed to this office for filing purposes.

be stricken out and a new clause inserted reading:

That members who wish to render services as a designer may do so on a salary basis and to receive $25 per day minimum.

And be it further resolved:

That the designers' contract be revised to conform to the above resolution.

And be it further resolved:

That all parts of the Constitution, By-Laws and Working Rules of the United Scenic Artists' Local 829 which may conflict with the above resolution shall be revised to conform with the above resolution.

YES ☐   NO ☐

THIS BALLOT TO BE RETURNED ON OR BEFORE
OCTOBER 15th, 1934.

1

1.2. Contract ballot, United Scenic Artists Local 829, 1934.
Box 4, folder 34, United Scenic Artists Records (WAG.065), Tamiment Library and Robert F. Wagner Labor Archives. Image courtesy of United Scenic Artists, Local USA 829, IATSE.

1934 and was affirmed by a vote of nearly three to one. Once again the designers organized an outside meeting to protest the model measure, precipitating a final standoff.

The union executive board met in December 1934, calling in designer Walter Walden to confirm the existence of a competing interest group. Designers Woodman Thompson, Jo Mielziner, and Simonson had just been elected as a head committee of another dual group, organized to "register a protest on the new legislation which was contrary to the wishes of the designers." Walden insisted that he represented a "younger group" of designers in attendance at the meeting, and he specifically named Sointu Syrjala, Mordecai Gorelik, and Arne Lundborg. At this meeting, the older men had signed a secret petition against the model law and agreed to fund an advocacy organization for the designers.[61] Thompson and Mielziner were immediately summoned.

Meeting minutes summarizing Thompson's and Mielziner's testimonies reveal the conflict. As Walden had done, Thompson objected to the union's treatment of designers, especially the new model requirement. The designers had also consulted an attorney. In these minutes, the chair (McLean, as Percival was out of town) marveled at the designers' bravado. McLean argued that "nothing had ever been asked by way of legislation which had been refused them. When they wanted minimum fees it had been enacted as law, contract forms had been established, publicity on programs, newspaper advertising etc had all come about as legislation and therefore any statement that they had not been treated fairly is erroneous."[62] Thompson simply replied that their protests had been ignored and that they had a right "as citizens" to see that their interests were protected, hiring legal help if necessary.

At Jo Mielziner's executive board hearing, the executive board probed his involvement in the splinter group. Mielziner said that the meetings had been going on for over a year.[63] He endorsed the subgroup and hoped that it could help designers interface with the executive board. "When they came into the organization ten years ago," Mielziner explained, "they came in as professional people and had the right to expect protection and have a guarantee that they would be protected." Though neither Thompson nor Mielziner directly threatened seceding from the union or initiating legal action outside the normal procedure for union grievances, they both invoked personal right to legal counsel. Mielziner's hearing concluded with an agreement that the board would meet with the designers' committee and hear their concerns. Minutes from subsequent meetings demonstrate continued tensions—designers still crossed out "models" and added the words "models or sketches" to their union contracts, for instance. The model issue was only resolved when the designers forced the union to retreat.

In 1935 a lawyer for the designers filed suit against union president Walter Percival for unconstitutional and illegal regulation. The suit concerned the model referendum and another rule, approved by the full membership in October, that changed the then-current sketch rate of $250 for accepted sketches and $100 for unaccepted ones to a flat daily wage of $25. Once again, moving from contract fees to time-based wages for design labor invited backlash. The designers' suit, *Andrews v. Percival*, contended that these rule changes had not been presented in accordance with bylaws. The suit argued that radical rules changes required the approval of the United Scenic Artists Los Angeles local, USA Local 235,[64] which had been defunct for years. The designers knew that polling a defunct local was impossible, and the legal costs and time delays necessary to amend the union constitution and to close Local 235 were impractical. In light of the significant legal costs, USA 829 granted Percival the power to negotiate a settlement or rescind the new legislation as he saw fit.[65] The lawsuit was dropped in November 1935 once Percival returned the payment scale for design sketches to its original form. This was done in part because of the high costs of defending against the suit, as well as uncertainty over union jurisdictions arising from federal changes to labor law that year.

There are several ways to interpret this legal drama. In one sense, it was simply an intraunion dispute over how design labor ought to be paid. Should the designers be obligated to pay assistants for model building or to hire new workers from union rolls? Given attempts by the union in 1933 and 1934 to strip designers of their ability to independently negotiate contracts, it is understandable why designers would protest out of simple economic interest. Another manner of interpreting this event is as a contest over the freelance labor paradigm itself: Is a designer's work equal to a painter's? Is that work interchangeable with the work of others, measurable in the same material steps, and better compensated through daily wages instead of contract payment? These questions presage a larger shift, during which designers embraced individualized professional organization rather than collective bargaining. Twice in his testimony Mielziner referred to the designers as "professional men rather than journeymen."[66] Together with the "class distinctions" described earlier, this conflict is best seen as a growing separation between the types of labor performed by the union's membership. The defense of contract fee payments was a defining feature of designers' freelance identity, one that distinguished them from their hourly-wage peers. Although the designers certainly recognized the strategic importance of allying with organized labor, they were unafraid to initiate legal action when their self-interest required it. When pressed, designers used the law and capital to their advantage.

Stability in the Freelance Model

After *Andrews v. Percival* was settled, scenic designers enjoyed a more stable professional status. They had successfully defended their gains from other factions in the group and in so doing seized control over their own working conditions. In addition, Federal Theatre Project (FTP) hiring in late 1935 and 1936 increased available work. FTP hiring was explicitly for out-of-work artists, and therefore workers on FTP rosters could not simultaneously work in union jobs. Still, the union encouraged its out-of-work members to seek employment with the FTP, and that hiring relieved some pressure on the union. Designers and painters were equally interested in federally funded jobs, and the union came together in advocacy for employing union men on projects in theatre, exhibitions, and public art. With more work available, the designers were perceived as less responsible for the decline in painting employment.

The union also faced external threats in the period following *Andrews v. Percival*. While the union was attempting to negotiate union-level wages on theatre projects funded by the Works Progress Administration, more work appeared at the New York World's Fair. Much of this work was not strictly theatrical, and the union was concerned that other unions, or non-union artists, would undercut USA 829's wage minimums. The union attempted to negotiate with World's Fair planners, and the union won partial jurisdiction over painting work, to be shared with District Council 9, a competing painting union representing exterior, industrial, and sign painting, organized under the BPDPA.[67] The two unions did not coexist peacefully. Challenging test cases proliferated, especially regarding dioramas, display work, and mural painting, all of which stood partially outside both unions' jurisdictions. As had been the case with the designers a decade earlier, USA 829's immediate response was to expand. This promised an increase in union membership (and finances). Scenic artists and designers, still in an uneasy truce, sensed a threat in the sudden influx of hundreds of new members.

To avoid losing their power within USA 829, the painters and designers revised their union contract in the summer of 1937 to include associate membership categories: diorama, display, and mural work; costume design; and costume painting. The associate level of membership limited artists to a single area of practice. The original scenic artist and designer members ("full members") were qualified for work in any union area. In return for a reduced membership fee and some local autonomy, associate members were barred from leadership on the executive board, barred from voting on the floor except as a bloc, and limited in their ability to adopt new regulations without approval. This second-class citizenship was frustrating but acceptable to some, especially to the costume design and costume painting members, who felt that partial union representation was better than none at all.[68] The costumers mostly wanted to distinguish their work from scenic designers, who had previously included costume design in their purview. They were willing to accept associate status in return for markedly higher fees and contract protections. The mural and diorama workers, however, immediately resisted the arrangement.

Dissatisfied with their associate membership status, the mural artists threatened legal action against the union in June 1939.[69] The union was frustrated too, due to a recent a ruling from the general executive of the BPDPA allowing that members of the house painters' union could also paint murals. The union no longer saw mural artistry as an area worth its energy. Most mural artists left 829 soon after the World's Fair opened in 1939, and the union put up little resistance. Diorama and display workers maintained associate status throughout this period and rarely caused much trouble. Associate membership categories persisted in the union until 1966, when a series of complaints by diorama, costume, and lighting members (lighting was added as an associate category in 1962) coincided with a federal Labor Department investigation into union election procedures. The full members settled their complaints and the investigation by abolishing associate status altogether.[70]

The problems presented by the World's Fair transformed the designers from adversaries of the scenic painter into allies, in part because the designers' previous arguments for valuing their intangible labor proved newly useful. In jurisdictional disputes, USA 829 had an advantage because it could claim to represent designers' creative labor as well as painting executed on-site. Mural artists, for instance, chose to organize with 829 because of that union's previous success in defending design labor and intellectual property, a claim that was less strong in District Council 9

the essence of a
stage setting
by
ROBERT EDMOND JONES

THE ESSENCE of a stage setting lies in its incompleteness. A setting is planned with great care to enhance the characteristic qualities of actors and their performances, and it does not really exist without them.

It is arranged around the particular happenings of the play. They are its focus, its central point. It contains the promise of a completion, a promise which the actor later fulfils. It is charged with a sense of expectancy. It waits for the actor, and not until the actor has made his entrance does it become an organic whole.

By itself it is nothing. In connection with the actor it can become a work of art, filled with dramatic life. ●

B. Pinchot

fine art of
variation
by
DONALD OENSLAGER

DESIGNING the scenery for a production is, perhaps, the Scene Designer's least important function. He has read the play, has discussed the action of it with its director, and has gathered together appropriate source-material from libraries and museums. Finally, he has designed the scenery, made sketches or models, or both, and his ideas have been approved by the Producer. At this point, the Scene Designer starts his real work, the work of a service institution, and, at this point, his office becomes a service station for all persons concerned with the visual aspects of the production.

Working drawings for the Carpenter are the Designer's next consideration. Blue-prints must be made of floor-plans, details and elevations. His office telephone starts ringing constantly. Also there must be blue-prints for painting, for lighting and for properties, and furniture and draperies must be selected. In the meanwhile, the Designer has made detailed color sketches for the Painter, and has shopped for flowers, accessories and hand-props. Supervision keeps him on-the-run, and rehearsals keep him at the theatre. Then dress-rehearsals begin, and scenery-rehearsals and lighting-rehearsals, and, because of his personal interest in his work and in the production as a whole, the Designer is obligated to give his full attention to all these things. Yes; the Designer is a very busy man!

There are as many kinds of settings to design in the Theatre as there are types of productions to be performed, and each type of production must be given a total background that is right and appropriate only for the particular play at hand. Hence, it is the author who really dictates the Designer's performance, and the Designer is the servant of the play.

As an humble servant of the play, the Scene Designer is called upon to work first as a craftsman and second as an artist. Sketches are easy to design; the chief labor is to translate them into the medium of scenery; and to make the scenery look like the sketches. The Designer must work as a tinsmith, a wood-carver, a florist, an (continued on page 29)

1.3. USA 829's 1941 *Almanac*, page 8: "The Essence of a Stage Setting" and "Fine Art of Variation." *Image courtesy of United Scenic Artists, Local USA 829, IATSE.*

costume's relation
to scenery

by

ALINE BERNSTEIN

D. Berns

COSTUMES and scenery perform the same function for a play. The scenery creates the mood, tells the story of the locale, and serves by its careful designing to contain the action of the play. The costume must be an aid to the actor's characterization, it must be the clothing of the character the author has written. The moment an actor appears upon the stage to play his part, he is in costume. His clothes are not the clothes of real life, but the clothes of his character; just as the words he speaks are not the words of his own life, but the speech of his character.

The scenery is still, and the costumes move before it in light. So the relation of the two should be perfect.

I believe it should be the work of one mind, certainly in a dramatic production. In musicals or spectacles, where the volume of work is so great that it is almost impossible for one person to handle it, there is a different problem. Although it can be done, for it has been done.

Every scenic designer should be able to design costumes. If he is artist enough to design scenery, he can do the costumes. He is representing the people of life instead of the things of life, and it is all the more fascinating for that reason. The problems of research are the same although the construction problems are different. But there is no magic to it, beyond the magic of good designing. ●

Blackstone

costume design

by

RAOUL PÈNE DU BOIS

THE PROBLEMS of costume designing are integrally interlaced with the problems of the production as a whole.

It is very often the case of placing the correct psychological emphasis on the characterization the actor and his director are trying to put "across the footlights"

Of course, there are comparatively simple but tedious elements of research connected with the job of a conscientious costume designer, but in my opinion, being correct chronologically is not sufficient. Costumes may be "in period", and yet add very little to the efforts of the scene designer, the director and the actor.

I would classify these elements in order of their importance. First—the mood of the play can be sustained or lost by the selection of materials and colors. Second—the lines and the masses of each costume have to correspond to, and emphasize the character of the actor. Third—the colors of costumes, in relation to each other and to their background, have to be kept in mind as a harmonious pattern. Fourth—costumes are almost always seen in motion and must be designed with this in mind. Fifth—the costume design, while so important in organizing a number, and in convincing the other members of the organization of this value of idea, is yet not the whole (continued on page 31)

1.4. USA 829's 1941 *Almanac*, page 10: "Costume's Relation to Scenery" and "Costume Design." *Image courtesy of United Scenic Artists, Local USA 829, IATSE.*

or other nonartistic unions. The World's Fair also provided an important venue for advertising union work. Publicity for good-quality painting and designing promoted the union well, and it was easier to advertise design than the labor of painting. This new value of design labor can be seen in the 1940–1941 *Almanac*, a publicity booklet published by the union after the fair. Short articles accompanied images touting the union's new services. Except for one article by Robert Bergman, the *Almanac* eschewed discussion of scene painting for the flashier aspects of the union's work: scenic, costume and makeup design; mural artistry; window displays and model-making; and product merchandising.[71] This booklet suggests that the growing celebrity status of Bel Geddes, Simonson, Jones, and Oenslager boosted public opinion of the union. The *Almanac* displayed designers' articles and headshots prominently. By 1940 the union recognized that being able to claim a variety of creative work under its jurisdiction was a valuable selling point for unionized labor.

World War II once again put the union back on its heels, as commercial production slowed and active membership waned because of war service. Tasked with keeping the organization afloat and its members working, the union struck a much more conciliatory tone with the designers who were still present. Newer, younger designers, including Howard Bay, Lemuel Ayers, Stewart Chaney, and Oliver Smith, took more active roles in union life, and as they had not actively antagonized the painters the decade before, their paths were smoother. Howard Bay's union leadership marked the most significant shift.

In the summer of 1942, the thirty-year-old Bay strode to the front of the meeting hall, taking the president's chair from Wood McLean. He embodied a new generation of designer and a new type of leader for USA 829. Previously the executive board had consisted of individuals coming from the majority core membership of the union: scenic artists. Perhaps due to their frequent absence from union meetings, or the disdainful attitude some held toward union politics, many older designers spearheaded designers' groups within the union but never served on 829's executive board. By contrast, Howard Bay, trained in the practical philosophy of the Carnegie Institute of Technology and a full decade younger than Mielziner and Oenslager, made union leadership a part of his career. Bay began designing on plays such as *Power*, *One-Third of a Nation*, and *Battle Hymn*, all produced by the FTP in New York, and he had recently expanded to Broadway and the World's Fair.[72] As his initial work was on relief rolls, his first jobs were non-union. Nonetheless, Bay had been a union member in good standing since 1934, and he regularly reported on FTP issues in union meetings.[73]

Howard Bay's pro-worker advocacy early in his career led fellow union members to see him as a designer sympathetic to labor concerns. Once he attained the vice-presidency in 1939, Bay used the position to advocate for designers' interests in closed executive board meetings. He was frequently a voice of reason on everything from contract negotiations to disciplinary actions, and in 1940 Bay became the designer member on a committee

1.5. Irene Rich and Howard Bay, backstage, *As the Girls Go*, 1948–1950. *Lucas-Pritchard and Lucas-Monroe. Museum of the City of New York, X2012.93.17.*

tasked with revising the scenic artists' standard contracts. In 1942, after war service had reduced the active general membership and shuffled the executive board, Bay rose to the presidency. The union gradually warmed to the idea of designers partially leading the organization, and so other designer members also took on leadership roles. Woodman Thompson, Peggy Clark, and Emeline Roche all took on greater responsibility in the union after 1942, following Bay's example.

As president, Bay had considerable power to set the tone of debate in union meetings. Often decisions were made by the executive board and only ratified by the members; this was especially true of disciplinary actions, exceptions to the rules, and contact with outside organizations. In 1944, in the third term of his presidency, union minutes exemplify Bay's ability to set the tone of debate favorably for the designers. Edward A. Morange, painter and shop contractor, challenged Bay's presidency on the grounds that designers had a managerial function. Owner-operators and contractors, such as Morange, were barred from union leadership, so Morange argued that designers should also be banned. Bay rebutted this challenge simply by quoting the then-established policy on the matter, which stated that designers were service employees on contract, as actors and authors were, not employers, and referred the matter to the floor for a vote. After a vote of twenty-one to two in favor of Bay's opinion, the meeting continued on to other business.[74] In this moment, Bay showed that the presence of a designer on the main governing body worked.

Bay's success was in part a factor of personality; Howard Bay exhibited a lifelong commitment to teaching and service, and he maintained faith in institutional change. In 1974 Bay wrote, "there is no sure palliative for the economic straits of our so-called glamour profession," but he agreed that USA 829, for all its faults, perhaps did not go far enough to protect designers' interests.[75] At the end of his first term as president, from 1942 to 1946, Bay left for Hollywood with words of wisdom for the union, as reported in meeting minutes: "Since this is his last meeting he spoke of the strength of the Union and the unusual combination of having journeymen and the publicity value of designers if everybody sticks together."[76] Bay's service to the union is remarked on by design historians but is often cast as a minor part of his career.[77] Seen within the context of labor politics, though, Bay's leadership concludes a chapter of struggle between painters and designers.

After World War II, film and Hollywood organizations were the main fronts on which the union fought its battles. Television studios on both coasts were reluctant to employ union painters and designers and certainly did not want to pay the higher New York local wages to California workers. The problem was compounded by the relative weakness of the scene painters' and designers' local union in California and by the relative strength of other unions, including IATSE, in the same shops.[78] In 1945 a jurisdictional dispute among Hollywood studios, IATSE members working in painting and art direction, and members of the Conference of Studio Unions (a carpenters' and painters' union) led to a six-month strike and work stoppage in Hollywood. USA 829 backed the Conference of Studio Unions owing to their shared affiliation within the BPDPA. Speaking in a union meeting in October 1945, Howard Bay said that IATSE was not only attempting to organize film production but also to make incursions into theatre design work on both coasts. His advice, approved by the union in a floor vote, was to provide financial support to the Conference of Studio Unions' cause but not to get involved with the strike.[79]

The immediate resolution of the dispute favored IATSE, though its labor wins were soon curtailed by federal restrictions on organized labor. Chief among these restrictions was the Taft-Hartley Act, passed in 1947 by an anti-labor Congress over Harry Truman's veto. It drastically limited the power of organized labor by outlawing closed shops, banning strikes over jurisdictional disputes, limiting the timing and authorization of strike action, and requiring all union leaders to sign anti-communist affidavits.[80] Given these marked reductions in union power, especially in the ability to expand union jurisdiction through strike action or closed shop tactics, USA 829 was put into a position of defending jurisdictions it had already accrued, rather than attempting to grow. The era of union expansion and labor power was over, and for much of the fifties, the union was in a position of defending designers' rights from external business and governmental threats.

Much of the designer's freelance professional identity was firm by the postwar Broadway boom. To take a well-known example: by 1948, when Jo Mielziner signed his initial contract for *Death of a Salesman*, the union remained the securer of labor and intellectual property rights for scenic designers. Though external threats continued in the following decades, the hybrid professional-union status of the designers was accepted and even cherished within the union. Mielziner could count on payment for all phases of design, in thirds, beginning with the signing of the contract and ending with the last third paid on or before opening night. Mielziner frequently had his business travel expenses paid for by producers and was assured billing in a style comparable to the director's. Many intellectual property rights to his designs were also guaranteed, including rights to licensing fees for subsequent productions, payment for television and film adaptations, and the right to refuse the sale of his scenic design for foreign production. Title to the drawings, and the right to exhibit them, remained with the designer and was enforced by union records and business agents. Furthermore, no work on the production could be started until a contract was filed with the union and payment posted in a cash bond, and Mielziner was guaranteed at least four weeks to design the production in advance of an eleven-week building and painting period. All this was standard language, and while Mielziner did occasionally add riders to his contracts and often negotiated higher fees, many standard contractual rights were available to all designers as a result of their savvy use of union politics.[81]

The development of social closure among theatrical scenic designers in New York was accomplished over the span of two decades, from 1924 until the mid-forties, due to the strong power of unions in the United States. During the interwar period, expansion of the unions and pro-labor New Deal policies allowed the designers to use unionism to develop a hybrid union-professional status. They sought many of the protections commonly associated with other professional groups: peer election and regulation of group norms, near-monopoly control over a type of work, social respectability, and the specification of domain-specific knowledge. They did so by walking a line between employee and independent contractor, between freelancer and wageworker. Remaining allied with the blue-collar scene painters was a challenge for some designers, but they acknowledged union membership as a necessary evil. The success of this advocacy was due as much to individual designers (and the occasional legal suit) as it was due to the historical moment in which designers began to organize their profession.

Counterpoint: Gender, Race, and Union Membership

Closure is, by definition, exclusion. Although the effects of social closure in the union created the new profession of scenic designer relatively quickly, the adoption of hybrid union-professional standing also brought negative effects. White male designers' tendency to keep work for themselves excluded women and Black artists, especially when USA 829 closed union rolls and suspended entrance exams during the Depression. As a counterpoint to the story of union closure, this section turns to the ways in which closure and professionalization contributed to gender and racial discrimination. The inductions of Aline Bernstein and Perry Watkins, in 1926 and 1939 respectively, illustrate that it was possible for a woman and a Black man to join the union but only with great effort. They had to apply social pressure, threaten legal action, and subvert union bureaucracy. For Black women, the situation was more difficult to overcome; the first African American woman to join the union was Louise Evans Briggs-Hall, who joined as a costume designer in 1953, according to historian Kathy Perkins.[82]

The stories of Bernstein's and Watkins's union memberships have been told before, but the narratives tend to be short and celebratory. In Carole

1.6. Aline Bernstein, 1933. *Carl Van Vechten (1880–1964) / Museum of the City of New York.* ©*VanVechtenTrust.*

Klein's retelling, Bernstein strode into a union meeting in elegant evening apparel, while the confused doorman announced, "Brother Bernstein!" Perry Watkins, in Kyle Rex's short profile on Blackpast.org, "was permitted to take the drafting and art exam for admission into the set designers' union."[83] Deeper research into the history of these artists' early careers revealed the amount of extra work that professionalism required of these artists. For example, both Bernstein and Watkins had to overcome secondary class status in the union. While they could have worked in associate or informal ways as painters or amateur designers, they could not work at the best-paid level of the profession. The creative authority of the commercial scenic designer was valuable to the in-group of white union men, and so the union protected it. It is untrue that times simply changed around these artists or that the union passively evolved or that theatre culture naturally became more inclusive. Bernstein and Watkins were not finally admitted because the union changed its heart. On the contrary, they enlisted the support of others, lawyers if necessary, and pushed their way in by force.

Aline Bernstein was the first woman designer to join the union, but she was neither the first woman member nor the only woman working in scenic painting. At least four women were working as scenic painters at the time Bernstein applied to the union, according to Donald Stowell. These women were not designers, however, and, in certain cases, not even members of the union; they were simply allowed to work for painting studios in an exception to the closed-shop rule.[84] Mabel Buell, daughter of scene painter Charles Buell, was the first woman member of the union, and she was allowed to join in 1917.[85] In the thirties, union records show that Buell had become an owner-operator of a painting studio. There were also several designers and painters who were not operators. Stowell notes that Lilian Gaertner was working at Urban's studio, and Millia Davenport and Emeline Roche were also doing regular paid painting work in the twenties.

Women did design and paint for the amateur theatre, as USA 829 did not claim jurisdiction over that work. Davenport partnered with Robert Edmond Jones on costumes and sets at the Provincetown Playhouse, and Aline Bernstein worked regularly at Alice and Irene Lewisohn's Neighborhood Playhouse.[86] The union would even look the other way when women were paid for commercial work, when it was convenient. Roche, Gaertner, and Davenport were permitted to paint Broadway scenery from 1918 well into the late twenties even without official membership in the union. Roche joined the union in 1927, Davenport joined as a costume associate in 1937, and Gaertner seems to have worked with Urban until his death in 1933, but she may never have been a member of the union.[87] Davenport has explained that ad hoc permission was given to women simply as a matter of convenience, as the men did not want to have to provide another bathroom in their union meeting hall.[88] (Peggy Clark partially corroborates this claim, as she recalled being passed over for jobs in the thirties because there were no women's bathrooms in some painting studios.)[89] Perhaps it was the authority that came with designing that gave members pause, or perhaps it was simply that men preferred having women as subordinates to having them as peers when it came to the commercial tiers of scenic practice. The effect of this exclusion by closure, then, was to maintain male dominance of the profession and to permit women by exception only.

Aline Bernstein needed to join the union because the Neighborhood Playhouse was reclassified as a non-amateur house. The newly organized scenic designers were ready to admit her, but her first application was denied in 1924. Her peers and her producer Gilbert Miller sent letters to the union, and only with these and the intercessions of her parents and her husband's family was Bernstein finally permitted to take the examination in the summer of 1926. She passed and was introduced that year at an often-remarked-upon November meeting.[90] Despite the celebratory tone of her introduction, Bernstein must have been aware of the effort she had expended in joining the union, and she was pragmatic about the continued bias she would have to face. Descriptions of Bernstein's professional life after 1926 at once praised her ability to blend in with male workers and also acknowledged (perhaps too sanguinely) the basic fairness of the union once Bernstein gained membership. "Aline proved that she could work on equal terms with the men. They were tough, they were truculent, but they respected courage and they played fair," wrote reporter Frederika Brochard in 1951. Bernstein biographer Carole Klein explains that the rank and file were "red-faced with discomfort when she'd slide past them to take her seat in the hall," but Bernstein countered with "warm and affectionate laughter. . . . [T]hey respected her courage in joining."[91] For many journalists profiling Bernstein—the best sources extant, as few of Bernstein's archives survive that cover this period—she was constructed within limiting gender discourses. She possessed beauty and determination but was embarrassed to enter the male-dominated union hall. The union, conversely, was characterized as fundamentally good, willing ultimately to accept a female "brother" if (and only if) she proved herself worthy and courageous.

Despite her exclusion, Bernstein mostly supported the craft union politics of USA 829.[92] To join, though, she had succeeded in part due to the intercessions of male peers and the application of financial, professional power from Gilbert Miller. This, as Watkins would also find out, was a language that unions could not ignore. Once in, Bernstein took to mentoring and "opening doors" for other women, including Emeline Roche, who had a long-standing relationship with Bernstein, discussed in chapter 4. But it should not be ignored that Bernstein pressed her way in. The majority of women in the union joined as associate members in costume and makeup, not scenic painting or design. This second-class membership status did not end until the mid-1960s. Gender disparities in those fields previously given "associate" status continue today.

Perry Watkins faced similar pressures of closure and exclusion. His application was prompted by comparable circumstances—a pending professional contract and an urgent need for union membership—and Watkins had to contend with similar secondary status. Ultimately, as had occurred with the scenic designers in *Andrews v. Percival*, it was the threat of legal action that finally convinced the union to consider Watkins's petition. As designer and historian Kathy A. Perkins has noted, Black designers were often excluded from commercial work in New York City, and so they frequently worked across fields (scenery, costume, lighting, sculpture, visual arts) and in venues outside the commercial mainstream.[93] Perry Watkins studied to be a fine arts painter in Rhode Island but found it difficult to get full-time employment. In 1936 he applied to the FTP as an artist and found success in the New York Negro Theatre Unit at the Lafayette Theatre. Watkins drafted, built, and painted sets and managed lighting for FTP productions, notably for the Orson Welles–directed "Voodoo" *Macbeth*.[94] After several years of work with the FTP, commercial Broadway producers approached Watkins to design their production of *Mamba's Daughters*. (FTP introductions also kick-started the careers of Abe Feder and Howard Bay.) Like Bernstein, Watkins was then obligated to apply for union membership, and it was a challenging process.

Racially segregated IATSE unions for stagehands existed as early as 1918, first in Washington, DC, and then expanding to other cities, including New York City (Local No. 1-A). These so-called Associate locals provided a way for Black backstage workers to organize and work in Black theatres, but the groups remained separate from and subordinate to their white counterparts.[95] No IATSE locals had jurisdiction over theatrical design or commercial Broadway work. Watkins first applied for membership

1.7. Perry Watkins, ca. 1939. Opportunity: A Journal
of Negro Life, *vol. 17, no. 2 (February 1939): 53.*

in USA 829 in 1937 and was accepted under "class B" scenic artist status.
Class B membership was another associate membership category with
restrictions similar to those placed on costume, mural, and diorama workers. It was for scenic artists working in "semi-professional theatres": summer stock, amateur, and community theatres. Class B membership came
with lower exam and dues requirements, but it also prohibited members
from commercial work unless they were to reapply for full membership.
Watkins passed the class B exam easily in the fall of 1937 while working
with the FTP.

In August 1938 Watkins petitioned the board for the opportunity to
design *Mamba's Daughters* on Broadway, produced by Guthrie McClintic.
After pleading his case before the executive board, the board met privately
and decided that Watkins would have to take the full member examination
at the next regularly scheduled time, which was not yet determined. (At
this point, the examination was being offered only once a year and was
occasionally canceled without being rescheduled, and a waiting list of
designers was growing.) By December, though, preproduction on *Mamba's*

Daughters had moved forward, and the union refused to accept Watkins's filed contract for the project on the grounds that he was not yet a full member and therefore not an authorized designer. To help manage this situation, Watkins sought advice from other working designers, including Lee Simonson, and acquired legal representation. The lawyer threatened the union with a lawsuit, which prompted speedier action. Simonson, also in attendance when the suit was announced, suggested either holding an immediate examination or making a one-time exception to allow Watkins to work on the production. Several board members objected. Wood McLean suggested that it was "an effort to get in under the wire" and was "unfair to the waiting list," and Woodman Thompson noted that Watkins "had been invited to take the examination in 1937 but had not availed himself of the opportunity." Rather than open up the examination, however, the board granted a one-time exception to Watkins, at the behest of Simonson and others who did not want "to make a racial issue of this" by fighting the suit.[96] Once again the union maintained closure for its white male members by making an ad hoc exception to the rules. Watkins passed the full examination in March 1939 and joined that August.[97] However, the examination fee of $500 proved to be a financial burden—and was perhaps the reason he had not availed himself of the exam earlier. According to Jonathan Dewberry, Guthrie McClintic and the producers of *Mamba's Daughters* paid half of Watkins's examination fee, and the other half came from a personal loan given by Fredi Washington, executive director and secretary of the Negro Actors Guild of America.[98]

Watkins opened up more opportunities for Black designers on Broadway once he joined the union.[99] The effects were not immediate. Watkins sent fellow designers to the union to apply for membership, but the union continued to turn away Black applicants because they were not considered serious artists.[100] Watkins remained the only Black member of USA 829 through the forties.[101] Later Black designers to join the union included costume designer Louise Evans Briggs-Hall and scenic designer Edward Burbridge; both joined in the fifties. So, while the efforts of Watkins and Bernstein to break into the union were noteworthy, they were both let in as special cases. It would take many years for women, Black, and other minority artists to gain significant representation in the union beyond the ad hoc exception.

Another difficulty in tracking these challenges to social closure, and part of the reason these stories are not often told, is that these artists pursued less linear career paths. Bernstein's and Watkins's institutional contributions were limited to those roles most acceptable to the white men in power. At times they worked within the union but often on issues seen to align with race or gender stereotypes. Bernstein headed an educational committee of the union, and Watkins was sometimes called upon when questions of race confronted the union in the forties and fifties. Importantly, both turned to theatrical producing later in their careers: Bernstein cofounded Helen Arthur's all-women production company Actor-Managers, Inc., which produced in Rhode Island and Michigan, and Watkins produced a number of Black productions in the forties on and near Broadway, including *Beggar's Holiday*, a 1946 musical featuring Duke Ellington's music. (It was also the first musical mounted by an integrated producing team consisting of Watkins and white playwright Dale Wasserman.)[102] Unfortunately, historians have previously overlooked these types of careers in the history of scenic design.

Design history must reorient its criteria for success and acclaim away from high-profile designs, long careers of prolific work, or steady production in one design discipline. Histories that challenge racism and sexism must note that past discriminatory practices erected many more obstacles for non-white and women designers. To rectify this, histories of the most frequently taught and anthologized designers should sit alongside those of lesser-known peers. Watkins and Bernstein should not be seen as unserious or less important by comparison because they worked in multiple venues or were not as productive on Broadway year after year. In fact, their work in production is notable for its creation of centers of theatrical activity outside the established practices of Broadway. It is important to avoid the conclusion that Bernstein, for instance, was "fortunate in not having to worry about building a professional reputation" because her writing life and marriage afforded her other means of financial support, as Donald Oenslager suggested.[103] As this chapter's discussion of the union might suggest, discrimination may not have been intentionally personal or mean-spirited, but the processes of social closure as practiced by unions (and other institutions discussed in this book) still had discriminatory effects. The story of progress here is not simply an opening up of the scenic design profession to new artists but rather the application of social, financial, and legal pressure to make a somewhat conservative institution such as USA 829 stand up and take notice. The credit goes to the individuals: Bernstein, Watkins, and their allied peers.

Conclusion

By 1950 the era of strong labor activism had ended, and designers main-tained their self-image as professionals distinct from the unionized wage-worker. Newer entrants to the field, such as Oliver Smith, William and Jean Eckart, Eldon Elder, and George Jenkins, tended to see themselves as independent artists within a field, rather than union members first. They could do this given the advances an earlier generation had made in professional practice. Established designers in the fifties, many of whom were still at the height of their careers, also began to take steps away from the labor unions to craft more diverse professional portfolios, expanding into architectural consulting and arts policy. Chapter 4 discusses these developments.

Specific claims against designers' professional status still periodically created difficulties for USA 829. For instance, in negotiations between the union and television networks in 1951, the networks countered the union's demand for weekly hour maximums by arguing that designers were exempt from such restrictions. The Fair Labor Standards Act of 1938 exempted professional workers from hours limits and overtime pay, so the networks demanded that designers work as many hours as necessary. Fearing that a firm federal ruling that designers were professionals would endanger their unionized status, USA 829 acquiesced to the networks' counterargument. Similarly, the Internal Revenue Service pursued the designers for unincorporated business tax payments in the mid-fifties, and only after several years did a court decide that designers as contract employees were exempt from the unincorporated business tax. In 1961 the Department of Justice found that the union's requirement that scenic design contracts be accompanied by union contracts in costume design and scene painting was illegal, constituting an action in restraint of trade. The union's response was to remove the provision, effectively allowing non-union designers and shops to work on union projects, if producers so demanded. Historian Philip Alexander holds that losing the closed shop and union-contract requirement was but a minor sacrifice, as "most designers sought union membership as a sign of professional status." Inter-estingly, none of these incidents resulted in a definitive ruling on designers' status as professionals.[104] The interest of the Internal Revenue Service and the Department of Justice in designers' working status does suggest that not only did designers increasingly see themselves as artistic professionals but so too did the federal government.

Social closure is a tactic shared by labor unions and professional organizations, Weber notes. The case of scenic design labor is an example of a hybrid approach to closure, one that exploited the strength of American unionism but that also had professional aspirations. Scenic designers increasingly modeled their professionalism on the careers of other applied artists of the time, such as architects, industrial designers, and advertisers. Many designers founded their own small firms and in some cases developed small offices with multiple assistants and staff. These new business arrangements were undertaken for a mix of reasons, ranging from financial and tax purposes to the development of personal branding. As the next chapter shows, alliances with other applied art fields and the remaking of designers' self-image on the basis of personality further advanced the notion of the theatrical scenic designer as independent, valuable, and professional.

2. THE CELEBRITY ARTIST: PROMOTING THE DESIGNER

Entertainment fans walking up to a newsstand in the 1920s would have found themselves surrounded by images. Film, gossip, and culture magazines filled the racks, drawing in readers with celebrity close-ups, exclusive backlot interviews, and photo spreads of Hollywood notables relaxing at home. Celebrity photographs were new and exciting. The studios' marketing machines spurred the magazines on, but technological developments also made celebrity photography possible. Lighter portable cameras, cheaper lenses, and faster photographic printing placed photojournalism at the heart of film fan magazines and also newspaper tabloids such as the New York *Illustrated Daily News*. For both the magazines and the tabloids, personality drove sales, and nothing sold personality quite as well as a great photograph. This new approach to media and promotion was successful because it cultivated what Joseph Roach has termed "public intimacy," or "the illusion of proximity to the tantalizing apparition."[1] Tantalizing profiles and photographs deepened Hollywood's overall investment in star culture, for while films presented the star, the magazine "could reach beyond the visual image and examine and reveal the 'real' personality."[2]

In addition to film magazines, theatre periodicals also began to publish more images of artists involved in production. Few theatre magazines were as large or slickly produced as those that advertised films, yet by the twenties the theatre press took a page from film and began to promote its stars through photography. As one might expect, actors received most of the attention at first. Yet some theatrical designers—especially those who dabbled in film—became celebrity features as well. For example, a 1920 feature in the film magazine *Photoplay* locates Joseph Urban at his Harlem film office, scripts piled on the desk, chatting with the reporter while hot black coffee is poured by a member of his staff: all conspicuous symbols of Urban's executive status.[3] A few years later, Norman Bel Geddes, a well-known designer of theatre sets and consumer products, was profiled for playing a "War Game" in his home with friends: Geddes had spent a decade building a cork topographic map, and guests commanded artillery, battalions, and airplanes by moving colored pins across its surface. The game was photographed by the *New York Times* and *Popular Science Monthly* and was covered in national press.[4] Eye-catching profiles such as these had a significant impact on the public "face" of the designer.

Scenic designers who sought careers extending beyond the theatre embraced celebrity journalism in the form of the feature article, profile, and photo shoot. In particular, Joseph Urban and Norman Bel Geddes

Urban's invasion of the movies has been accomplished from a General Headquarters some twenty by fifteen feet in size.

Marietta Serves Coffee

By
JULIAN JOHNSON

And on the other side of the small blacks sits Joseph Urban—last year the greatest constructing artist of the theater, and now of the movies.

I may seem strange to you that I am giving the coffee so much prominence, but you would see for yourself —were you there—how important it is.

Urbanly speaking, it occupies the same social position that the cigarette has long since achieved among the rapidly revolving Mexicans, and is as much of a formality-killer as was that archaic salutation, "What'll you have?" among our four-finger fathers.

Joseph Urban's invasion of the movies has been accomplished from a General Headquarters some twenty by fifteen feet in size, on the second floor of a rambling and ponderous cement building near the Harlem River, on the northeast corner of Manhattan Island. The structure has been the International Film studio only since last autumn; before that it was a Casino, alternately jazzed and shot up by dancing clubs more than one member of which could give a movie cowboy a couple of rings on the pistol target and then beat him twice out of three.

Like most film arenas, there is nothing especially aesthetic about the place until you come to the cave wherein Abu Hassan Urban—since they gave us our numerals we can borrow at least a figure of speech from the Arabians—keeps just a few of his artistic jewels.

It is all white, with highly-curtained windows that keep one's eyes off the grime of the adjacent streets; occupying almost all of one end is an L-like combination of desk and table and work-bench; around the walls, framed in orderly rows, are little paintings and drawings, made by Mr. Urban for books, or else colored sketches of scenery for dramas or grand operas or female extravaganza; there are deep, hugely comfortable chairs of black and white wood—striped like a lady's cape or a stout gentleman's trousers; one end of the room is entirely engaged with shelves bending beneath art-books in half a dozen languages or the universal pictorial appeal, and the other end of the room has a window both deep and high, opening upon the afternoon sun and the upper strata of the Second Avenue elevated.

Joseph Urban is usually to be found as a rotund wedge driven into the angle of the L-like table. No matter how well he may know his guest, no matter how obscure that guest may be, he does not request the visitor to take a chair; he proffers it himself, though it entails a trip across the room and back. This is merely a sample of his old-world courtesy that now strangely hovers over a corner of a rough old pile but recently devoted to malt, hops and stray shots. And

2.1. "Marietta Serves Coffee," 1920. *Photoplay, vol. 18, no. 5 (October 1920): 33.*

cultivated a version of design celebrity that blended the professionalism of architecture with the new press strategies of film marketing and advertising. Urban and Bel Geddes needed celebrity to parlay their early work in stage design into broader design careers, and both men were successful in their bids to generalize their design expertise from the stage to mass media. Urban's name was synonymous with luxury goods in the twenties, and in the thirties Bel Geddes was among the most famous industrial designers, placing his stamp on everything from consumer objects and vehicle designs to compelling futurist predictions on film and in World's Fairs.[5] Their personae introduced the American public to the idea that a stage designer could become a celebrity.

Scenic designers such as Robert Edmond Jones, Lee Simonson, Jo Mielziner, and Donald Oenslager did not cultivate celebrity with the fervor of Urban or Bel Geddes, but they did embrace personality-based journalism on a more limited scale. Many designers found that press attention raised their social and economic standing, so they permitted themselves to step briefly into the spotlight to talk about their work. Feature articles on scenic designers became commonplace in the 1930s in New York newspapers and theatre-focused periodicals. Some designers used personality-based media as an opportunity to help shape the public's view of the scenic designer's labor. They explained what, precisely, a designer contributed to theatre production. However, the new expectation that designers participate in personality journalism discriminated, too. Certain designers, particularly gay men, were reluctant to let the media into their lives, and they resisted the turn toward self-exposure and personality journalism in the thirties. After the thirties, profiles of designers continued in a more subdued fashion, but the claim had been made: designers were not simply performing a job but were doing so as an artist in their own right. As an artist, their personality was a subject of public interest.

Urban's and Bel Geddes's self-promotional strategies were versions of what film scholar Emily Carman has referred to as "professional agency." In her book *Independent Stardom*, Carman shows how certain women film stars constructed a freelance identity, independent of long-term film studio contracts. Such stars publicized "their labor as actors and their unique creative public personae—their 'celebrity' images—to attain increased professional visibility in the Hollywood film industry." Barbara Stanwyck, Constance Bennett, and Miriam Hopkins, among others, became "architects of their own images."[6] They sought out relationships with producers and talent agents outside the studio system, pursued a diverse range of leading roles to avoid typecasting, and worked for multiple studios at once. At the same time that this independence was being declared in film, industrial and theatrical designers were also engaged in processes of self-promotion. Inspired by Carman's study, and especially her concept of freelance artistic labor as a means by which stars actively shaped their careers, this chapter suggests that the professionalization of the scenic designer depended on a new type of self-promotion.

Adopting this new self-promotion strategy was viable for Bel Geddes and Urban because of a changing journalistic environment. The *New Yorker*, for instance, initiated its "Profiles" section when the magazine launched in 1925, and by the early thirties, the feature was a fixture in the magazine and in New York culture. As further developed by writer Alva Johnston beginning in 1932, the *New Yorker* profile became a form with "real literary and journalistic weight" and "the first to combine a natural wit and a sense of storytelling with the legwork of a first-class newspaperman."[7] Celebrity culture from Broadway captured American interest nationwide with the syndication of Walter Winchell's gossip column in the *New York Daily Mirror* in 1929, and the next year Winchell began a radio program that similarly exposed the fascinating and often seedy side of theatrical production.[8] The *New Yorker*, in particular, did much to carry the designer into public consciousness; Joseph Urban was profiled in 1927, and Henry Dreyfuss and Robert Edmond Jones were both profiled in 1931.[9]

Larger sociological factors also account for the shift in journalism toward celebrity. As cultural historian Warren Susman notes, "personality" was a new cultural value of the twentieth century, supplanting "character" as a general, shared public goal. Personality, or the "quality of being Somebody," was manifest in arenas from self-help literature to high-culture hobbies. The need for distinctiveness permeated early twentieth-century culture, especially among artists. Professionals, including "painters, architects and politicians, all depend upon a numerous and faithful body of admirers. Emancipation, self-expression, excellent work are all meaningless unless such gifted individuals have the support of a following."[10] Michael Denning agrees, and identifies Susman's turn to personality as "the product of a new middle class of managers, professionals, and technicians."[11] A good amount of this turn to personality was accomplished through the celebrity profile. Enthusiasm for the celebrity as an "intimate stranger" had begun in the nineteenth century, but it peaked in the teens and twenties, alongside the dominance of film and tabloid journalism. Celebrity journalism then spread from sensational papers published by

James Pulitzer or William Randolph Hearst to middlebrow publications.[12] Urban and Bel Geddes intentionally hitched their careers to the media engine of celebrity.

Celebrity and personality-based journalism was important for scenic design professionalization because it showed that designers could win fame. Doing so cast designers as artists of a kind similar to actors, directors, or playwrights—figures of public interest and parties responsible for the success of theatre productions. Although occupying a position as a public figure was not a necessary element of professionalization for all designers, many designers did make the leap into the public eye. The existence of high-profile designers such as Urban and Bel Geddes accelerated acceptance of the designer as a professional knowledge worker. Younger designers later relied on public understanding of the designers' job as first publicized by Urban and Bel Geddes.

Embracing Design Celebrity

Both Norman Bel Geddes and Joseph Urban welcomed celebrity journalism and developed consistent self-promotional practices. Their innovations were the first applications of an overt strategy that focused on the artist himself as a calling card and not on one of the artist's designs. As historians have noted, Urban's and Bel Geddes's designs for the stage, opera, industry, and public exhibitions remade modernism in America, and the career paths of later industrial or industrial-scenic designers were much inspired by their work in the twenties.[13] This chapter adds the observation that their promotional press changed the way that later scenic designers mobilized their personae. Although scenic design historians have framed Urban and Bel Geddes as less influential precisely because of their work outside the theatre, this chapter shows that their effects on the design professions endured precisely because they pursued broad fame.[14] Their embrace of product and industrial design, in particular, induced them to see their job as one more in line with advertising. Both men knew that they were the product.

US press about Joseph Urban began in 1912, immediately upon his arrival from Vienna. Features during this time, when he was lead designer for the Boston Opera, emphasized the products of Urban's creativity and less often the man himself. Reporters gave some attention to the Swampscott studio where Urban worked, which was notable both for its unusual, Continental methods of scenic painting and for the full staff

2.2. Portrait of Joseph Urban, ca. 1916. *Genthe photograph collection, Library of Congress, Prints and Photographs Division.*

of German-speaking artists Urban had assembled. Many opera articles in the *Boston Evening Transcript,* for instance, focused on the music and the performers, yet interest in Urban's foreign methods and charismatic personality soon grew.[15] In 1915 a feature on Urban in *Vanity Fair* initiated the new coverage of his personality. The article's subtitle, "A Glimpse at the Scenic Obstacles Surmounted by Joseph Urban," and photograph portrait of Urban highlight his innovative work on his first Broadway production, Edward Sheldon's *Garden of Paradise.* The article describes Urban's general method of approaching a scenic design through sketching, rendering, and modeling phases.[16] This production proved influential for Urban's career, as this fantastic, largely underwater setting prompted Florenz Ziegfeld Jr. to offer Urban a design contract for his *Follies* that same year. Later features in 1915 also paired Urban's face with images of his realized stage designs.[17]

Urban innovated in the canny placement of his image. Beginning in Boston, Urban allowed magazines and newspapers to reproduce images of himself, his workers, and his working space. When he moved into film work, Urban furnished a headshot to be placed alongside the headshots of directors, producers, and main actors in ads and in front-page stories. The newspapers complied. The inclusion of the headshot introduced the designer as a key creative mind behind film production, associated Urban with Cosmopolitan Productions' in-house team, and, perhaps most importantly, put a face to the name. Few other profiles of designers in theatre magazines used images of the artists, and in fact many theatrical designers were reluctant to seek attention in the press at the time. Urban was different. When a headshot was too formal or unavailable, cartoons fit the bill; in the early twenties, cartoons and caricatures of Urban satirized his distinctive facial features and imposing size.

Urban did not attempt to hide or resist caricatures of himself, perhaps because their inclusion helped construct his celebrity. These led to other cartooning of scenic designers in arts publications. By the mid-twenties, cartoons accompanied most *New Yorker* profiles, and other publications used them as well. In the June 1923 issue of the arts magazine *Shadowland*, for instance, Urban, Jones, Simonson, and James Reynolds are depicted in caricature in front of watercolor renderings of their most famous scenic designs.[18] Portals sit behind Urban, Jones towers over a stairway reminiscent of his design for *The Birthday of the Infanta* (1920), and Simonson impatiently waggles his pencil above a thumbnail sketch of a set for *Back to Methuselah* (1922). Images like these cast designers as a unique professional class and, in this case, capitalized on the name of Urban to introduce art-theatre designers who may have been less well-known outside New York.

Urban boosted his public recognition, too, by diversifying the types of work he accepted and by seeking relationships with well-known, socially influential benefactors. In 1915 Urban expanded his work for Boston operas to include Broadway productions, a new partnership with Ziegfeld to design the *Follies*, and designs in progress for the 1916 community masque *Caliban of the Yellow Sands*. Throughout these projects Urban provided direct quotations and interviews about his work to the *New York Times* and

"With Stage Settings By:"

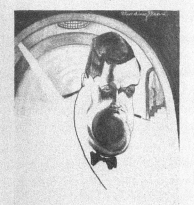

JOSEPH URBAN

ROBERT EDMOND JONES

LEE SIMONSON

JAMES REYNOLDS

2.3. "With Stage Settings By:," 1923.
Shadowland, *vol. 8, no. 4 (June 1923): 41.*

Theatre Arts Monthly.[19] The rapid success of his work in multiple theatrical venues, from the *Follies* to opera to civic entertainment, allowed Urban to craft a public image of a designer independent from any single organization. Urban turned to film in 1920, signing a five-year exclusive design contract with Cosmopolitan Productions, a studio owned by William Randolph Hearst. After his film work, Urban supervised interior renovations and new architecture for New York theatres, office buildings, universities, hotels, and, famously, Marjorie Merriweather Post's estate, Mar-a-Lago.[20] Urban's name came to connote a luxurious style of design (prominently featured in the *Follies*) that could be highlighted among producers and purchased by consumers. Such brand-name identity made Urban the first modernist theatrical designer in the United States to develop a visual style widely recognizable outside theatre circles.

Urban sought such a diverse set of commissions in part due to his background. Before coming to Boston, Urban had supervised many projects in Austria with significant architectural components. His European work included interior architecture and exhibition design. After early success in competitions, well-connected patrons invited Urban to design residential interiors and festival buildings and to organize and design exhibits for the Hagenbund art collective in Vienna.[21] He also staged twenty-five designs for theatre and opera in Europe. Coming from a multidisciplinary group of artists with wealthy noble patrons, Urban viewed his role as a designer and interior architect as that of an artist serving the public, within a network of peers. He was uninhibited by medium. American theatre design and architectural practices, on the other hand, struck him as foreign. In the United States, architecture, theatrical design, and exhibition design were conceived as separate professions, and few artists crossed over these groups on account of custom, licensing law, or union regulations. Urban simply continued to operate as he had done in Vienna: he sought diverse applications of his artistry, aligned his work with wealthy patrons, and insisted on a guildlike organization of applied artists.

Joseph Urban's work across fields necessitated a more direct media approach than had been employed by other theatre designers. Coverage of Urban's output noted his "ambidextrous" facility for multiple styles of design as early as 1917. By the twenties, Urban's move to film led to features in more than theatre-focused periodicals.[22] The *Photoplay* feature (whose opening page appeared early in this chapter) stands as an early example of Urban's fame: Urban, photographed at his desk, sits surrounded by books and designs, while a staff member, in a sidebar image, pours a cup of coffee. The title of the piece, "Marietta Serves Coffee," reinforces Urban's professionalism. The feature goes on to explain and perhaps exaggerate his fame to the magazine's film-obsessed readers: Urban was "the most distinguished master of environment, light, and color that we Anglo-Saxons know in the theatre. . . . Rheinhardt [*sic*] is practically unknown in America and but little known in England, and [Robert Edmond] Jones is still a matter of metropolitan fame." It quotes Urban's views on trends in film, theatre, and Ziegfeld's *Follies*, and Urban speaks as though he were a corporate executive. This article, and others appearing in the similarly popular-interest, theatre- and arts-focused *Shadowland* magazine in 1921 and in newspapers such as the New York *Sunday World* and Los Angeles *Evening Express*, all centered Urban's executive authority and creative mind.[23]

As both an architect and a stage designer, Urban was something different. His approach to press was more aligned with the star system of Hollywood than with the restrained, stiff press that architects allowed themselves. Historian Mary Beth Betts argues in her study of Urban that he "successfully exploited public interest in his biography and personality as a set designer and was willing to use that interest in order to promote his architectural practice."[24] As examples of Urban's pioneering self-promotional scheme, Betts points to Urban's early adoption of profile journalism, including a 1927 piece in the *New Yorker*, and his willingness to publish images and descriptions of his office. It was similar to the way film celebrities used their homes; such an approach was common among film and tabloid celebrities but anathema to the more reserved profession of architecture. Few other architects' offices, Betts notes, approached Urban's performance of modern practicality. Simple wood chairs; a subdued color scheme of white, black, and red; and a large work table gave the office a lived-in quality. The décor also had what one profile called "an atmosphere of efficiency."[25] By the beginning of the thirties, Urban had established an image of himself as a multidisciplinary designer, a maker of high-status goods and interiors, and a popular cultural figure. Such a view is epitomized in press such as the *Brooklyn Eagle*'s 1930 feature on Urban, "Excels Because He Does Not Specialize." Unlike his press in the teens, this feature describes and demonstrates the different types of design Urban executed, and it places the artist, not the work, at the center. "We are living in an age of the specialized, but there are exceptions," journalist Frank Cadie wrote, "Joseph Urban . . . is more than an exception, he is a paradox."[26] This article, like a similar Norman Bel Geddes feature published by *Fortune* in July of the

same year, firmly planted the personality of the theatrical-industrial designer in the center of a constellation of useful, diverse projects.

In the late twenties and early thirties, Urban became comfortable in his
position as an authority in matters theatrical-architectural. Having completed work for the stage, for theatre and cinema buildings, for film, and
for architectural interiors and exteriors, Urban claimed general authority
in the applied arts. In 1928 the *New York Times* published a rendering of
his designs for Max Reinhardt's new theatre, which was never built, along
with a treatise on practical theatre architecture. The article, "Wedding
Theatre Beauty to Ballyhoo," crystallized his pragmatic approach to theatre
design, one that took the necessity of electrically illuminated advertising
into account. "Architecture and advertising—the two outstanding practical arts of America—were bound to collide," Urban wrote. His rendering
featured a sleek theatre façade of black vitrolite, lined with golden fire
escapes providing horizontal sign space and a tall, golden, grilled central stairway tower.[27] In characteristically Urban fashion, he embraced
commercialism; the Reinhardt theatre design transformed the needs for
advertising space and audience safety into a unified, elegant structure.

2.4. "Excels Because He Does Not Specialize," 1930. Brooklyn
Daily Eagle, *Brooklyn Public Library, Brooklyn Collection.*

Unlike other New Stagecraft artists, who either begrudgingly accepted the needs of the commercial stage or attempted to forget them entirely, Urban encouraged future designers and architects to beautify business. Similar tones animated both Urban's book of proposed theater architecture, *Theatres* of 1929, and several articles describing Urban's designs in trade publications as diverse as *Sales Management and Advertisers' Weekly, National Hotel Review, Mosaic Messenger,* and *Lighting.*[28] While some articles are interviews with Urban about his projects, and others display and report on his contributions, each positioned Urban as a practical, well-known artist with direct relevance to businesses' decorative needs.

After Urban's sudden death from a heart attack in 1933, his innovations were absorbed into other New Stagecraft practitioners' methods. While he was alive, his name was shorthand for an integrated artistic practice, a sense of luxury, and a cunning understanding of the relationship between art and business. After death, his multivalent design career was quickly written off as frivolous; during the worsening Depression, the luxury of elite fashion, hotel interiors, and Ziegfeld-era displays of wealth were at best reminders of times lost and, at worse, evidence of profligate consumption. This, too, is a likely cause for the omission of Urban from design histories. In a lengthy remembrance published in *Architecture* in May 1934, Deems Taylor observed, "his extraordinary many-sidedness . . . has made it difficult to put him into any convenient category. . . . [B]ecause he stood for more than a single phase of his art, he could not be trade-marked, and a man who cannot be trade-marked is at a disadvantage in an era of specialization."[29] Urban resisted categorization and specialization because his output spanned categories and specialties. He was, in Taylor's words, a "sort of one-man guild." Urban's lasting influence on his peers, then, was not in the persistence of his forms or styles—although his signature color persists in theatre memory, particularly in the lighting gel that bears his name: Roscolux R81 Urban Blue. But he was much more than a colorist. Urban reconceptualized the scenic designer as a type of celebrity artist-professional.

From Celebrity Journalism to Public Relations

The most insistent imitator of Urban's promotional style was Norman Bel Geddes. Like Urban, Bel Geddes seized the opportunities presented by a changing print media environment. Bel Geddes was, according to Innes, a "Napoleon of self-promotion [who] consciously constructed his own persona."[30] From his beginnings in stage design, Norman Bel Geddes became best known for industrial and exhibition design work in the thirties and forties and for developing the "streamlined" visual style. His stage work included a high-profile collaboration with Max Reinhardt in *The Miracle* (1924), for which Bel Geddes transformed New York's Century Theatre into a Gothic cathedral, audience and all. His significant Broadway productions included a self-directed *Hamlet* (1931) and *Dead End* (1935), written and directed by Sidney Kingsley. Bel Geddes was more widely known, however, for the objects and concepts that came out of his industrial design firm, Norman Bel Geddes & Company. The firm designed for IBM, Chrysler, Standard Gas, Ringling Brothers, and many other corporations. Its most famous works were the 1939 World's Fair exhibits for General Motors, *Futurama* and *Highways and Horizons*. These immersive exhibits displayed a model of the future, a United States of 1960 transformed by highways and motor vehicles, and together were one of the most well-attended attractions at the fair. Bel Geddes's concepts have been cited as a major influence on the US interstate highway system. His designs, some remaining unrealized, were his largest legacy, preserved in his books *Horizons* (1932) and *Magic Motorways* (1940).[31] By the end of his career, Bel Geddes had made his name as a designer of sleek products and possible futures, though his work connoted a much more middlebrow consumer sensibility than that of his Austrian predecessor.

Initially, Bel Geddes simply sought fame for himself, through the same sort of celebrity profiling Urban encouraged. The need to develop a public image roughly coincided with Norman Bel Geddes's shift from a predominantly theatrical design career to one based in industrial design. Such a concurrence is not surprising, as building a clientele for industrial designers depended on much more public and business community recognition than what the smaller New York–centered theatre market required. Before 1927, press about Bel Geddes tended to focus on specific projects, exhibitions, or designs completed. For instance, Kenneth Macgowan's 1924 feature "Introducing Mr. Geddes" used Bel Geddes's design for Max Reinhardt's *The Miracle* to provide audiences with a history of Bel Geddes's career. The closest Macgowan tacked to a discussion of personality came with a brief mention of Edward Gordon Craig—specifically, Bel Geddes's claimed independence from the British designer's theories. As was the case with many other features from this early phase of his career, the traditional approach was retrospective: it began with a current accomplishment and

2.5. Norman Bel Geddes. *Photo by Vandamm Studio.* ©*Billy Rose Theatre Division, The New York Public Library for the Performing Arts.*

then introduced the artist by narrating an artistic curriculum vitae from birth to the present day.[32]

Bel Geddes began to build his celebrity by appealing to broad interests. He wanted to be known in the press for more than his completed projects. Like Urban, he featured his face and his drawings, not merely his scenery. Early on, Bel Geddes drew satirical cartoons for *Vanity Fair*,[33] and beginning in 1925 he provided photographs and sketches of his face for publication. Comments on his appearance and manner began to appear at the start of feature articles, and large images of his face accompanied announcements of his presence at lectures or exhibitions. Only Bel Geddes and Urban engaged in this type of celebrity by face recognition. The

New Yorker caricatured him in 1925, and in 1927 Bel Geddes published his own cartoon self-portrait alongside a self-authored feature in a theatre program for the Broadhurst Theatre.[34] While other scenic designers only reluctantly allowed their images or caricatures to be printed—and often, only in theatrical outlets or New York–based society pages—Bel Geddes embraced placements of his image and images of his work in the mainstream press.[35]

By 1930 Bel Geddes was known for far more than stage design. He had designed floats and costumes for the Macy's Thanksgiving Day Parade in 1926, founded an industrial design office the following year, and was named an advisor to the architectural commission for the 1933 World's Fair. His public image was already carefully crafted; the 1929 press on the "War Game" cited near the start of this chapter is one such example. In 1930 Bel Geddes published versions of his designs for theatres of the Chicago World's Fair in the *New York Times Magazine*, and a feature article in *Fortune* magazine displayed his architectural and product drawings with the headline "Advertiser and Artist, a Portrait of Bel Geddes." In 1931 journalist Arthur Strawn's headline on another feature simply read, "Norman Bel Geddes, Jack of All Arts, Deserves Name of Genius."[36] Both of these features paired Bel Geddes's young, rakish face with his newest designs. He provided ample opportunities for new photographs to be taken, often posing at work over a model or a drawing. He kept photographs of his designs at all stages—drawing, model, and finished product—and readily provided these images for feature news written by others or by his office staff (with a Norman Bel Geddes byline, of course).

Once Bel Geddes decided to leave theatre design for industrial and product design, he developed new self-promotional strategies. The model of design celebrity he inherited from Urban was no longer sufficient to support a growing business network. Taking a page from corporate advertising, Bel Geddes began to engage in a conscious process of public relations to build his press image. Such construction was mostly managed by writers, editors, and managers hired for this purpose. When Bel Geddes first assembled an office for industrial design, he had already hired several associates, draftsmen, and secretaries to help with publicity work.[37] As the office grew, Bel Geddes maintained staff who collected his promotional press, managed articles "written" by Bel Geddes, and arranged for publicity around new and recent projects. In this way he emulated the architecture or advertising firm more so than the solo stage designer. Bel Geddes's office grew throughout the thirties, and by the forties he employed 150 workers. The enlarged staff allowed for specialization within the firm, and it also gave Bel Geddes the manpower to actively pursue a public relations strategy. Notably, his office was a pioneer in the use of public relations, and the approach of Bel Geddes, Inc., would soon be adopted by the rest of the "Big Four" industrial designers: Walter Dorwin Teague, Henry Dreyfuss, and Raymond Loewy.[38]

Norman Bel Geddes, Inc., maintained extensive clippings and promotional files that became the center of its public relations strategy. This archive held both finished copies of published materials, often from news clipping services, as well as prepublication materials from the firm's press relations office. In many cases Bel Geddes (or his staff) edited articles in colored pencil both pre- and postpublication; these edits generally cut words, creating slimmer, punchier prose. Geddes's edits resisted attempts to define his profession as anything other than simply a designer. He repeatedly crossed out the terms *industrial designer, scenic designer,* or *theatre designer* in advance copies of profiles and interviews because no qualifying term accurately described all of his work. On a *New York Times* review of his book *Horizons*, blue markings reduce the text "Norman Bel Geddes, stage designer, architect, and more recently an industrial and commercial designer" to "Norman Bel Geddes, designer, architect." A *New York Herald Tribune* profile later explained that "if any single word or phrase can sum up his manifold qualities, it is 'designer,' in the specialized sense that he is willing to undertake the sale of any bill of goods through decorative or artistic media."[39] The archive is unclear as to the purpose of these annotations. Some annotated copies are obviously advance copies of yet-to-be-printed material, but not all are. Since this was an active file for the publicity and sales departments, other articles, especially notable features such as those from the *New York Times* or *Fortune*, were likely edited and kept to guide later output.

His most direct self-promotion took the form of memoirs and feature articles. Released in 1932, *Horizons* outlined a possible, elegant future of American products and industry. It combined Bel Geddes's personal history with a hopeful, visionary view of transportation and modern life—and it sold the work of Norman Bel Geddes, Inc.[40] The operational practices of his office, in an archived employee manual dated 1945, indicated standardized, bureaucratic procedures for researching and outlining, for the management of Bel Geddes's edits and comments, and for the secure control of business information before, during, and after publication.[41] The company also made it standard practice to use the press to establish Bel Geddes's authority before approaching a new client. The press relations department would compile drawings and images from its files, then commission an article by an external hired writer to secure the company's place in the pages of a trade magazine the prospective client was likely to read. The firm's first in-person conversation with this client would refer back to the published article.[42] In the trades, many of these articles took the form of case studies, in which both the final product and the design process of the designer were discussed and documented.[43] Feature articles on Bel Geddes, in addition to case studies, began as early as 1928, and by 1932 Bel Geddes and his products had appeared both in trades (*Pencil Points, Product Engineering, Industrial Engineering, Modern Cinema Technique, Architecture*) and in the general press (*Fortune, Time, Christian Science Monitor, New York Herald Tribune, Today*).[44] Over the coming decades, many other design firms would follow Bel Geddes's example.

In thinking about the legacy of the designer in the press, it's useful to distinguish between celebrity journalism and public relations. Bel Geddes engaged in both, but Urban was primarily a figure of celebrity, and he did not engage in much formal public relations. Typically, public relations are managed business functions, undertaken either internally by a firm (as Bel Geddes did) or by some contracted external entity. This differs from celebrity journalism, which is simply the practice of reporting on the lives of the famous, often in a private setting. In the case of celebrities, the two functions have become blurred; in the twenties as well as today, celebrities did hire publicists to manage relationships with the press, especially to pitch features, interviews, and photo sessions. However, the discipline of public relations was founded by agents such as Edward Bernays to promote his clients to businesses, not to individuals. The main differences between the two fields remain in place today, in both the audience sought (business contacts versus the lay public) and in the high degree of planning and overt promotional behavior of public relations.[45]

Further complications emerge in the case of applied artists, who may at once be a celebrity themselves and the head of their own business. For instance, Urban was a famous artist and the head of his own small architectural office, and Bel Geddes was a well-known designer and the head of a large design firm. Were they engaged in celebrity journalism, public relations, or both? Urban sought celebrity journalism but did not engage in public relations. Many of the profiles he authorized helped him attract high-status clients and maintain his air of exclusivity. He attracted work through personal contacts, and his life can be tracked through society pages. Urban did not hire his own press agency. Bel Geddes began his career in the same way, but his work on corporate products soon led his firm to engage in overt public relations practices. Bel Geddes was especially familiar with the need to design desirable products and to stimulate consumer desire. He participated in public relations efforts, then, on two fronts: to sell his own design services to companies and clients, and also to sell his designed products to consumers. At the same time, he encouraged celebrity journalism, as he himself became the face of his own company brand.

Once Urban and Bel Geddes changed the self-promotional image of the designer, others followed. Few, however, would be as bombastic or systematic as Bel Geddes's in-house public relations machine. Perhaps because scenic designers did not have large firms to support or seek to gain national corporate clientele, they let fame come to them. They capitalized on their position as modest celebrities when possible. Around 1930 Lee Simonson began to broaden his design expertise by making window displays for Macy's and writing *The Stage Is Set*, a book of scenic design history and theory. This accompanied his own increasing celebrity, as seen in several articles in general readership newspapers explaining the job of scenic designers and the difficulties they faced.[46] In both these efforts, Simonson managed his own press. With the exception of other stage designers who turned to industrial work, such as Henry Dreyfuss, scenic designers tended to remain in theatrical circles. Nonetheless, attention to the scenic designer as a possible figure of public interest provided Simonson and others a platform on which to advocate for their own new professional standing. In doing so, they harkened back to Urban's and Bel Geddes's careers, as well as to the fields from which Urban and Bel Geddes drew their inspiration: architecture and advertising.

Architecture and Advertising as Professional Models

The self-promotional wave in the theatrical press of the thirties was inspired by larger trends toward celebrity and public relations in the applied arts fields of architecture and advertising.[47] These two fields' attitudes toward self-promotion raised questions of professionalism. Is it ethical for professional architects to promote their work? Can an advertiser advertise? Urban and Bel Geddes created their celebrity journalism and public relations strategies from their knowledge of these related fields.

They charted new modes of self-presentation that were foreign to stage design but were rapidly becoming commonplace in industrial design and advertising. Architecture, too, started to embrace self-promotion, though it was slower to do so because of its longer history as an elite profession. One question remained at the forefront of these disciplines' professional claims, however. For applied artists and designers, what amount of celebrity press or self-promotional activity was appropriate?

Architecture was the most reserved and traditional of the applied art professions, largely because of its historical development. In the United States, architecture's first national association was founded in 1857, state licensing of architects began in 1897, and the first school of architecture was founded at the Massachusetts Institute of Technology.[48] Moves to consolidate the strength of the profession in the early twentieth century included the creation of the American Institute of Architects (AIA) and the beginning of reciprocal agreements between state licensing boards.[49] Most important, however, was American architects' reliance on the French École des Beaux-Arts model of the profession, which saw architecture as a lofty pursuit, built on high aesthetic ideals and inherent class separation from construction workers.[50] The architectural product was meant to be beautiful as well as functional, and both schools and professional organizations emphasized that architecture's true aim straddled the aesthetic and the practical.[51] As individuals with the necessary knowledge, class privilege, and resources to provide aesthetically pleasing buildings, architects enjoyed the most thorough professional organization of applied arts fields in the United States during the interwar period.[52]

American architects viewed professionalism within fairly narrow constraints. American architectural training taught students to work as building designers only, and within concepts of professional decorum. Schools instituted fundamentally conservative values of aesthetics, public service, and self-sacrifice, especially in those that used Beaux-Arts pedagogy. The hierarchy of the architecture firm also structured professional ideology. Salaried workers in firms saw themselves as middlebrow professional workers, while the owners and partners of firms claimed a high professional class status similar to other artistic, legal, or medical elites. (This was especially true of architects in large cities.) Independent practice was a career goal, either in partnership or individually; this model encouraged younger architects to envision themselves within a professional ideological framework.[53] Finally, codes of ethics banned competitive business practices. Ethics codes, first adopted by the AIA in 1909, enforced norms by sanctioning and even fining errant members. One of most notorious banned practices was commercial self-promotion, either by giving discounted or free advisory work or by disseminating advertising material or images.[54]

A ban on advertising and self-promotion protected architecture's careful balance between business and fine arts, but this would change over the twentieth century. In the nineteenth century, ethical code bans on architectural advertising attempted to rein in the then-common practice of firms garnering business by distributing pamphlets, sketches, and advertisements.[55] Under the ideology of professionalism, good work was meant to be its own reward, and successful architecture alone led to further clients and commissions.[56] In the twenties, though, architectural press was permissible, so long as it was directed at the profession and fairly critiqued or explained notable work; such articles were commonplace in the journals *Architectural Record* and *Pencil Points*. Promotion directed toward the public remained distasteful. Restrictions further lessened by midcentury, as architecture recovered from the Depression and the professional ideal shifted from the Beaux-Arts model to a more business-minded, managerial view of the architect.[57] Architect and historian Peggy Deamer notes that distrust of overly commercial business practices remains today.[58] Serious architects, in the view of the AIA, and with a few notable "starchitect" exceptions, avoid creating a "brand," "persona," or other marketing of their business.[59] Urban and Bel Geddes, neither one trained in the tradition of American architecture, did not abide by such standards.

Many scenic designers saw a natural link between the work of the architect and that of the theatrical designer. For one, there was a strong historical link between the two in European practice, since many influential stage designers were also known for their nontheatrical architecture.[60] Scenic designers worked in a manner similar to architects—at some supervisory remove from construction—and produced similar types of drafted design documentation. Scenic designers also aspired to the prestige of architecture. At the time, architecture continued to fashion itself as a pursuit of elites and was still perceived to be a "gentleman's profession" for those from wealthy backgrounds.[61] It was dually removed from commerce and from manual labor, especially for those influenced by the Beaux-Arts training model. Architects considered public taste in their designs, but they sold their work to clients rather than directly to the public. Designers found this professional remove attractive, and so they attempted to adopt the labor model of the practicing architect. They made studios that looked like those of architects, sought fee-based payment instead of wages, and regarded themselves as the heads of small independent firms, sometimes assisted by staff. Scenic designers also cultivated the same cultural biases that architects had developed: suspicion of overt self-promotion, subservience to the client's wishes (here, the producer), and a freelance professional identity centered on the studio and its accompanying sketches, blueprints, and models. In these ways, scenic designers adjusted their studio working environment to make it analogous to architecture's.

The other professional model for designers came from advertising. Unlike architecture, advertising (along with illustration and graphic design practiced in advertising) had comparatively little professional organization. Advertising executives similarly sought greater autonomy over their work in the twenties, and they longed for professionalization. Roland Marchand, historian of American advertising, has identified two divergent models that mirror the changing professional ideas in architecture. One saw advertising as a potentially elite pursuit and supported the development of schools, a service outlook, and ethical standards. Another set of advertisers, drawn predominantly from business, argued that modern professional advertising should be focused entirely on the client, which could best be achieved by maximizing profits. In this second model, discussions of service ideals or aesthetics took time away from maximizing sales and keeping an eye fixed on client needs.[62] Over time, advertising moved away from the older model of elite professional practice and began to embrace sales, client service, and managerial thinking.

One notable element of advertising's self-promotion is its "dual audience" perspective. Marchand notes that one of the distinctive aspects of advertising is the way in which it must appeal to two audiences simultaneously: the client and the public. The client pays for the advertiser's services, so a significant component of an advertising firm's energy should be dedicated to sales to clients and to building relationships with client businesses. However, successful advertising—and therefore the likelihood of holding on to a client business long-term—is dependent on the public at large. This created two "theatres" in which advertising firms worked: one "inside" the business world and another facing the public. Advertisers bragged of their effectiveness in trade and business publications but presented a more naïve front to consumers.[63] Such "tricks of the trade" are elements of professional groups, Marchand notes, and the dual-audience situation is most prevalent in advertising and promotional occupations.

How could an advertising firm promote its effectiveness to one set of clients, while keeping its trade secrets unknown to the public?

A dual-audience situation also confronted scenic designers. Audience response determined whether a show would run or close, yet scenic designers mostly sold their services to producers and directors. New Stagecraft designers attempted to demonstrate that their more modern style of design was a worthwhile investment for a production. However, they only needed to promote their appeal as a designer for hire within the theatrical press. As a result, trade- and art-focused magazines such as *Theatre Arts Monthly* or *Variety* discussed a designer's working life and the economics of theatrical production much earlier than general-interest periodicals. When designers did talk about their own work, many attempted to link architecture's professional remove with advertising's consideration of multiple audiences. Therefore, the scenic design profile is at once a piece of personal celebrity (or near-celebrity) journalism and also a document of the ambivalences many designers felt about their newly professional occupation.

Shared Values in the Scenic Design Profile

By the 1930s both Urban and Bel Geddes designed for the theatre much less frequently. Their press continued, but it mostly reported on their nontheatrical design work. Other designers, though, picked up where they had left off. Around 1930 the theatrical press regularly mentioned the names of around ten scenic designers. This consolidation of the field was due to the decreased availability of high-paying commercial scenic design jobs between 1930 and 1934 and the closed-shop policies enforced by USA Local 829.[64] In the 1934–1936 seasons, for instance, Jo Mielziner would open as many as eleven Broadway shows in a single season, alongside other projects. Since five to eight designers were getting most of the available work, feature articles emerged that promoted multiple shows by the same designer. While the previous decade had seen more variation among designers, and less press on each individual, the combined effects of the tightened market and of the change in the media environment around scenic designers created a small group of designers who shared similar contacts and working methods.

Scenic design profiles in the thirties departed from criticism of stagecraft and design as an artwork and moved toward a celebrity- and labor-based discourse. Profiles first appeared in theatre-focused periodicals like *Theatre Arts* but quickly expanded to other New York City–based magazines of general interest such as the *New Yorker* and to newspapers including the *Times* and *Herald Tribune*. Journalists pointed out the prevalence of new billing lines such as "Settings by Mielziner," a byline that one reviewer noted "has been repeated so many times in so many different theatre programs . . . that some account of this young scene designer may be interesting to theatregoers weary of reading about actors."[65] Similar acknowledgments of the ubiquity of designers' work can be seen in articles about Donald Oenslager and Lee Simonson. Sometimes editors or reporters penned articles focused on scenic design as a part of their publications' regular theatre coverage; in other instances, designers themselves submitted opinion pieces for newspaper publication.[66] Lee Simonson frequently published his ideas on theatre economics in the *New York Times* in the early 1930s, while Jo Mielziner penned articles on theatre architecture in the forties. Another frequent type of feature described designers together, introducing a new class of artists. In these articles, critics not only compared the designers' work but also contrasted their working styles, choices of material, and even their studio environments.[67] In the later thirties and early forties, naming, describing, and interviewing a cohort of scenic designers became a subtheme in Broadway-focused theatrical press for the first time.

In these features, artists responded to the celebrity they saw around them by introducing scenic design to the theatergoing public. Designers explained their specialized design labor and its complexity, and they advocated for fair compensation. Journalists and critics agreed and began to discuss designing as another type of professional activity. For instance, in the middle of an interview article on Donald Oenslager, sympathetic stage manager and critic Norris Houghton constructed an image of seven designers busy at work, scattered throughout the city, working with shared purpose:

This business of "setting a show" which has been described as Donald Oenslager's method is one which every designer working in the New York theatre practices. It has been outlined in detail this once because it has seemed unnecessary to repeat it all with each designer discussed. For while Oenslager is rooting through a property shop on Forty-Third Street, Robert Edmond Jones is no doubt searching for a Victorian urn, Lee Simonson is selecting chintz, Jo Mielziner is going through an auction house in the Forties or an antique shop in the East Fifties hot on the trail of a French Empire bed, Raymond

Sovey is doubtless on the paint frame at Bergman's Studio, Mordecai Gorelik is shouting above the noise of a saw at one or another construction company, and Stewart Chaney is pinning velvet at a costumer's. Their paths will cross and recross as they go on their way plying the craft, for their paths lead them all to the same doors. . . . These designers are men who do more than handle a camel's-hair brush or a scale rule.[68]

Houghton presented this digression in the fourth installment of an eight-part interview series in *Theatre Arts Monthly*. Houghton had proposed a series on designers to follow the journal's series on directors at work, and he took it upon himself to interview designers, report on their methods, and contrast their working lives. The last line quoted above—these "men . . . do more than handle a camel's-hair brush or a scale rule"—can be read as Houghton's own description of designers' heightened class standing. In this digression, he draws attention to designers' ability to manage diverse types of work and to supervise scenic painters and carpenters. In Houghton's writing, and in other multi-production features on designers in the thirties, the claim that designers did "more than" others helped justify the creation of an elite professional group.

When they were profiled or interviewed, scenic designers did not phrase their contribution as Houghton did. Mostly they struck a balance between the celebrity of Urban and Bel Geddes and workmanlike anonymity. They acknowledged the particular skills of the designer and enjoyed the fleeting celebrity offered by the feature. They used the interview feature to explain their labor and perhaps attempted to increase their public acclaim; some may have imagined they could ask for a higher fee on their next contract. At the same time, though, they did not linger in the spotlight; most preferred simply to get on with their work. Designers managed their ambivalence over dual-audience marketing by creating a sort of rhetorical middle space. This middle, wedged between craft and artistry, allowed designers to cultivate name recognition, but they never completely abandoned the idea that they were working for higher ideals of the theatre: the play, the concept, the director. Four main themes recurred in this new discourse of the middle space. Each theme was taken up by more than one designer, which suggests an emerging shared ideology among the small cohort of designers at the forefront of the field. Furthermore, they all implicitly supported freelance professional ideals. Their shared themes can be summarized as the themes of the craftsman-worker, the reflective practitioner, the self-abnegating artist, and the working day.

The first theme—that the scenic designer was predominantly a hybrid craftsman-worker of the theatre—was most commonly expressed by Donald Oenslager, who wrote it into his design curriculum at Yale. Oenslager called the scenic designer "not a decorator, a painter, or an architect . . . [but] a craftsman possessing a working knowledge of all these arts." In his view it was important to distinguish the new scenic design from previous applied art fields by appealing to its assemblage of necessary skills. This view was not limited to the classroom lecture, though. Robert Edmond Jones similarly referred to the scenic designer as a "jack-of-all-trades . . . an artist of occasions," one who can be called on to apply any number of ancillary arts—decoration, upholstery, sculpture, sewing, metalwork, painting, or interior decorating.[69] For Oenslager and Jones, the notable quality of scenic designers was not that they excelled in any one art but that they possessed generalized expertise across art fields, combined with sufficient competence in both arts and trades.

As all of these themes do, the craftsman-worker theme upheld the values of professionalism. It emphasized that scenic design was not fine artistry, nor was it primarily technical as scene painting had been characterized in the past. By emphasizing arrangement and vision over the essential practice of any one art skill (drawing, painting, drafting, etc.), designers claimed a more abstract basis for design work than the pure arts, crafts, and trades. Because the work of designers like Oenslager and Jones was based on discretion and expert managerial skills, discussion of the designer as a craftsman-worker or "artist of occasions" also privileged the intangible qualities of design work. The separation from the visual fine arts was particularly strategic; painters and sculptors accustomed to solo work and gallery exhibitions often fared poorly when they tried to transfer to Broadway, precisely because they lacked practicality in their designs and the ability to collaborate well with backstage workers. Insistence on the dual nature of design allowed scenic designers to differentiate scenic design from other theatrical arts, and this foundation supported their later claims to a separate, elevated status through professionalization.

With respect to the second theme, the reflective practitioner, designers interviewed for features were reluctant to lay claim to having any set method of working. "How do you work?" was frequently the first question interviewers asked them, yet rarely did a satisfying answer follow. Rather, designers refuted the premise or went on to talk about their latest design without claiming that the procedures used on that project were indicative of a general method. The reasons for their reluctance to discuss their working method varied by designer, but most reasons aligned with ideas of professionalism. For one, the reluctance to explain method was a way of protecting expertise; as members of a growing professional group, they had an interest in maintaining control over their practices. For another, some designers saw themselves first as artists, especially Jones but also Bel Geddes, and so they interpreted their work as predominantly creative and therefore resistant to any statement of basic principles or methods.[70] Other designers who did follow a more regular pattern of stages in their process, such as Lee Simonson or Jo Mielziner, still refused to characterize their work in any systematic way because each script or production might call for a different working method.

The "no set methods" theme might be seen as an expression of learning theorist and philosopher Donald Schön's "reflective practice," a shared characteristic of many professional fields. Rather than applying a procedure or set of tasks to a given work process, Schön has argued, professionals distinguish themselves by the application of expert judgment and a history of practice to impose order on indeterminate situations.[71] A professional diagnoses a problem and determines the best treatment or course of action and then provides that service based on skills and experience. No set methods exist because each instance of professional practice is a "conversation" between a problematic situation and a skilled practitioner.[72] As professional rhetoric, it was advantageous for designers to point to the indeterminacy of their practice. Like the craftsman-worker theme, claiming to have no set method allowed designers to occupy a middle ground between craftsman and artist, and between tradesman and white-collar professional. To preserve this hybridity, many scenic designers avoided explaining their methods and instead claimed that their work responded to the needs of the play, their expertise and background, and creativity.

The third theme derived from the beginning of the New Stagecraft movement. Design historian Orville K. Larson identified a shared "theory of self-abnegation," that is, the tendency of designers to decline attention paid to them for their work.[73] Instead designers position their work as being at the service of the playwright and the production. Lee Simonson wrote in 1932 that the designer was a "necessary workman . . . as one interpreter of the script," and Robert Edmond Jones wrote that after the set was created, both designer and set itself ought to recede so that the actors, playwright, and story could become the audience's main focus.[74] Other designers similarly placed their work "below" that of playwright, director, and actors in their interviews. In a period when novel designs and celebrity designers were emergent, designers' first impulse was often to reject praise.

Perhaps more importantly, though, from the perspective of professionalism, a stance of self-abnegation allowed designers to claim that their work was a type of service. Though their products may be beautiful, even art in themselves, the designers who created them were simply doing their job. Such a stance distinguished the applied nature of scenic art from the visual fine arts, and it also subtly made scenic design necessary through its integrated effacement. If designers' work is only one component of a playwright's vision, a subsidiary art to the main art of theatrical playmaking, then scenic designers were providing a needed service. Service, as chapter 4 details, justifies professions' claims to a privileged status in society by subordinating professions to a higher good and to societal need.

Finally, as a fourth theme, in several self-promotional features and interviews, designers discussed the work of the designer in day-to-day, minute-to-minute terms. In speaking of their working day, they often emphasized the many simultaneous and various responsibilities of scenic designers and the exhaustion those tasks produced. Robert Edmond Jones was known for his tendency to scour shops for fabric and antique props, and Lee Simonson and Jo Mielziner stressed the amount of travel and coordination required of a designer to manage his own studio, attend technical rehearsals, visit shops, and complete other supervisory duties.[75] This theme was most frequently presented in theatre-focused periodicals, such as *Theatre Arts Monthly*, though both Simonson and Mielziner explained their daily working lives in the *New York Times* as well, when they felt that the wider public ought to sympathize with the scenic designer's workaday life.

When they elaborated on this theme, designers emphasized the managerial quality of the designer's labor, and they attempted to dispel the assumption that scenic designers simply worked at a drafting table fulltime.[76] The new model of designing was of a freelancer on the go, caught between appointments and rehearsals and openings and their own studio work on the next production. The discussion of the uptown-downtown nature of new design work—rehearsals and shops in midtown, perhaps a studio uptown, shopping downtown—aligned designers with a middle-class, professional-managerial identity. By giving an account of the working day of the freelancer, scenic designers showed that their work exceeded the tasks of a trade illustrator, painter, or artist. They likened their work to other types of applied art or to the self- or firm-employed workers of advertising or architecture.

The four themes in the rhetoric of scenic design labor each supported ideologies of professionalism and aligned scenic design with other emergent applied art professions. Architectural historian Andrew Shanken argues that it was architecture's "uncertain status in the period—somewhere between a profession and a trade" that caused architects' hybrid self-concept: as being "artist or craftsman, engineer or technician, doctor or scientist, manager and businessman."[77] While the dual status of architecture and scenic design are related, the uncertain professional status in scenic design was both a liability and an opportunity. Many designers positioned their work as a unique and essential link between the paired polarities Shanken enumerates: artist/craftsman, engineer/technician, manager/businessman. By doing so, scenic designers could claim the privileges of artistic creativity and the benefits of professional organization without fully sacrificing their connections to trade work.

Such in-between placement required a delicate balance of ideas. Artistry became tempered with managerial functions. Designers took on more responsibility for planning and supervising designs and also became responsible for managing their own small businesses. These new managerial concerns prompted designers to talk about their work differently. For instance, in a 1937 *Stage* magazine article, a critic blamed rising production costs on the bidding process, in which producers negotiate building costs with scenic studios, overseen by the designer. "With the bargaining over," the writer continued, "the designer gets back into his smock; but always with it he must wear the executive's brass hat."[78] Once designers picked up the work of the manager and executive, caring about cost and promotions as well as the artistry of the matter, they could not put it back down.

Counterpoint: Transparency and the "Open Secret"

Not all scenic design profiles express the same ideas, however. Comparisons of feature articles on designers whose work spanned this period reveal important differences in their degrees of transparency. Some designers, such as Simonson, only became more public over time in their mobilization of persona. Others, such as Robert Edmond Jones, permitted feature articles and celebrity early in their careers, but they stepped back in the thirties and gave vague answers to interviewers.

Twenties-era profiles of Robert Edmond Jones, for instance, reprinted photographs of his drawings and detailed Jones's biography. In the *New Republic* and *Theatre Arts*, critics Oliver Saylor and Kenneth Macgowan placed Jones's production of nonrealist scenic designs in the context of early twenties "new movement" aesthetics of plasticity and abstraction. By contrast, in 1931, the *New Yorker* found a reluctant Jones: "In a profession notorious for its quick intimacies, in a period of self-exploitation and bally-hoo, Robert Edmond Jones, a master of the theatre and a man profoundly at home in his age, has chosen to live quietly, almost obscurely."[79]

The profile press of Lee Simonson provides a stark contrast. Early profiles simply connected him to the growing New Stagecraft movement and to Jones's and Urban's modernist innovations. Later, Simonson gave many more interviews, and he often turned articles about his work into attempts to theorize scenic design. "Scenery is really a plan of action," Simonson opined in 1923; "the scenery must direct and canalize that movement."[80] In 1929 he added the designer's role to the mix, writing that "the function of stage scenery, and hence the job of the scene designer, is . . . to stimulate the kind of seeing which is believing."[81] Soon Simonson became a subject of interest in and of himself—not only for his theories or for his designs but also for his pugnacious, activist stance toward design labor.[82]

This section counterpoints the celebrity inherent in designers' profiles by highlighting designers who resisted the pull of the profile genre. Simonson took it upon himself to advocate for designers through transparency, challenging the profile by transforming it into a work of labor activism. On the other hand, Jones and fellow designer James Reynolds chose discretion, obscuring their labor and avoiding celebrity-style profiles.

After Simonson succeeded in his advocacy for designers' rights within the union (see chapter 1), he transformed himself into an advocate for designers in print. In the early thirties, he opined on the reemergence of touring on the road, on the economic risks of Broadway production in the Depression, and on the reluctance of scenic designers to exhibit or otherwise document their designs in 1932 and 1934.[83] A series of letters between Simonson and producer Brock Pemberton published in the *New York Times* illustrate Simonson's later approach. Pemberton's January 1933 editorial singled out scenic artists and designers for "demand[ing] minimum fees that are ruinous."[84] One week following Pemberton's letter, the *Times* published Simonson's reply, in which he detailed the necessary components of a design, the on-call, frenetic process of sourcing props and supervising construction and painting. "For from four to six weeks of the most grueling and nerve-wracking kind of work he gets the 'ruinous' minimum ... which is slightly less than the weekly salary of a competent press agent, and about equal to the salary of a second-line actor or the weekly pocket money needed by a first-line manager when north of Havana."[85] To bolster his point, Simonson connected the dire straits of the designer making minimum fees to systemic exploitation within the theatre industry.[86] If costs were going up, it was not because designers got paid too much; it was because producers shared too little of their profits. Reorganization would not be done by the "Big Laissez-faire boys" of theatre production, he argued, but only by a national overhaul of theatre's profit-making motives.

Simonson's eloquent defense of artistic labor punctured Pemberton's inflated rhetoric while inadvertently illustrating the particular economic problems of professionalism. He was the only New Stagecraft designer to publish the daily costs of his work, down to the cab rides and the rent he paid for his working studio. To advocate for the professional designer meant, for Simonson, showing how one designer really worked and then leaving it to the reader to determine whether the seemingly ruinous compensation was fair once his expenses and duties were considered. Simonson felt that transparency might be effective politics; by standing up for his own work, and presenting his daily life in the papers, Simonson attempted to turn his celebrity into new professional advocacy. This exchange was the only time Simonson published his business finances in the *Times*, though. Apparently, his dollars-and-cents argumentation was not the persuasive strategy he imagined it to be outside theatre circles.

Simonson's candor is set in relief by other designers' reluctance to speak about work. For instance, Robert Edmond Jones was comparatively silent on his labor. Earlier in his career, before his name had become familiar, Jones was more inclined to weigh in on matters of technique, coining concepts (the artist must "make his work unobtrusive") and standing up for the value of his self-consciously theatrical design style.[87] After 1930 Jones said little about how he worked or how he created his art, in stark contrast to his philosophically inclined lectures. Jones was occasionally profiled, but he took to this outlet less enthusiastically. Gilbert Seldes found his reticence unsurprising since "to Jones, brought up in the silent intimacies and the silent animosities of rural New England, there is nothing extraordinary in this lack of words."[88] As press on designers increased, Jones's career was beginning to wane, and he never felt the need to share personal details or or explanations of why or how a particular set design worked. In a 1936 interview, Jones redirected interviewer Norris Houghton to consider not his methods or his labor but the "essence" of the designer. "The important things are the deeper ones, things that have to do with our ideas about the theatre. . . . [Y]ou must try to extract the essence of each of us."[89] Houghton admitted to being "magnetized by a kind of electrical discharge" from Jones, the theatrical visionary. But Jones's methods did not make it into the article.

This reservedness can be conceived of as both an accurate reflection of Jones's approach to art and perhaps as its own media strategy. Jones repeatedly remarked that his designs come "all at once," rather than through architectural logic and stepwise planning, as Simonson worked.[90] Given his background as a costumer and multidisciplinary designer, this is not surprising. It may also be that Jones preferred to view art as separate from concerns of labor and economics. Jones was, by all accounts, economically well-off and making a living in stage design. He showed relatively little interest in teaching except through apprenticeships, especially early in his career. Nor did he call for economic reform of the theatre; where money matters impinged on his design process, they were to be attacked with creative thinking and artistic solutions—a new style, a simplified line—not institutional reform. In his press Jones repeatedly reframed questions of method or labor as questions of theory or vision, and by so doing he maintained his poetic outlook. Because of his transitional position in scenic design history—a career largely built in the late teens and early twenties, before profiles helped catapult designers' careers, and a career largely built off-Broadway rather than on—Jones avoided the creation of a persona.

The dissimilarities between Jones's press and those of other designers may stem from the somewhat-open secret of his homosexuality. Rumors of Jones's orientation were common among his acquaintances and have been examined by scholars as well. Jane T. Peterson has argued that Jones's latent homosexuality plagued his professional life and can be seen in the incompleteness and disorder of the Jones archive, expurgated posthumously by his family and executors. This point of view is disputed by Christin Essin, who has suggested that tension over professionalization or the open life of Greenwich Village, not his sexuality, is what led to Jones's truncated personal relationships with other designers.[91] Although the matter of Jones's sexuality is likely not a fully determinant factor in his professional history, the emergence of the scenic designer magazine profile would have added new pressure to be personally vulnerable. Did the new self-promotional style of scenic design journalism select against those who did not want to share personal details with the press?

In his resistance to self-promotion, Jones's career counterpoints the narrative of scenic design celebrity and self-promotion in this chapter. In this, Jones is similar to another designer who is largely omitted from New Stagecraft histories, James Reynolds. Reynolds was a costume and scenic designer who, early in the movement, was frequently mentioned along with Jones and Simonson and who provided designs for Ziegfeld alongside Urban's more well-known creations. Reynolds was also an out gay man in theatrical circles, and he never married as Jones did. Jones and Reynolds resisted the profile's prying eyes, and both ended up with less robust careers in the thirties.

In the early 1920s, Reynolds's work was well publicized on the pages of *Theatre Arts Monthly*. His costumes and sets appeared onstage in the early 1920s in John Murray Anderson revues. John Peale Bishop touted Reynolds's promise in the January 1921 issue of *Theatre Arts* as "the youngest among the moderns," and he lamented that unlike Jones, whose alliance with Eugene O'Neill and Kenneth Macgowan boosted much of his early work, Reynolds had not yet found a signature creative partnership.[92] Reynolds was not interested in such an alliance and instead gravitated toward dance and revue designs. By 1921 Reynolds had already completed two full sets of costumes for the Greenwich Village Follies and was under exclusive contract with Ziegfeld for 1923 and 1924.[93] He was critiqued again in two issues of *Theatre Arts Monthly* in 1924, which included images of his renderings for Rostand's play *L'Aiglon*. Reynolds's renderings feature costumed figures either against a blank background or in relationship to a scenic piece. His lines are broad, nearly cartoonish, exaggerating detail. Both costume and scenic renderings show a high degree of contrast, using very dark and very light shading in the same figure or compositional element. Reynolds was particularly drawn to Romantic themes, and frequently he worked with symbolic elements in his designs or represented mythic Greece or Ireland.

Living as an out gay man was probably a liability for Reynolds, whereas Jones's more conservative approach to his personal life—and his better-connected network—afforded him more success. In comparison with Jones, Reynolds's work in the twenties is less easily traced by theater historians because he often worked across genre and geography. Reynolds became the art director of the Ram's Head Players in Washington, DC, in 1924, a position he held for several years but one for which he received little press in New York City. Like design peers Norman Bel Geddes and Lee Simonson, Reynolds also allied himself with direct sales to department stores; in 1926 he licensed his costumes for reproduction and sale through Lord & Taylor and the Brooks Costume Company. A hundred costumes from his string of recent Broadway successes were displayed, made into a line, and distributed nationally.[94] He designed a series of five productions for Charles Dillingham in 1926 and 1927. As most of Reynolds's work was for commercial Broadway productions, and the art theatres with which he was associated were neither in New York nor particularly innovative, Reynolds's significant contributions to scenic design in the twenties (at least thirty productions between 1919 and 1930, by Orville Larson's count, and likely more) made him a familiar name in the arts pages more than the theatre magazines.

Reynolds's life involved several more turns. In 1933 Reynolds felt that he was "beginning to repeat himself" and left the profession for Europe. He spent the last twenty years of his life living an eclectic life: traveling, "judging horse shows, staying with the very rich or grand while he painted their horses on the walls of castles or country houses."[95] He designed textiles and lectured on interior architecture trends, and he wrote and illustrated several books on horses, the ghosts of Ireland, and fiction of his own. Most of these books were published between 1945 and his death in 1957. Reynolds was in a terrible car accident the year before his death that left him immobile and in pain. He died by suicide, according to his friend and fellow costume designer Millia Davenport. His *New York Times* obituary referred almost exclusively to his accomplishments in publishing and illustration; his theatrical and textile work was only mentioned in a final sentence.[96]

The timing of Reynolds's departure from the field was like that of other artists whose love affair with artistic expression in the experimental twenties became hard to sustain during the Depression. Although Reynolds did some Broadway commercial work, he preferred to work as a relatively autonomous artist, as Jones did too later in life. This explains his penchant for ballet and pantomime, art forms, he said, that "aim above all for a visual effect. It thus provides the surest inspiration for the designer." A Broadway musical designer, he noted in 1928, "encounters an intolerably intelligent point of view" in the audience and even in collaborators, which obstructs the designer's fancy."[97] After Reynolds left New York, he spent several years living with "the gorgeous son of a Scandinavian sardine king," whom Reynolds met while the son was studying in the United States. Davenport recalls that "his and Jimmy's friendship lasted his lifetime. He needed an heir, married a German baroness and had a son; Jimmy was his godfather, and they all lived together until the Scandinavian died."[98] Reynolds was provided for in his friend's will by a trust that employed Reynolds as a tutor for young European artists. Reynolds's pursuit of alternative artistic venues came to overshadow his contributions to performance design, and his identity as a gay artist probably closed doors. His work was primarily in non-text-based performance, and this too has made his archival traces hard to recover.

James Reynolds's name was often included in lists of designers working in the twenties, yet full articles on Reynolds were scarce outside *Theatre Arts Monthly*. Reynolds's departure from the union and the field of scenic design occurred in the early thirties, the same period when more overt self-promotion was becoming prevalent. Reynolds was not famous or well connected enough to be profiled in the *New Yorker*, nor did he seek out a defining role in the union or in education. Such a path is not less worthy or effective, though it is more difficult to pinpoint than the well-publicized careers of Bel Geddes or Simonson. As the years passed, those designers who discussed their careers defined the profession, at least to the lay reader. Those designers who, because of either disposition or social prejudice, were reluctant to share a version of their "selves" on the page had less access to media as a tool of professional development.

Conclusion

Through self-promotion, designers leveraged aspects of celebrity to highlight what made themselves and their work special. Through feature articles and photography, readers learned that scenic designers were partially responsible for successful theatrical productions. It was no longer uncommon for a designer to take top billing in a newspaper or magazine feature, especially for a particularly spectacular production. While scenic spectacle had previously been attributed to a producer-director like David Belasco, and only secondarily to the producer's staff designer, after the thirties designers came to be seen as creative authors. Feature press began in newspapers such as the *New York Times* and the *Herald Tribune* and spread to other outlets across the nation. Designers and their work were profiled in the *New Yorker*, highlighted in *Scientific American*, and discussed on the pages of *Vanity Fair* and *Mademoiselle*.[99] Those designers who actively promoted their work across fields, extending beyond the theatre to include industrial or product design or film art direction, garnered the most recognition. Self-promotional press also allowed this group of designers to take control of the market for scenic design, since in-demand celebrity designers contributed to increased ticket sales.

After World War II, feature articles on design continued to be published, but there was no longer such a pressing need to "sell" theatrical design to the public. Most younger designers seemed to prefer Jones's self-abnegation to Bel Geddes's bombastic self-promotion. The main elements of designers' self-promotional writing after 1950 included the occasional self-authored article in *Theatre Arts* or *Educational Theatre Journal*, or the single or group profile after a major production or season.[100] Drawings and production photographs continued to decorate the pages of trades like *Theatre Arts* throughout the 1950s, but designers wrote far less frequently than they had in the previous decades. Simonson, Mielziner, and Oenslager did continue to publish books collecting their work, but designers who came after them have generally not published their memoirs.[101]

Promotion of designers by others remained a part of the media landscape. Features had become a common article genre, and managing one's profile was an important part of a designer's professional practice, even though by the fifties a designer's reputation in the field was more important than name recognition by the public. A survey of articles illustrates that designers were still readily furnishing photographs, drawings, and sometimes self-portraits for reproduction in newspapers. For example, several *New York Times* features in the late fifties published images of scenic designers at work (Jo Mielziner, Donald Oenslager, Howard Bay, Peter Larkin, Boris Aronson, and Raymond Sovey) alongside their drawings or models.[102] Features periodically highlighted postwar designers such as Oliver Smith (*My Fair Lady, West Side Story*), William and Jean Eckart (*Mame, Damn Yankees*), and Ming Cho Lee.[103] In interviews these designers discussed the particular challenges of scenic design, the difference between fine arts painting and applied theatrical designing, and their opinions on the state of Broadway. It is notable how little they make a case for designers' authority or labor. Later designers already had models for expert authority, freelance artistry, and self-promotional press, and many designers simply operated within that framework.

Self-promotional publication in newspapers, magazines, and books was an occasion for designers to demonstrate their expertise. It afforded designers recognition separate from any single production or working relationship. Publication also allowed them to specify the types of work designers did as distinctive from other creative acts in the theatre. The specification of knowledge took place in other venues, as well, notably in university design programs. As the next chapter explains, designers taught these skills to students at the same time as they promoted them to the public in the media. Book publication, in particular, was often aimed dually at students and at interested theatre audiences. Affiliation with universities was one of the most enduring legacies of scenic design professionalization, mostly due to the institutional permanence given to design once it was ensconced in a curriculum, degree program, and department. Both promotional publication and educational expansion intertwined as designers came to view themselves not merely as one cog in a theatre-making machine but as independent freelance professionals.

3. THE TEACHING ARTIST: BUILDING UNIVERSITY CURRICULA

A student walking into Yale's Drama 112 course in the fall of 1937 would have encountered a tall man with a round face and commanding authority. Donald Oenslager—the "O" to some students, "Uncle Don" to others—had reviewed their drawing ability ahead of their enrollment, but most students probably had not seen much of Professor Oenslager until they took his course. Though he was only in town once or twice a week, Oenslager's fame on campus was bolstered by the fame of his recent Broadway productions. Nine Oenslager-designed shows had opened in the fall of the previous year, among them Moss Hart and George Kaufman's *You Can't Take It with You* and a Cole Porter–penned star vehicle for Jimmy Durante, Bob Hope, and Ethel Merman titled *Red, Hot, and Blue*.[1] The thirty-five-year-old Oenslager was working at peak capacity and had been teaching at the school for over a decade.

In the course's opening lecture that year, Oenslager spoke of the theatre as "a common infection"; a shared enthusiasm for theatre had successfully transcended the anti-theatricalism of the past. At present, Oenslager pointed out, Yale offered a forward-looking educational program that could develop artist-craftsmen through university study. Throughout the lecture, though, Oenslager emphasized that Yale was simply a step toward a professional career. The students were not there to study "the theatre of old books and libraries, but the daily living theatre of the new season in New York. That is your homework. Transition Yale to New York."[2] These students were enjoined to become "the artist of the theatre of the future." This artist was much more than simply a competent worker; this artist was someone who would "do the world over after your own heart's desire." After speaking about history, hope, and homework, Oenslager sent out the young designers with a reading list and a set of assignments for the term.

Oenslager repeated this orientation lecture for many years thereafter, and each time he emphasized what would become the main tenets of his educational philosophy at Yale. A designer should, in the words of Robert Edmond Jones, maintain "some images of magnificence" and seek artistry that would not only serve the needs of the play but would improve the art form. At the same time, Oenslager emphasized that designers could be called upon to work in any one of many craft areas, from upholstery to sculpture; in his lectures he intentionally blurred the lines between craft and artistry, between trade labor and designing.[3] Oenslager later recalled his insistence on "practical demonstration and an imaginative approach to teaching," and he continued to emphasize problem-solving as well as historical and theoretical knowledge in his work.[4] Student designers learned to think practically about their careers, too, by keeping their eye on the commercial theatre of New York City and aligning themselves with the "living theatre of the new season." Although he explicitly trained skilled artists, Oenslager implicitly trained his students to be emerging professionals.

Through his teaching Oenslager established a model for scenic design education in the United States. As he wrote in 1949, "there was no established order for teaching Scene Design" in the country when he started at Yale, and despite the existence of competing models at other institutions, Oenslager's system has endured.[5] The resilient success of the Yale School of Drama is due to many factors, and Oenslager's innovations and his long tenure at Yale are primary among them. Yale Drama also embraced a professional graduate school model of education, refusing from the start to place itself under the purview of the English or Speech Department. For these reasons, Yale's system has been influential in both the history of design professionalization and university theatre education. Yale placed scenic design education within an influential and well-funded American university, and this soon led to the incorporation of theatre design at other universities as well. Moreover, it impressed a particular vision of scenic design labor in the minds of students, who then promulgated the individualism and intense, commercially driven style of freelance labor that Oenslager embodied.

The story of the Yale School of Drama, which until 1955 was the Department of Drama in the School of Fine Arts, begins with its founder, George Pierce Baker. Baker came to Yale's faculty after years of not-so-benign neglect of his teaching methods at Harvard, where Baker taught the playwriting course, English 47, and an accompanying theatre production seminar, 47 Workshop. This workshop culminated in performances of student-written plays for a subscribing Boston audience. Baker wanted to test student playwrights' work on stage, but the workshop's technical and production needs quickly expanded beyond the space and resources of Harvard's Massachusetts Hall and exhausted the patience of Baker's deans and English Department colleagues.[6] Yale enticed Baker away from Cambridge with fine arts dean Everett Meeks's vision of a home for professional theatre education. The offer included funding for a new theatre building, provided by benefactor Edward Harkness.[7] Yale gambled on graduate-level theatre education, and the department was soon a success. Baker found that the administrative structure of Yale's School of Fine Arts was more supportive of his educational philosophy than Harvard had been.

When Baker joined Yale, Meeks had recently risen to the deanship (appointed in 1922). During his tenure, Meeks reinvigorated Yale's professional education for architects in the Beaux-Arts mode. He also fostered close collaborations among other departments in the school such as Painting, Sculpture, and, after 1925, Drama.[8] For Baker, the new building, the practice-friendly school, and the opportunity to teach graduate pre-professional classes were invigorating; his curriculum for dramatic writing quickly expanded to include other theatrical areas, including design and production. The venture soon attracted many students eager to participate in the buzzing Broadway market and growing Little Theatre movement, for which a Yale certificate of completion would provide a useful credential. Oenslager, a former student of Baker's, shared a similar opinion: the true purpose of study should be to train first-rate theatre artists, competent in skills but also prepared to begin a career.

This chapter argues that universities helped professionalize scenic design by providing it an institutional home. It adds to studies of university theatre by Susan Harris Smith, Shannon Jackson, and others by taking a close look at Oenslager's pedagogy, its inspirations, and its legacy.[9] Much of what Oenslager taught was closely aligned with architectural education, especially the Beaux-Arts model, because it emphasized theoretical knowledge, studio practices, and competition. As designers left Yale, they took Oenslager's concepts to other educational institutions and into their professional lives. Some of this influence depended on Oenslager's consistent Broadway production, which exemplified freelance professional success more clearly than any lecture could.

Other models of design education also flourished at Yale and elsewhere, but they had a more limited effect on freelance ideology. This chapter examines two types of counterpoints, one institutional model at Carnegie Tech and two individuals whose design careers diverged from Oenslager's Broadway-focused professionalism. A decade prior to the establishment of Yale's Department of Drama, Thomas Wood Stevens founded a Department of Drama at the Carnegie Institute of Technology (now Carnegie Mellon University) in Pittsburgh. Stevens's department provided much-needed education for technicians, actors, and especially those who wanted to teach or direct theatre in universities or venues of the Little Theatre movement. Carnegie Tech's model, however, emphasized practice heavily and so repeatedly denied students the chance to create at the highest levels of production authority, such as directing, designing, and playwriting. The first design and painting educator of the department, Woodman Thompson, developed a scenic design course sequence in the 1920s that appeared as though it might rival Yale's model, but it could not sustain itself as a preprofessional educational philosophy. Turnover on the faculty—Thompson himself left the program for a New York-based career in 1922[10]—and overemphasis on practical technique meant that Carnegie Tech's educational legacy would be eclipsed in later years.

Oenslager's commercially driven artistry and individualistic professionalism was not the only path in education that student designers could take. Oenslager's co-teacher for Drama 112, the costume designer Frank Bevan, chose a more university-focused career and limited his work mostly to Yale classes and productions. While his students have remembered his classes as useful and challenging, Bevan's teaching did not model the same type of professional practice that Oenslager's did. The other individual whose design career diverged from Oenslager's professionalism was Woodman Thompson, who in his later career instituted testing for period-style knowledge on the union's entrance exam. By holding designers to high educational standards, the union exam worked alongside the Yale model to refashion the role of the scenic designer into one partially based in abstract knowledge. Both of these men educated designers and pose a counterpoint to Oenslager's professionalism: Bevan in his quiet, scholarly teaching and Thompson in his use of testing and tutoring, rather than university classrooms, to train emerging designers.

The Oenslager Educational Model

When Baker invited Oenslager to come to Yale in 1925, there were classes in "theatre production" in at least eight schools, including Stanford, Howard, and Brigham Young.[11] Carnegie Tech offered basic "technical practice" in its acting and directing/production curricula. Before Yale's Drama Department was founded, however, there was no sustained formal course progression in theatre design. A narrative history of Yale's drama program, compiled by the department's historian Alois M. Nagler for internal use in 1965, noted that Oenslager created his own teaching materials, drawing from his studies at Harvard and his own observations of European stagecraft from a tour of Europe funded by a 1923–1924 Sachs fellowship.[12] As a designer steeped in New Stagecraft praxis, the twenty-four-year-old Oenslager also drew from his professional experience. New Stagecraft theory held that designs should be used to transform the playscript into a theatrical event, and simplicity, suggestion, and selectively realistic settings should highlight a play's action and language. To these ideas Oenslager added training in professional behavior and the study of historical theatre design practices. Like fellow designer Lee Simonson, Oenslager saw theatrical design as a process of problem-solving: devising a series of solutions to problems presented by the playwright, the theatre, and available technology. He made his stamp on Yale's program by teaching New Stagecraft philosophy, historical awareness, and a practical preprofessional orientation to design.

3.1. Donald Oenslager. *Photo by Friedman-Abeles©. The New York Library for the Performing Arts.*

Both the organization and the method of instruction in Oenslager's courses emphasized the applied, contingent, and exploratory nature of design work. In his first year he developed three courses for design students pursuing the MA in design: The History of Stage Design, Practice and Theory of Stage Design, and Advanced Stage Design. The first two courses lasted a half year, and the last a full year; later, the half-year courses were combined into one course: Background and Practice of stage design. (In the first years of the drama program, a two-year MA rather than an MFA was offered. The department transitioned to a three-year MFA in the 1930–31 academic year.)[13] These courses were required only of students in design and technical production (stagecraft and stage engineering).

The history class emphasized written and visual knowledge of past design styles and techniques, while the later classes were project-based. A 1930 catalog confirms that Oenslager began with a historical approach by examining "the relation between the actor, audience, and stage in the Greek, medieval, Renaissance, and eighteenth-century theatre." Students also surveyed the "fine arts as background for theatre practice" and the "problems of design in stage decoration: color composition, grouping, planes, scale, etc." Oenslager considered "plays of each period," both "from the point of view of their contemporary method of production and with all the possibilities that the theatre of to-day presents."[14] Students studied past designers' solutions to the problems presented by certain playwrights, and after working through those problems, they created their own designs.

More advanced classes in the design sequence continued a "problem" orientation.[15] In 1930 the second-year course Problems in Stage Design (Drama 22, later 122) simply assigned projects on "various types of plays" and for the department's main productions, while the third-year course Principles of Stage Design in 1942 taught "the problems involved in translating the designer's sketch into terms of stage scenery."[16] This third-year course was added to the curriculum in 1930–31, the same year that the program expanded to a three-year MFA. The course consisted of "different long projects from each student according to his particular need."[17] Across his Yale course material, Oenslager referred to the "problem" of design, echoing terminology emergent in industrial design, architecture, and other applied arts fields.

Oenslager did not write a textbook on design, and the teaching materials of his that still exist are mostly notes, slide lists, and prepared lectures from the last few decades of his career. In the first design course, Drama 112: The History of Stage Design, Oenslager arrived for each class with multiple pages of lecture notes and thirty to forty slides. The slides ranged from images of theatre sets (renderings, models, photographs) to paintings, sculpture, and architecture. For instance, a slide list from the 1966 iteration of Drama 112 contained forty slides for the first lecture of the course, "Sketching for Scene Design." This lecture introduced the idea of the sketch as the key component of the design idea and featured images of designs from Adolphe Appia to Boris Aronson. Subsequent lectures taught the history of visual representation in theatre through architecture and painting. Frequently, exploration of past styles would conclude with current interpretations of those periods, such as Norman Bel Geddes's 1924 *The Miracle* in relation to French Gothic architecture or Inigo Jones's seventeenth-century masques in relation to contemporary musical theatre.[18] These lectures demonstrated how different designers approached similar scenic challenges.

The class was divided into combined historical and studio units, meeting for two hours on Tuesdays and Thursdays; Oenslager taught on Thursdays, and Frank Bevan, a faculty member in costume design, taught on Tuesdays. Each Tuesday class featured about an hour of history instruction, taught through slides and lecture, and another hour of studio teaching on topics such as perspective, foreshortening, relief and chiaroscuro effects, or designing for thrusts and arenas. Though Oenslager was not present for both days of Drama 112, and probably did more lecturing than teaching of technical skills, narrative evidence suggests that students saw him as the leader of the studio and their major scene design mentor.[19] (Bevan was Oenslager's student in the early twenties, so he likely adapted his teaching to Oenslager's already established methods.) Drama 112 only required that students purchase watercolors, pencils, paintbrushes, papers, and tools; Oenslager's course was one of the only design courses offered at the school that did not have accompanying textbooks.[20] Written examinations were simply less important than the demonstrated skills of modeling and drawing, which were assessed in frequent critique sessions.

Oenslager's "crit sessions" had a project orientation. This studio technique of evaluation emulated the pedagogical model of art and architecture schools, in which student work was assessed in-person by a panel of experts. At the end of a project period, Oenslager brought the class together and asked students to question the proposed designs from the points of view of technical staff, directors, lighting designers, and playwrights. The narrative history of the department described the question-based method of Oenslager's teaching: "Through the years Mr. Oenslager's teaching methods have changed little. The class is given a play to design. The students' renderings are then discussed in a 'presentation.' Mr. Oenslager leads the discussion by asking directors in the class if such a set would 'work' for a director, asking lighting designers how a particular lighting effect could be achieved, and himself pointing out merits and difficulties."[21] Oenslager was also responsible for "hiring" designers to work on school productions. The history continued: "The opportunity to design major productions is awarded in competition. After a discussion with the director and playwright, each third-year designer prepares a rendering. Then in a second joint session preliminary designs are discussed. Lastly, on the basis of a final rendering, the designer is selected by the director, playwright, and Mr. Oenslager."[22]

"Bid sessions" for the right to design major productions attempted to replicate commercial practices. Oenslager required advanced students to prepare competing designs for the chosen plays, in a process not dissimilar to working "on spec," which professional designers had resisted in their accession to the scene painters' union in 1924. These bid sessions, however, served a pedagogical purpose: exposing students to the demands that would be placed on their designs by future collaborators and producers. Competitive criticism was Oenslager's primary teaching tool, one that he saw as necessary for students' development.[23] Speaking about his teaching later in his career, he reflected on the need for professional behavior: "In my teaching and my work I have always stood for theatre traditions, cultivated standards of craftsmanship, emphasized the values of style and personal taste, and above all practiced discipline. By my own strict way of work I have insisted that schedules be met, and also that rigid deadlines be met by students. This insistence established the close rapport so essential between designer and apprentice."[24]

Discipline and the apprenticeship model lay at the core of his pedagogy: students were to be trained to become not only theatre workers but fellow members of the design profession. Oenslager's curriculum emphasized discipline and perseverance, an ability to cultivate personal taste within established styles, and high standards of craftsmanship.

As the Yale Drama Department changed in the thirties and forties, Oenslager's design sequence remained relatively stable. After Baker's retirement in 1932, subsequent leadership of the school argued for tightened admissions standards, adopted a more academic approach, and added a PhD in dramatic literature directed by Allardyce Nicoll. The acting, directing, and playwriting curricula were in flux through the war years, yet design remained a highlight of Yale's program. For example, a 1945 internal memo from directing professor Frank McMullen to fine arts dean (and ex-head of the Drama Department) Boyd Smith frankly admits that "the place has been going down hill gradually during the last ten years," with directing and playwriting as the weakest programs, but "the design and technical departments have suffered little of this criticism."[25] Perhaps this was because design and production enjoyed steady leadership, unlike the directing and playwriting programs, which had undergone significant and frequent changes of faculty. The design curriculum also maintained its status because it remained connected to the profession through the employment of working designers and visits from prominent speakers. It was a testament to Oenslager's vision and execution of the scenic design curriculum, in collaboration with Bevan and lighting designer and technician Stanley McCandless.

Long before the teaching artist model was accepted in undergraduate theatre education,[26] Oenslager built the curriculum at Yale in such a way that he could keep residence in New York and maintain an active Broadway design career. This differed from the norm at other universities, which asked artists on faculty to work full-time on campus. Oenslager's unusual request brought rewards. He was the most active professional on Yale's faculty in the early years, and he continued to be engaged in the New York theatrical design scene throughout his fifty-year teaching career.[27] He brought in a steady stream of Broadway contacts and speakers to work with his students. Regular contact with professionals kept students up to date with industry developments, and Oenslager drew from the newest productions in his lectures. He also maintained a sizable collection of slides, drawings, and models in his New York office, and often he brought students to the city to work with the collection, meet guests, or view current Broadway productions. In his choice to commute, Oenslager became a powerful model of professional practice at a high level. At the same time, though, Oenslager was less available to students on a daily basis, and he relied on other faculty to teach foundational classes and skills. Other design faculty such as Frank Bevan (costume) or Stanley McCandless (lighting) did not pursue commercial careers on Broadway; they instead chose other avenues of professional work.[28] Oenslager's model of university participation distinguished Yale's program, yet it also raised one version of design work above others: the hectic, freelance professional life of the Broadway designer.

Finally, the lasting influence of Oenslager's educational philosophy coincides with the spread of the Yale Drama pedagogical model nationally. The best evidence of this spread was published in a series of "Baker Maps." These maps illustrate Baker's influence and have been extensively analyzed by Susan Harris Smith.[29] Approaching these maps from the point of view of design shows that design pedagogy spread in more limited patterns than those seen in other disciplines. In 1925, the year Yale Drama opened, *Theatre Arts Monthly* published a map of George Pierce Baker's influence drawn by McCandless. The map listed playwrights, directors, and designers who had studied in the 47 Workshop with Baker at Harvard. The only designers listed were assigned to New York City, and they consisted of well-known figures in the New Stagecraft movement: Lee Simonson, Robert Edmond Jones, Rollo Wayne, and Donald Oenslager. Baker's reach in other fields, though, was far-flung; his students had gone on to teach or work in little theatres across the country.

Eight years later the July 1933 issue of *Theatre Arts Monthly* celebrated Baker's retirement from Yale. The editors reprinted McCandless's map and supplemented it with a new "Yale map," demonstrating "how quickly other younger men and younger colleges in various parts of the country are building their own new theatre worlds."[30] The Yale graduates placed on this map were concentrated in the Northeast and Midwest, with only a few working in Texas, California, and the South. As before, the map noted the primary occupation of each graduate, and a similar geographic distribution emerged: most of the designers worked in New York City or nearby. There were emergent clusters of designers around art theatres, such as the Goodman in Chicago, or at large theatre-focused universities such as the University of Iowa, which by 1933 had built up a production area within its theatre department. From these maps, several conclusions can be drawn: first, that Baker (and Yale generally) was aware of Yale's growing influence as a generator of a "new" national theatre network through its graduates and, second, that Yale's influence was also strong in universities and Little Theatre companies. Professional designers, however, remained in urban theatre centers.

In the years to follow, the success of the school would be demonstrated best by its network of alumni relations. Alumni lists and surveys were collected as soon as 1930, and reports of significant alumni activity, likely emerging out of internal reports to the dean, were circulated to alumni as early as 1936.[31] A formal alumni association started in 1938, and after a brief war hiatus, it became a robust network with fund-raising appeals, newsletters, and an annual benefit dinner in New York City.[32] Even though the Department of Drama would not be institutionally reconstituted as a school until 1955, Yale Drama alumni functioned as an independent, supportive body of theatre benefactors and professionals from at least the mid-forties.

Oenslager was aware of his influence through alumni, too. Oenslager and other established Broadway designers hired Yale graduates as assistants, and a few prominent ones would eventually become influential designers themselves.[33] In his 1974 essay "U.S. Stage Design, Past and Present," Oenslager listed a number of "new arrivals on the scene" in the thirties and forties. Of the nine designers named, four had graduated from Yale, including Stewart Chaney. A similar group listed by Oenslager for the fifties were "applying their therapy to the Broadway scene." Of seven names listed, four were Yale graduates in scenic design.[34] Of the non-Yale-educated names listed, most had derived their experience from either coursework in architecture or apprenticeships at theatres outside New York, followed by assistantships with major designers in New York; they were not alumni of other university programs. Given the sequential design education Oenslager taught and the significant professional networks he curated for students inside the school and after graduation, Yale had a commanding influence on the education of American theatrical designers.

Professionalism, Testing, and University Education

Oenslager's pedagogy merits deeper analysis, but it is worth considering first the relationship between the university and professions more generally. Yale was not narrowly interested in theatre education when it founded its Drama Department; something much more valuable was on Dean Meeks's mind. By embracing graduate theatre education, Yale hoped to begin a mutually beneficial relationship between the theatre profession and the university. The Drama Department would distinguish Yale's School of Fine Arts from other such schools, and the school might see more of a return in prestige than it paid out in resources. This bet paid off. In fact, this type of professional school gambit was one that many US schools made in various professional areas in the early twentieth century.

Most professions enjoy a symbiotic relationship with higher education. Once a profession convinces a university that a professional school for its field is worth an investment, the university then allocates resources to the study and development of professional practice. University affiliation is not necessary for professional organization, but it accelerates the process, as the university provides much of the space, money, and personnel stability a profession needs to develop quickly.[35] For its part, the university gains prestige, faculty expertise, and increased student enrollment by professional-graduate students. Some professions are well represented among universities—architecture, medicine, and law—but with other professions, universities may seek to distinguish themselves by funding large-scale investments in a new area. To name just a few, Columbia's School of Library Economy and the University of Pennsylvania's Wharton School were attempts to claim early dominance in the 1880s, and Georgetown's School of Foreign Service and Michigan's School of Public Policy (now the Ford School) were attempts to stake claims in the 1910s. Although the theatre arts were a later addition to the university, their inclusion in schools such as Yale's School of Fine Arts cemented scenic design as a professional pursuit.

Much professionalism ideology depends on education at the university. As theorist Magali Sarfatti Larson has noted, professionalism consists of "structural links between relatively high levels of formal education and relatively desirable positions and/or rewards in the social division of labor."[36] In countries where universities provide postbaccalaureate professional education, as is true of the United States, the role of universities is integral to the concept of profession: professions are careers one studies for.[37] As more occupational groups gained dedicated professional schools throughout the twentieth century, the status of the occupations they represented rose accordingly. This "structural link" was co-constitutive: universities came to (partially) define their mission as providing a home for professional education, and professional education afforded new occupations a means of professionalizing.

The legitimation of professional practice in the university allows professions to gain cultural acceptance quickly, because the university serves not only the profession itself but larger cultural values as well: knowledge, good work, self-development. Andrew Abbott argues that the legitimation work of the university provides a link between the individual professional practitioner, whose work is relatively private, and "central values in the larger culture," which might include health, safety, or quality of life. The university commits capital investment, labor, and expertise to projects that serve these values, and so incorporation into the university legitimizes newly professionalizing fields.[38] In theatre, university departments added legitimacy and status to the pursuit of "show business." Donald Oenslager's curriculum, in turn, foregrounded professional values: on one hand, aesthetically pleasing designs, and on the other, work produced with a certain rigor, selflessness, and seriousness.

Another key role that educational institutions play in professionalization is in providing pre-licensure or test-preparing education. Examination for certification or licensure is rarely done by universities themselves. Rather, it is usually administered by another organization, as in the case of the designers' union membership exam, or is delegated to a nonprofit agency that handles licensing, as in the case of US medical board exams. University education, while not a substitute for legally binding certification, becomes a common path for practitioners to acquire the skills and content knowledge necessary to pass their profession's qualifying exam.

There are a variety of potential control mechanisms for regulating labor, including licensure, liability and malpractice laws, mandatory group membership (such as unionization), or nonmandatory but generally recognized certification. Harold Wilensky points out that no typical pattern existed in midcentury among legal protections, examinations, or licensing systems and the other components of professionalization. Some professions organized in conjunction with universities or professional organizations before licensure laws, and others did so in the reverse order.[39] Julia Evetts has noted that market closure through education and licensing is particularly important in early phases of professional organization, when closure is needed "to endorse and guarantee the education, training, experience and tacit knowledge of licensed practitioners."[40] Eliot Freidson adds that university degrees create "sheltered labor markets," wherein the university degree and later exam-based certification constitute "a labor market signal" that allows new recruits access to previously unavailable work.[41]

For this reason, it was important that scenic designers establish standards through a union membership exam; the examination guaranteed that only skilled practitioners could join the union. Later, the exam helped the union regulate its labor supply as well. Schools played a part, too. School curricula helped codify what testing covered, especially Oenslager's curriculum at Yale. His emphasis on knowledge of period styles, problem-solving through playscript interpretation, and refined skill in drawing, painting, and drafting were each tested on USA Local 829's exam. The union exam was not the only way, however, by which Oenslager's pedagogy spread professional ideals; his teaching embodied professional tendencies, particularly in his adoption of studio pedagogy.

Studio and Beaux-Arts Pedagogy at Yale

Oenslager's pedagogy was innovative because it embraced studio-style, Beaux-Arts-inflected education, encouraged students to view themselves as independent artists, and cultivated professional behavior. Most of these skills were taught in a new type of learning environment, at least new to theatre studies: the design studio. Here, *studio pedagogy* refers to an educational mode with roots in design, architecture, and related fields. Such roots reach back centuries. It began in European arts academies in the sixteenth and seventeenth centuries, and then inspired the spread of the atelier method, the "democratization" of arts instruction in US public education in the nineteenth century, and the creation of new academies devoted to artistic movements such as the Beaux-Arts and Bauhaus schools. In the late nineteenth century, American universities began to develop their own art and architecture education programs modeled on European art schools. These programs awarded academic credit for courses in the humanities and letters alongside studio courses where student artists acquired skills.[42]

Versions of the studio course have continued at American universities, especially in arts, engineering, and design-focused programs. In a contemporary context, the studio approach has been studied by psychologists and learning science researchers in order to identify the skills and competencies it teaches. In *Studio Thinking*, for instance, cognitive psychologists Lois Hetland, Ellen Winner, and their coresearchers identify elements of studio technique and justify the benefits of studio education without resorting to instrumental arguments.[43] By asserting that the value of the arts in education stands on its own, this study of student learning helps explain the move taken by Oenslager and, to a certain extent, Baker in founding Yale's design curriculum and the place of design in the department.[44]

Studio Thinking refers to the intrinsic benefits of education in the arts as "habits of mind" encouraged by the studio. Some of these habits of mind include engagement and persistence in tasks, envisioning phenomena not currently present, expressing a personal vision, focused observation, and metacognitive reflection.[45] These habits are not taught through direct instruction. According to the coauthors, they are learned through an instructor's coaching, experimentation, and skillful management of the studio space. The coauthors also note that studio pedagogy has a distinct rhythm. It uses a combination of demonstration lecture, coaching throughout working periods, and critique sessions. An iterative A-B-A structure emerges. Instructors demonstrate in short bursts of lecture, often accompanied by tools or a demo of the art medium at work. They then encourage students to work on assignments (the "studio" time) while instructors give individualized feedback or brief group reminders. Most units end with a critique of student work, which in Hetland and Winner's observations was often done in front of all students.[46]

In his design classes Oenslager adopted a teaching model similar to Hetland and Winner's studio. His projects and critique sessions taught crucial skills of observation, persistence, vision, and exploratory analysis. Oenslager and Bevan used the A-B-A structure in classes, particularly in Drama 112; they balanced lectures and skills development sessions weekly and repeated the process throughout the semester. In more advanced classes, Oenslager might assign one design per week, with weekly criticism sessions as well. Final projects came in for the longest and most intensive criticism.[47] This allowed students to practice skills in progression, while at the same time learning the habits of mind that afforded them the persistence and self-awareness necessary to survive as a working theatre artist.

When making the new Yale curriculum, Oenslager also drew from his Harvard education, which was possibly his first introduction to Beaux-Arts pedagogy. Oenslager did not have a studio-based education at Harvard as part of the regular curriculum; he attended Baker's 47 Workshop and participated in its active critique and mounting of plays, but he did not have dedicated design classes. Oenslager and other students requested that a seminar in "visual theatre" be taught to augment their studies, a class ultimately taught by fine arts professor Arthur Pope.[48] Pope's teaching "merged theory with practice, emphasizing the importance of first-hand experience and practice with different techniques and materials to complement study of theory," and Pope's example likely introduced Oenslager to studio teaching.[49]

Harvard's Department of Fine Art and School of Architecture worked together closely during the years of Oenslager's study, roughly 1920–1923. Both were using Beaux-Arts pedagogical models with their students. Harvard's faculty recruitment in 1921 and its competitive prize system, similar to the system in place at the Parisian academy, attest to the university's attempt to emulate the French model. Beaux-Arts-style education was becoming fashionable at many elite universities, and Harvard wanted to become the main American center for the Parisian style of architecture education. Dean George Harold Edgell wrote in a 1922 alumni bulletin that he wanted to create a "situation in architecture in Harvard and Boston [that] would resemble that of the Beaux-Arts in Paris."[50] In his final years there, Oenslager would have experienced these changes to Harvard's architecture pedagogy.

The Beaux-Arts system was a French form of education associated with the architectural school that shared its name. The most significant elements of this method were an allegiance to a studio (atelier) run by a practicing architect, the development of skills through increasingly demanding projects, and competitive yearly prizes for which students submitted elegant sets of drawings.[51] This pedagogical model also assumed a problem orientation to designing. For instance, it used the *esquisse* system, which was required for longer projects. In this system, a student began a project by completing a timed initial sketch, and these sketches were held by the school. The student's final set of plans, two months or more in preparation, some with fully realized renderings, would need to match the student's original sketch. In the school's eyes, this was considered "a substitute for restrictions of client and site encountered in real life."[52] The Beaux-Arts system also involved major jury review and prize contests, both preceded by famously grueling multiday preparations, or *charrettes*.[53] Before facing the jury's critique, students would devote "all waking hours to the production of project drawings." Juries determined a student's future in the program, and prize contests rewarded students with renown, opportunities, and travel. (The most famous such prize, the Prix de Rome, paid for several years' study in Italy on the French government's dime.)

The ascension of the Beaux-Arts system in American higher education was a late nineteenth-century phenomenon, and it was particularly influential among elite private schools. It departed from earlier forms of training for architects in America, which had taken the form of either apprenticeship in a firm's offices, where drawing and engineering skills were emphasized, or more traditional university education. The architectural curriculum at the University of Illinois stressed liberal arts and manual skills, while Cornell's program of study emphasized what would today be called engineering: study of mechanics, heating, and materials.[54] The Beaux-Arts method emphasized aesthetics above all, particularly the theoretical concepts of beauty, spatial organization, and historical reference. This approach to schooling took root at the Massachusetts Institute of Technology and Columbia University in the mid-nineteenth century and soon thereafter at Harvard and Yale. Given that American architecture in general was still looking across the Atlantic for aesthetic inspiration, the Beaux-Arts educational system was a useful way for universities to separate the profession from other building trades: draftsmen, engineers, and builders.

As was the case at Harvard, Yale's School of Fine Arts had also been teaching by Beaux-Arts methods. The Yale Architecture Department—one of the most respected departments in the Fine Arts School—was founded under the philosophy in 1869. When the Drama Department was formed in 1925, Dean Everett Victor Meeks, trained at the École des Beaux-Arts, was already at work expanding Beaux-Arts methods at Yale. Two of Meeks's changes upon his arrival in 1922 were to create joint collaborative projects among architecture, painting, and sculpture students, and to invite successful practicing architects to join juries to critique student designs.[55] The Yale Architecture Department also had a version of the part-time teaching artist.[56] Because professionals could be hired ad hoc to teach or critique student work, Beaux-Arts reforms saved money, while the school boosted its preprofessional orientation. Perhaps the existence of a teaching artist model in architecture inclined Baker and Dean Meeks to acquiesce to Oenslager's 1926 request to live and work in New York and commute weekly to New Haven.

In developing his own scenic design curriculum from scratch, Oenslager likely borrowed from architectural education. Although there are no documented direct links between Oenslager's curriculum planning and the Beaux-Arts movement, several elements of Oenslager's pedagogy resonate with Beaux-Arts' emphasis on design, theory, precedent, and competition. Like Beaux-Arts architects, who were trained to see the practice as fundamentally individual "matters of personality, talent, creativity, and convictions,"[57] Oenslager's introductory course in the MFA curriculum (Drama 112) focused on the identities of specific designers and on "'problems' which are as similar as possible to those encountered by professionals in the field."[58] By studying how notable designers solved problems of script, site, and spectacle, Oenslager cast the answer to scenic design problems as fundamentally a matter of approach and ingenuity—problems that ought to be solved by one individual, on paper. In Oenslager's later courses, students were given plays to design, and their results were subjected to critique by peers and faculty. The crit sessions mirrored the juries of Beaux-Arts, and the "prize" of production was given to the student who provided the best design for a given production.

The ideology of professionalism espoused in Beaux-Arts pedagogy allowed architects to claim a more elite status than they had otherwise enjoyed in American building industries. Scenic design took a similar path, in that the move away from the paint floor and the grounding of education in the drafting room helped to construct a professional identity around new design behaviors. However, Oenslager himself would never have explicitly referred to his education as professionalization. In fact, few designers working in the theater at the time, especially those with fewer industrial design contacts, referred to themselves as anything more than a craftsman. Oenslager said as much in 1935, and his educational strategy emphasized the craft of design over artistry.[59] Nonetheless, Oenslager conceptualized the designer as a sort of meta-craftsman, not "a painter, a decorator, or an architect" but rather a "craftsman possessing a working knowledge of all these arts."[60] The designer's creative and managerial function is to select which of the many arts available to apply to a given situation. "Good scenic design is good thinking," he wrote, "with freedom of imagination supplemented by reasonable performance in execution."[61] To unpack this precept: the selection of the correct approach to a given scenic problem was a sort of expert diagnosis. What kind of problem does the script present, and how can it best be solved?

The idea that "good design is good thinking" connects Oenslager's teaching to professionalism. Oenslager's restraint in calling his work artistry was admirable—after all, he was trying to instill workmanlike rigor and responsibility in his students—but his pedagogy also hints at a professional class standing. Like architects, doctors, or lawyers, Oenslager taught his students to approach design as a type of problem with many possible "treatment" options; finding the best solution—that is, what to design in which types of situations—constituted good practice. The best answers were found as a result of an abstract process of diagnosis (script analysis) and the application of creativity through expertise. Such framing was one way that Oenslager's teaching produced freelance artist-professionals rather than craft workers.

A problem orientation was not only key for designers' education, but it also constituted professional behavior in and of itself. Such an approach resonates with theorists' views of professionalization, especially that of Andrew Abbott, who has argued that a process of diagnosis, inference, and treatment characterizes many professional practices when encountering difficult, ill-defined problems.[62] Doing design is, in effect, a way of solving problems that are difficult to diagnose and solve. Working from philosophy and learning theory, Donald Schön has linked his concept of reflective practice to design. According to Schön, reflective practice is a "competence by which practitioners actually handle indeterminate zones of practice."[63] In *Educating the Reflective Practitioner*, Schön notes that, in design fields, reflective practice is most often taught through informal studio-based classes organized around problem-solving. Design courses contain an "intensity and duration long beyond the normal requirements of a course," and "students do not so much attend . . . as live in them."[64] Projects can be intentionally structured in such a way as to develop student expertise and can be supervised by knowledgeable, established professionals who are focused on education, not production. While Schön's analysis surveys architectural education, his immersive, studio-based model bears much resemblance to the way in which design has been taught in other disciplines.[65] By instituting studio pedagogy, developed out of the Beaux-Arts tradition, Oenslager helped teach professionalism as well as design.

Finally, in addition to the organization and skills of studio pedagogy, Oenslager taught by personal example. He lived his life as a teaching, practicing professional. As an artist continuously working in New York—the only one among Yale's theatre design faculty to do so—Oenslager modeled the career to which many students aspired. He demonstrated that scenic design, at least at the Broadway level, required fierce independence from any institution, producer, or employer. Oenslager's once-a-week presence on campus reinforced the idea that a designer ought to juggle multiple projects and travel among job sites. In a sense, it modeled the transformation of the scenic designer into an architect, who would visit the building site for supervision but who did not work on the site daily.

To make his schedule work, Oenslager coordinated teaching with his colleagues, especially costume design professor Frank Bevan. When they co-taught Drama 112, Bevan's consistent presence on campus gave Oenslager the freedom to commute there once a week. Bevan taught many of the studio sessions, particularly later in Oenslager's career, when he made fewer trips to campus other than his Thursday commute. Bevan's career has gotten much less attention than Oenslager's, likely because his designs and teaching legacy are mostly limited to work at Yale, with only a few Broadway credits to his name in the forties. It is important to recognize, though, that Bevan's instructional role at Yale had its own benefits for students and did not simply reinforce Oenslager's teaching. Bevan came up through Oenslager's system of teaching design professionalism; he joined the Yale faculty in 1929 at the age of twenty-seven, immediately after completing Yale's two-year program under Oenslager's tutelage. In addition to the knowledge he had gained from Oenslager, Bevan also applied ideas from his apprenticeship with Robert Edmond Jones and a brief stint working for David Belasco. Bevan preferred an academic milieu to the commercial Broadway scene. Scenic designer John Ezell, a student of Bevan and the executor of his estate, recalled leaving his class with reams of notes. Elia Kazan, in his autobiography, remembered Bevan as "scholarly, rigorous, and precise about his work."[66]

It's possible, even tempting, to compare the careers of Oenslager and Bevan and find Bevan lacking. Even in articles that have attempted to recover Bevan's life, such as one penned by Daniel Robinson in 2013, Bevan's students framed his life with deficiencies. Bevan was, according to Ezell, "not particularly adept at self-promotion," "a very private man," "rather formal," and a victim of "the early struggles for costume design to gain professional acceptance."[67] It is useful, though, to consider Bevan's career as a counterpoint to Oenslager's more public approach to blending design and education. Without a strong teacher and rigorous scholar present in New Haven, holding students to their work and their study of history, would Oenslager have been able to spend as much time on Broadway? How might Bevan's teaching demeanor, scholarly and precise, have complemented Oenslager's prepared slide lectures and crit sessions? And to what extent did the flashier career that Oenslager enjoyed imprint on students a model of professional practice that benefited from the work of assistants, apprentices, and former students such as Bevan?

The lack of attention paid to Bevan's career is similar to biases faced by marginalized groups in theatre design. These biases are compounded in parts of production that scenic designers saw as "supporting" a scenic vision. Costumes and lighting assisted scenic design in the early twentieth century, and the secondary status of these areas created tension in the union and in the profession. Such issues were frequently overlaid with overt sexism, too. Because of costume design's proximity to the actor's body, and the association of clothing and textile work with femininity, domesticity, and care work, Bevan's support of Yale's design program deserves recognition as another type of professional labor, one that comes into clearer focus when design history moves beyond commercial successes.

How can professional work directed toward students be acknowledged? Feature articles on Bevan in *Theatre Design & Technology*, the journal of USITT (United States Institute for Theatre Technology), have provided one approach, but seeing Bevan and Oenslager as a dyad—at least from the point of view of students in Drama 112—provides another. Oenslager was a celebrity out in front, both when teaching at Yale and when Yale promoted its faculty's work outside the institution. Bevan, in Ezell's memory, taught quietly. Writing about Bevan, Robinson points out that while Bevan completed few high-profile jobs off campus, being "out of the professional limelight . . . gave him the room to innovate without the pressures of the profession affecting his work."[68] Robinson sees this leeway as freedom from the often-conservative and budget-conscious motives of Broadway; add to this the fact that Bevan had freedom from high expectations for production, for continuous self-promotion, or for opening as many as nine shows in a single season. Students probably learned that there was more than one way to be a professional designer, while they also saw that the theatre field—and the university—rewarded Oenslager's entrepreneurial, independent approach with more obvious material gains.

Through his teaching, Oenslager showed that a designer was a distinct type of artist. His curriculum and teaching schedule separated theatre design from its execution. The model of the distanced designer may seem completely natural today, especially to designers working simultaneously on multiple projects in different cities. In fact, this model was taught. Oenslager taught his students that commercially oriented designing was the proper model of professional practice, and he accelerated the acceptance of freelance professional ideals by younger generations. Oenslager took the commercial model of Broadway to Yale, and through his students, he passed that model on to other universities and into the profession at large. Few other universities would equal Yale's influence in theatre education, as Yale had a favorable administration, generous alumni backing, proximity to New York City, and the advantage of being the vanguard of graduate-level theatre study.

Counterpoint: Competing Models of Design Education

In 1914, a full decade prior to Baker's move to Yale, T. W. Stevens founded a department of drama at the Carnegie Institute of Technology in Pittsburgh. This new school, the first such department in the country, would provide comprehensive education in all the arts of the theatre through an extensive production program. Long teaching days featured liberal arts classes in the morning, art technique classes in the afternoon, and rehearsals and crew work in the evenings. As Yale would do a decade later,

Carnegie Tech highlighted "professional" training, but mostly for its student actors. Actor Charles Dennis McCarthy remembers that "from the beginning . . . Stevens had it in mind that we must soon make a living in one of the most demanding professions, and he drove us to learn our jobs." (The parallelism between "demanding professions" and "to learn our jobs" suggests here that McCarthy means simply non-amateur performance and not the class ideology of professionalism.) And, in fact, the majority of theatre students attending Carnegie Tech in the department's early years did intend to become actors.[69] Stevens considered the economics of theatre labor in his decision to focus on acting and technical work rather than on design or other leadership roles. As he saw it, the theatre needed more actors than it did directors or designers, and Carnegie Tech would serve students better by preparing them for the market's demand.[70]

As a counterpoint example of theatre design education, Carnegie Tech held a different set of career values. At the time, Carnegie Tech was not an elite research university but was instead a technological institute offering strong vocational training. It tended to view its students—and especially its few designers—as workers in training, not as professionals in the way this book has conceptualized them. Designers were not like architects as they were at Yale. They were craftsmen and working artists. This orientation can be seen in Carnegie Tech's curriculum, production schedule, and network of alumni. The first decades of the department did produce a great many working performers, teachers, and technicians, yet they did not embrace the same kind of professional identity that Oenslager cultivated at Yale. To be fair, many graduates did not need such a professional outlook to find work, especially in educational, community, and other theatres outside New York City. Neither, though, did these alumni have a large effect on scenic design's national leadership and occupational self-image.

The curricular differences between the two theatre departments' philosophies were stark. George Pierce Baker's program at Yale built on his English 47 Workshop at Harvard, in which production ultimately served the playwrights and their study of dramatic structure. In established narratives of the two schools, Yale was heady and theory-driven, while Carnegie's commitment to technical training meant that hands-on experience fueled the study of drama in Pittsburgh.[71] Seen from the lens of design pedagogy, however, a different picture emerges. Carnegie Tech emphasized production experience instead of studio learning, and its design curriculum neither formalized design pedagogy nor encouraged designers to see themselves as professionals. Design was taught almost exclusively through practical work in rehearsals, with few classes in either design history or technique. While Yale developed designers as artist-craftsmen with inside knowledge of a changing field, Stevens's curriculum taught theatre generally, covering techniques and skills of theatre production rather than approaching theatrical design as its own distinct type of intellectual labor.

As did Yale, Carnegie Tech first modeled its theatrical design curriculum on its architecture department, though it chose to emphasize the basic skills of the theatre artist (drawing, modeling, fabricating) over an approach that conceptualized design as creation or problem-solving. But the initial Beaux-Arts pedagogical influence faded quickly.[72] Most of the plays produced were canonical texts and contemporary works, rather than student scripts. Both technical work (set construction, rigging, props, etc.) and scene painting were taught from the school's inception, but the formal recognition of design as separate from scenic painting did not occur until 1949. Only acting, playwriting, and production were offered as concentrations before then, the last of which combined directing with design and technical direction. Conversely, at Yale, scene design existed as its own separate subject from the start of the department in 1925.

In Stevens's mind, everything that could be learned was taught by putting up nearly thirty productions a year.[73] Most direction and design was done by faculty, though occasionally students would take on design responsibilities. The key difference between Carnegie Tech's and Yale's educational modes, which perhaps maps onto their respective undergraduate and graduate missions, was Carnegie Tech's commitment to teaching design by having students take part in mounting productions. Students at Carnegie Tech spent most of their time working on fully realized productions—building scenery and costumes in crews, learning specialized techniques of voice and armed combat, and acting on stage. The initial idea for a drama department, as envisioned by Carnegie Tech's president Arthur Hamerschlag, had been for education in stagecraft and the technical arts of theatre. Stevens's counterproposal was "not [for] a school of scenery and lighting, not for applied design in the narrower aspect, but for a school of the arts of the theatre—something more comprehensive and more difficult."[74] A trained painter, Stevens "saw the training of the mind *through* the trained hand and eye." The vision for Carnegie Tech's department was to create a workshop environment where theatre production was the testing ground. Rather than teach the artistic products of design through problems or sequences of exercises in the studio class-room, Stevens applied a technical institute philosophy of trade education to theatrical study.[75]

Stevens's approach was effective at sending students into the the-atre world as actors and technicians, but it did not encourage them to see design as a discipline with subdisciplines. Stevens's curriculum de-emphasized specialization in curricular tracks; he firmly believed that "whatever the major interest of the student—acting, directing, writing or designing—he must learn to know [sic] all phases of production. . . . [O]nly in performance on a stage, working with others before an audience, can the student develop completely."[76] Yale, too, required students to take classes in other disciplines, but both the official curricular descriptions and the pedagogical methods encouraged designers, in particular, to think of themselves as a category of theatre artist, different in kind from their collaborators. Perhaps as a result of this philosophical difference, Carne-gie Tech's graduates tended to become generalist theatre practitioners or director-teachers associated with Little Theatre companies after gradua-tion, not New York design assistants. Moreover, its location in Pittsburgh put geographic distance between Carnegie Tech and the profession of theatrical design in New York City. A "Carnegie Map" published in *Theatre Arts Monthly* in July 1939 provided quantitative evidence of its distance from the world of New York theatrical design. Of the approximately 125 names listed, only three were identified as a "Designer," including How-ard Bay of New York City.[77] Many more design-focused individuals were listed as either "Educator" or "Technician," including Lucy Barton, Lloyd Weninger, and Abe Feder. (This map shows bias against costumer Barton and lighting designer Feder, who are glossed as Technician and Educa-tor, while Designer is reserved for scenic designers.) In comparison with Yale's alumni mapping, the Carnegie Map demonstrated different results: success in creating actors, technicians, and teachers but not in graduating many designers who went on to achieve national renown.[78]

The contrasts between Yale's studio approach to teaching design and Carnegie Tech's production-heavy model hinged on the role of the de-signer as a professional. Stevens's model, especially in the first two decades of the department, did not assign specific intellectual skills or tasks of design. Designing was part of putting on a play, so-called play production, but it wasn't framed as a distinct artistic identity. Further adding to the difference was the sheer number of productions put on at Carnegie Tech, most of which were fully mounted; in early years of the department, few if any design students completed projects for criticism on paper. Though Stevens drew his initial inspiration from the Beaux-Arts pedagogical model in use in architecture at Carnegie Tech, his emphasis on realized performance could not conceptualize design as a stand-alone subject. Yale's model, conversely, saw design as its own art with methods that could be taught separately. By dividing design from production, as Oenslager did, Yale led new theatre designers to think of themselves more like an architect, a professional freelancer, and less like a scene painter, a technically skilled artist executing another's plan.

As other counterpoints so far have shown, there is a form of professional exclusion at work here as well, an exclusion based in class and access. In building its Department of Drama, Yale linked graduate theatre education with the capital (financial, intellectual, social) of an elite private research university. Carnegie Tech created artists who embraced professionalism to a lesser extent because the school's leadership, from T. W. Stevens to its deans, was more practice-based in its approach to education. The institute's geographic separation from East Coast cultural centers, New York above all, accorded with Carnegie Tech's vocational emphasis and reputation for creating workers for industry, not professional artists. The Department of Drama was a recent addition to the institute and found itself at odds with the university's founding philosophy. At its incorporation as a four-year-degree institution in 1912, Carnegie Tech had planned a School of Fine and Applied Arts, but it did not include drama. The school would offer "mainly courses to produce skilled engineers and art workers in the industrial application of the plastic arts."[79] Carnegie Tech theatre students had less access to elite spaces and networks, and this meant that its designer graduates were less likely to identify their work with professions such as architecture. Perhaps just as important, there was also no direct faculty link to Broadway.

Eventually the idea of design as artistry distinct from production spread to Carnegie Tech. This transition began with the hiring of a number of Yale graduates in the late thirties and early forties, including Arthur Wilmurt, who had assisted Oenslager. Before then, when the first generation of its teachers moved on, Carnegie Tech tended to hire its own graduates once they had achieved prominence in a little theatre or commercial theatre. Lloyd Weninger headed the design and production program from 1930 until 1961; he was a Carnegie Tech graduate, although his degree was from the Painting and Design Department, not Drama.[80] Notably, the Yale-educated Henry Boettcher began his tenure as head of Carnegie Tech's Drama Department in 1936. Boettcher reduced the production schedule to give more time to "specific educational exercises," a vague statement indicating perhaps that Yale's less production-heavy style was taking hold. Carnegie Tech continued to benefit from Yale's educational model well into the seventies, especially with the design expertise of W. Oren Parker, a Yale faculty member who moved to Carnegie Tech in 1963.[81] He reorganized the design curriculum and penned a textbook that was widely adopted.

Yale and Carnegie Tech were not the only options for theatre design education in the twenties and thirties. At the undergraduate level, theatre was widely taught in universities; courses in acting and play production were spreading in the twenties, and by 1930 three-quarters of American universities offered at least one course in theatre, typically acting.[82] Most, however, were either practice-based, similar to Carnegie Tech, or thoroughly grounded in the liberal arts, often taught in a department of literature or speech. Few schools made theatrical arts a course of major study. By 1930 only three institutions were home to a department of drama at any level, Yale included.[83] The other two departments were at Carnegie Tech and at the University of Iowa, the latter a literature-based drama department that also offered a PhD. Yale and Carnegie Tech were the only schools to emphasize preparation for professional work rather than theatre study tied to a humanities-based degree in English, education, or speech and oratory.[84]

Several new design schools opened their doors in the twenties, awarding professional certificates instead of university degrees. The University of North Carolina hosted the Carolina Playmakers, established 1918, and taught production in a playwriting certification program focused on "folk plays" inspired by the history of the South. The Art Institute of Chicago allied with the Goodman Theatre to open a drama school along with its professional repertory company in 1925, and the Pasadena Playhouse added a theatre school to its little theatre operations in 1928. Thomas Wood Stevens left Carnegie Tech to start up the Goodman school, instituting a curriculum based on Carnegie Tech's in which students could specialize in design through a sequence of three courses within a generalist program.[85] Schools that were unaffiliated with universities, however, tended to offer shorter programs of study and were hampered by the need to balance education with the finances of a producing theatre organization. Stevens, for example, left the Goodman in 1930 after disputes over increasing deficits, and financial pressures plagued the Goodman school until its closure in 1975.[86] The support of a large university kept drama departments stable, especially in times of economic recession.

At the same time, programs in scenic design were offered by several smaller institutions looking to duplicate Yale's model, often with the attraction of Broadway designers or a close alliance with New York studios. To take one early example, the Dramatic Workshop of the New School for Social Research, founded by Erwin Piscator in 1940, featured a nine-course sequence in design for the theatre. Mordecai Gorelik chaired the area and taught two advanced courses in practice and theory, with foundational skills and history taught by Paul Zucker, a German architect and designer. Full-time students would spend two years in this school, which was billed as "a link between academic education and a professional career." It imitated Yale's approach, in that an established working designer headed the program, another artist taught mostly "practical problems" in its introductory classes, and the sequence prioritized "practical work for advanced designers" in higher-level classes. The New School curriculum also taught New Stagecraft philosophy's overarching claim that "the designer's business is not merely to create a stage picture but to make an indispensable contribution to the meaning of the production," and a full course was given over to the study of "the role of design in developing the line of the play."[87] The Dramatic Workshop did not function as a university department, however, and ran into trouble after the New School's separation from the Dramatic Workshop in 1949. Piscator's departure in 1951 left the school without a strong leader and identity. Today, the school is best known for its development of acting technique and its later workshops by Judith Malina, rather than its success in training designers.

Carnegie Tech, Yale University, and (later) the Dramatic Workshop were the three most notable schools offering scenic design education in the thirties and forties. State institutions such as the Universities of Wisconsin, Iowa, and Texas at Austin had established generalist programs in theatre or drama and sought established designers to join their faculty. Iowa attracted Yale-educated scenic designer Arnie Gillette immediately after his graduation in 1931,[88] and Texas hired the Carnegie Tech–trained costume designer Lucy Barton in 1948.[89] In 1939 Wisconsin attempted to hire Lee Simonson, who declined because he did not want to move to Madison; Wisconsin's negotiations with Woodman Thompson also faltered, according to Paul Leitner's review of Thompson's papers.[90] In any case, such programs had courses at the undergraduate level, not the graduate level, and did not seek to provide preprofessional education with specialization in a single design area. These schools were trying to increase the quality of education given to undergraduates with generalist majors in theatre or drama.

Some students bypassed the university and sought individualized schooling or apprenticeship, and designers occasionally chose to develop their own school-like bodies outside university settings. Norman Bel Geddes, for instance, taught scenic design workshops intermittently from 1922 to 1927,[91] trading on his name recognition rather than a university affiliation. Woodman Thompson took on private students from 1940 until 1951, as the next section describes. Lester Polakov developed his "Studio of Stage Design" in 1958 after leaving a temporary appointment at Columbia. Polakov's studio employed scene designer George Jenkins and lighting designers Jean Rosenthal and Tharon Musser (both Yale grads) to teach in the mid-1960s; its main scenic design sequence was a series of four courses based in "demonstrations, lectures, and critiques of student work," and it moved from "assigned projects" to "more advanced and complicated design problems."[92] For these private schools, the goal was more career-driven than the liberal arts education of state university programs. Like Yale and Carnegie Tech, they aimed to teach new professionals how to work effectively: passing a union exam, building a practice, getting hired as an assistant or apprentice.

The full national embrace of the studio model in higher education began in the fifties. American universities increased the number of MFA degrees they offered in theatre, and more long-standing designers sought university affiliation in their later careers. These included designers such as Gorelik, who followed up his Dramatic Workshop teaching with a position at Southern Illinois University beginning in 1960, and Howard Bay, who was among the first faculty hired in a new MFA program at Brandeis University in 1966.[93] Both of these schools followed Yale's model by seeking a leading professional to head an area of design. However, they differed in that the schools offered both master's and undergraduate degrees, and they emphasized a liberal arts basis to their (undergraduate) curriculum. In one version or another, Yale's studio-based university pedagogy caught on and became a popular way for young designers to attain the knowledge necessary to practice their art.

Abstract Knowledge on the Union Exam

The shift toward studio education was further institutionalized by revisions to the union entrance exam. As chapter 1 explained, the union achieved significant social closure by regulating entry into the group. Therefore, the designers who developed and graded the exam had a significant, though less direct, influence on design education. Revisions to the examination in the mid-thirties made schooling even more essential. Schools such as Yale and Carnegie Tech aimed to produce working professionals and measured their success in part by graduates' employment. As Yale's model spread, the union exam required more abstract and more period knowledge from designers, precisely the type of information that was most often taught in university classes. By 1950 it was difficult for newer designers to pass the union exam without some structured education, either in theatre departments or through private tutoring.

The examination for designers was first created in 1927. In winter of that year, designers had agitated for the formation of a "designers committee" within the union that would write, administer, and grade the exam and then recommend new designers for membership. The committee would recommend "only those candidates having artistic ability (without prejudice as to school), professional technical ability, particularly scale drawing[,] and actual experience in putting on plays on a professional scale."[94] A new examination specifically for designers soon followed. A handful of completed examinations still exist from this early phase; Vincente Minnelli's 1931 entrance exam, for instance, was archived.

His exam tested the applicant primarily in the areas requested by the designers in 1927: scale drawing and experience. The exam consisted of eight questions. The first two tested basic math (calculation of fractions and scale) and modern art knowledge, while the remainder asked Minnelli to sketch, draft, and detail an interior setting with specified architectural features, and to develop sketches and a costume design plot for *Romeo and Juliet*. The exam also included questions about experience and past employment, which likely influenced the decisions of both the examining committee and the union's membership voting to admit examinees. The exam was to be completed in two hours. (Minnelli passed and was admitted to the union.)[95] In its first version, the examination stressed pencil skills, freehand and assisted by drafting instruments, yet did not test painting skill or knowledge of period style beyond basic interior architecture terminology. There may have been an in-person test of scenic

3.2. Union examination page, by Vincente Minnelli. *Box 1, folder 30, United Scenic Artists Exam Designs, *T-VIM 2011-256, New York Public Library. Image courtesy of United Scenic Artists, Local USA 829, IATSE.*

painting technique as well, but union minutes refer to testing "on the paint frame" inconsistently, so it is possible that designers' testing deemphasized scenic painting over time.

The union's examining committee significantly revised the exam in 1934. In those revisions, Woodman Thompson, the new chair of the body, elevated recall of knowledge *about* design over producing examples *of* design. Slide identifications, mostly of period style in costume and interiors, appeared for the first time. The design skills tested on the examination expanded too. Beyond drafting and rendering a set in perspective, later exams additionally required full-color renderings in watercolor or gouache. These were, it seems, painted on the spot.[96] Many core design competencies endured, such as perspective drawing, the creation of ground plans, and costume sketching, yet designers of the thirties through the fifties were also tested on their color selection and painting skills (on paper). With these changes, scenic design further diverged from the skills required of a union scenic artist.

The standing union committee also graded the tests, and extant grading sheets illustrate the exam's exacting standards. In the areas of furniture, architecture, and costume, the exam asked for fine categorization of periods. Many of the errors, marked in Thompson's hand, were one period easily mistaken for another; for instance, students confused late sixteenth- and early seventeenth-century costume, or Directoire and Biedermeier architecture.[97] Thompson's blunt corrections suggest that he used slide identification and knowledge of period style as a sorting mechanism. Though the original purpose of the exam was to measure artistic talent "without prejudice as to school," knowledge of the details that distinguish one style from another, especially on slides, required at least some schooling. Period identifications were far more likely to be encountered in a formal education setting than in on-the-job training. Schools such as Yale and Carnegie Tech had already developed curricula that taught period styles, and in its revisions to the exam, the union formalized this body of knowledge for its own use.

Woodman Thompson served as committee chair from 1934 until 1951, when scandal prompted his resignation. He was the chief grader of examinations, and most archived exams bear his handwriting and occasionally his initials. Three other members of the examining committee endorsed the exams, as membership applications show, but these measures were not enough to guard against corruption and potential bribery.[98] Thompson took on private students who wanted to study for the exam, and a main subject of his tutoring was historical and theoretical knowledge—precisely what might not be taught in an apprenticeship. Thompson received many letters in the forties and early fifties from prospective students asking to study with him, especially from those who did not have an extensive background in visual design history. Letters to Thompson dating from 1950 to 1952 referred to the "historical background which is important in order to meet the requirements of the examination," to "adapting and extending my knowledge," and to "how much technical knowledge I am in need of for scenic work."[99] This tutoring provided income for Thompson, whose tailored instruction prepared students well for the examination that he would later grade.

Thompson's control over the system led to allegations of bribery. His critics argued that students were effectively forced to pay several thousand dollars for the privilege of studying with Thompson. Paul Leitner has suggested that Thompson resorted to this stream of income owing to the increasing difficulty he faced in finding scenic design employment or a teaching job at a university. Thompson's style of design emphasized the unit set and was considered out of date by the fifties. Designers interviewed by Leitner, including Peggy Clark, Lester Polakov, and Emeline Roche, recalled that an inquest into Thompson's tutoring led to his resignation from the examining board in 1951.[100] Thompson may have given in to the financial temptation of being both a private tutor and the union gatekeeper. Examinations graded in Thompson's hand demonstrate that he had significant control over who was judged to be sufficiently skilled and knowledgeable. It was not uncommon for applicants who did not pass the examination to gain membership on appeal to the union executive board.[101] Nonetheless, Thompson's tutoring substituted for university education in some ways, by filling the gaps in students' historical knowledge. As designers professionalized, individuals in power at legitimizing institutions had a significant degree of influence over new entrants to the field.

The entrance exam, then, functioned as an adjunct to university education. It allowed scenic designers to insist on testing skills particular to their discipline and to regulate union admission based on those skills. However, in practice, the exam also exhibited the negative effects of social closure, namely, a tendency toward discrimination and the temptations of power for those holding high positions in a professionally necessary institution. Attending a university program may not have been a requirement for younger designers, but graduate study did become a common path to professional status among designers by midcentury, in no small part because university curricula complemented new union exam requirements.

Conclusion

The historical influence of Yale's design curriculum was twofold. First, it provided a strong model of design education and practice, reinforced in its studio courses and in its continuous production program. For some, Yale taught them how to work; for others, it taught them what to expect as a designer in the commercial theatre. Second, as the first extended curriculum in stage design in the United States, Yale's studio practice became a model for other universities. Carnegie Tech adopted more of Yale's model after Stevens's departure by increasing its concentration on classroom exercises. Few new programs had the numerous advantages Yale enjoyed, yet many looked to Yale's education as one example of how theatre, and theatrical design, could be taught to benefit both the university and the profession.

The influence of education on the development of design professionalism was not limited to Yale. Other schools, independent designers, and the scenic designers' union all took on educational roles. The growing dominance of university education troubled designers and union members. During the forties, an educational subcommittee of the union sponsored classes for members and students. An announcement sent to union members in 1943 explained that the subcommittee's purpose was "to educate our own members, to refresh ourselves in our work, and . . . to educate the younger people." "It should not be necessary to send students of the theatrical arts to universities," the memo continued; "their educations should be our responsibility."[102] Members taught classes in everything from painting and reading blueprints to designing costumes and sets. Teachers included Lee Simonson, Aline Bernstein, and Robert Bergman, who donated use of his shop for painting classes. This wartime initiative was a way of making use of a downturn in business and, perhaps, was a covert swipe at the more expensive training given by Thompson and Oenslager. This group, chaired by Bernstein and employing several designers who were not in war service, privileged informal education and a social atmosphere based in the union, not the university. They did not see their instruction as preparing professionals for a career; rather, they were elevating scenic work "to the position of the craft guilds of the past."[103] The educational subcommittee's classes were only offered during the war, however, and the subcommittee disbanded once normal business resumed.

It is also interesting to note that the 1943 educational subcommittee was run by a prominent woman designer, Aline Bernstein, who bridged the design subdisciplines of costume and scenery. More women taught in union classes than in universities, especially in design areas. Women were frequently hired to teach costume design but not scenic or lighting design. (Gendered labor is discussed at greater length in the next chapter, in particular the career of Emeline Roche.) World War II provided an opportunity for career advancement for these women. In many cases, though, opportunities presented themselves to women designers in different terms and tempos than they did for the men discussed in this book. As a result, differing trajectories of professionalism emerged for women theatrical artists.

To conclude this chapter on theatre education, it is worth stating that education remains a strong means of establishing and enforcing professional closure today. Universities provided stability and finances for design education, and theater programs located at higher-status universities and in or near a major city, especially New York City, have been the most successful in producing large numbers of alumni who work in the profession. This history may be seen as mostly positive, in the sense that Oenslager's pedagogy transformed a diffuse artistic field into a replicable course of study, or as mostly negative, in that its closure tended to reify institutional power and classist peer networks.

Pedagogy is a chief means by which disciplines organize, legitimize, and proliferate knowledge, and so a history of professionalization among scenic designers must take the university into account. Yale and Carnegie Tech fed the regional theatre movement and other movements for a national theatre. Graduate and undergraduate training for theatre in higher education became a source of stable employment for designers (and actors, directors, and playwrights, too) by the middle of the century. As occurred in other areas, the students who enrolled in design classes transformed the field. Those students internalized lessons from their teachers and, in so doing, promulgated a professional ideology that comprised formal classroom training as an early career milestone.

4. THE CONSULTING ARTIST: SERVING THE NEEDS OF OTHERS

Lee Simonson, reflecting on his career in a 1943 portfolio memoir, came to a blunt and telling conclusion about the design profession. Scenic design, he wrote, "tends to become an avocation or a part-time job for most of its practitioners. Otherwise it remains a profession for young bachelors, men with rich wives or independent means, or artists with some other source of professional income. At best it is a profession for part of a lifetime."[1]

In this memoir, *Part of a Lifetime*, Simonson attributed the precarious career trajectory of many designers to inconsistency within the field. He blamed the "box office rhythms" of commercial theatre, the union's over-supply of qualified artists, and the "overcentralization of . . . professional play producing in New York."[2] As a result, scenic design saw an overrepresentation of the young, the well-off, and those able to turn previously established theatre networks into "some other source of professional income." For designers working in the commercial theatre, stable professional income came from a diversified portfolio of work. Income from other types of design and design-adjacent work mitigated some of the career uncertainty inherent in theatrical employment. This approach predated the war and was firmly in place by the late forties. Donald Oenslager, for one, agreed with Simonson: "After World War II I was taking on all kinds of extra-theatrical activities. This was the moment when interior and industrial design, store and window display, and packaging too, were turning to the theatre in search of fresh directions. Before long they were 'dramatizing' and 'theatricalizing' right and left."[3] Looking to industrial design was just one answer; architecture projects, interior design, film art direction, industrial theatre production, and exhibition and fairground design also filled designers' pocketbooks.

Many designers blended their extra-theatrical design work with a concept of public service. This chapter focuses on theatrical work that, while mostly paid, implicitly served a public good and was undertaken outside theatre production proper. It conceptualizes this subset of extra-theatrical work as service, both as a nod to the academic-professional roots of its justification and because designers themselves saw such contributions as valuable for the betterment of American or world theatre.[4] Such a claim invokes what professionalism theorists have called the "service ideal." Just as professions claim allegiance to higher secular and civic values—beauty, safety, health, justice—scenic designers too found that highlighting the public service aspects of their work allowed them to support claims of having specialized, useful expertise. Oftentimes such projects were paid contract work, and therefore not strictly service in the academic's sense of unpaid work to promote a field, but their close association with the promotion of the American theatre allowed designers to make claims of serving a greater good.

Hidden within Simonson's lament about the part-time nature of designing, however, is a subtle gender critique. Scenic design being a career for "young bachelors" and "men with rich wives," women were structurally excluded from Simonson's view of the profession.[5] Though Simonson's omission of women might be typical gender bias for its time, his formulation sustains those biases by neglecting prominent women colleagues and fellow union members. As this chapter attends to the ways in which service allowed designers to professionalize, it also relates some history of those expected to perform service—here, women—to show that, though they occupied service roles, women's design service was less valued by men in the field.

A civilian volunteer spirit permeated the United States during World War II, and as a result many scenic designers applied their skills to the war effort. Some male designers served as camoufleurs, makers of camouflage, in the US military, while women served on the home front by taking up additional service work with military support organizations. Both of these new avenues for design work helped initiate the service ideal of design professionalism. After the war, men and women designers continued to engage in acts of service, but their service led to differing results.

Several well-known male designers parlayed their design expertise into consulting jobs, particularly in building new theatre architecture for regional and university theatres. The concept of the designer as consultant provided a new late-career path and income stream for those who could transform expertise into lectures, symposia, and consulting contracts. Women, on the other hand, found that their service was seen through the lens of volunteerism: useful but not remunerated by significant fees or increased prestige. In many cases the field encouraged women to perform service that sustained existing organizations and projects, service that journalists and scholars have viewed as less notable or revolutionary. Service work and consulting rounds out this book's history of design professionalism because it occurred later than other efforts. As previous chapters have shown, extra-theatrical work in unions, in the media, and in education provided legal and cultural recognition of the scenic designer's new labor status. Service, however, functioned as an *ex post facto* justification for the social closure and occupational control that the designer had already accrued.

Wartime Service in Camouflage and the Stage Door Canteen

World War II had a more significant impact on scenic designers as individuals than it did on scenic design style or approach. While production slowed on Broadway, younger designers mostly filled in for those who shipped out. Many working designers did join the war effort; in addition to Jo Mielziner and Donald Oenslager, scenic designers Frederick Fox and Harry Horner and lighting experts Abe Feder and Stanley McCandless also volunteered.[6] They found their way into camouflage work alongside other applied artists, including architects, sculptors, and civil engineers. By applying their scenic design expertise to a real-world war problem, a process Mielziner referred to as "the exact antithesis of stage designing," designers discovered a new, more civic-minded outlet for their talents.[7] Women designers also served the war effort. Their work was more often in civilian institutions as replacements for absent men and in roles that maintained morale. Both arenas of service have been only lightly discussed by theatre design historians, perhaps since the temporary and applied nature of wartime design service strikes historians as a curious footnote. And, indeed, many designers did see war service as different from their everyday jobs, as outside their normal careers.[8] Yet, seen from the point of view of a developing professionalism, a service ideology remained a part of designers' concepts of their career after the war ended.

The designers who joined military service wanted to serve in camouflage. US armed forces had previously hired artists to create and execute camouflage in World War I,[9] and they sought out similar constituencies for World War II service. Since the 1910s, camouflage practice had moved away from painting-based approaches, such as the "dazzle" patterns meant to frustrate enemy identification of ships. Increased air combat in the

1940s made three-dimensional camouflage more important. Scenic designers emerged alongside modelmakers, landscapers, film art directors, sculptors, and architects as the new World War II camoufleurs. Other types of scenic design service contributed to the war effort without requiring designers to enlist; for instance, Norman Bel Geddes produced a number of scale model photographs depicting the Battle of Midway and other battles for *Life* between 1942 and 1946.[10] Lazlo Moholy-Nagy and Jay Doblin, students of Raymond Loewy, worked on civilian contracts for state and federal defense projects.[11] For Oenslager and Mielziner, however, military camouflage service was how they applied their design expertise to the theatres of combat.

In 1942 Mielziner, Oenslager, and eighteen other working designers founded the Camouflage Society of Professional Stage Designers, a civilian group dedicated to the study of camouflage. According to Frederick Fox, "If we were going to go in the army we might as well do the things we knew how to do. We each paid $50.00 for membership so we could rent an office in which to hold classes and to pay the guys . . . who would be teaching us camouflage. A Russian officer, the Baron [Nicholas Cherkassoff] was the main teacher, and he sold us copies of his camouflage book for $25.00 each."[12] The group hoped that prior training would allow them some control over their wartime assignments. Fox attested to their collective optimism: "the class met one night per week and lasted six weeks. After that, we marched *en masse* to the induction center at Church Street." Behrens further noted that, of the twenty or so attendees in the group, only Oenslager and Mielziner received an officer's commission. Several others enlisted, and not all served in camouflage-related posts.

The group's Statement of Aims and Policy, written by group treasurer Donald Oenslager, explained the links that group members saw between scenic design and camouflage:

Camouflage Authorities consider Stage Designers among those best qualified for Camouflage Service. Their reasons are many. The Stage Designer requires a working knowledge of painting, sculpture, architecture and engineering. He understands the principles of optics and psychology. He works in three dimensions, creating imitation and deception by an arbitrary use of form, color, light and texture. He specializes in portable and collapsible construction and in unusual materials, creating the utmost in illusion with the least possible outlay of materials and labor. He personally supervises the execution of the actual production working with sub-contractors on a basis of budgets and schedules. And above all the Stage Designer is a practical craftsman accustomed to working with responsibility, accuracy and imagination under conditions frequently most trying. To the Stage Designer Camouflage is "scenic science" adapted to the task of National Defense.[13]

This statement reads dually as a justification for scenic designers' unorthodox approach to military volunteerism and as an ideological bridge between New Stagecraft practice and the perceived needs of wartime camouflage. It articulates the transferrable skills of the scenic designer, both in terms of visual and craftsman-like talents, and of managerial functions: "He personally supervises the execution of the actual production . . ." The group achieved press recognition, as well. For instance, the society was named among other professional groups of civil and heating engineers as contributing to camouflage development in a *Popular Mechanics* feature in December 1942.[14] By banding together and drawing on scenic designers' distinct talents, the Camouflage Society enjoyed modest success in its goals of achieving better army placement for Mielziner, Oenslager, and a few other designers.

The designers' actual work was not publicized during the conflict, as their designs were considered war secrets. Publications after the war revealed that Oenslager was first involved in camouflage training programs for bomber crews at Scribner Army Air Field in Nebraska and then later was transferred to Guam, where he worked in Combat Intelligence. Oenslager's modeling, construction, and lighting expertise served him well. He specialized in the creation of realistic camouflage and in the use of fluorescent pigments and ultraviolet lighting to convey information in briefings. One area he camouflaged was deemed "too dangerous for trainee bomber runs. . . . [T]hey couldn't find the fields!"[15] One photograph of his work at Scribner's Camouflage Demonstration Building shows a young Oenslager holding a long wooden pointer before a map of Japan; others show him with army officers erecting camouflage netting, inspecting tufts of fake grasses, and discussing plan models before an informational display titled "Draping Heavy Bombers." From the evidence of Oenslager's memories and these photos, the scenic designer's talent for realistic modeling and visual communication was clearly put to good use.

Jo Mielziner also served abroad as a commissioned officer. Like Oenslager, he was occupied with aerial camouflage; he disguised runways with both paint and three-dimensional camouflage, turning military bases into farms or suburban neighborhoods.[16] Mielziner's contributions are less

4.1. Photograph of Donald Oenslager during his army
service in camouflaging, Jefferson Barracks, St. Louis,
MO, 1942. *Donald Oenslager Papers and Designs, Billy
Rose Theatre Division, The New York Public Library.*

well documented than Oenslager's, but his approach to camouflaging as
a type of applied scenography comes through in interviews in the forties.
In 1944 Mielziner theorized camouflage as inverted scene design. Rather
than fulfilling the need to "tell the audience as quickly as possible who
the characters are, and how many; where the play takes place; what kind
of a play it is," the designer takes rules and "operate[s] them in reverse"
when camouflaging. When "you have an installation you can't possibly
disguise," he advised, "make it look like anything except what it is." In the
interview Mielziner went on to promote the professional competencies

of the theatrical designer; he cited the designers' "sense of color" as more valuable than the "engineer's mathematical experience" and praised designers' ability "to adapt themselves to what is called 'field expedient'— which means improvising quickly when the scheduled camouflage material doesn't arrive."[17] In 1946 a review of Mielziner's war service concluded that "his intimate 'know how,' gained in the theatre, was just the right equipment for an expert who had to be intimate with the 'chemistry' of lighting, the principles of landscaping, architecture and hasty improvisation."[18] In his camouflage work, Mielziner demonstrated that scenic design was a flexible, portable set of competencies that could be equally useful in nontheatrical applications.

Another form of design-related war service occurred at the Stage Door Canteen, an outreach arm of the American Theatre Wing, which provided entertainment for departing US servicemen. The Canteen was a social venue and nightclub staffed by volunteers from the theatre business; it featured free food, women hosts who conversed and danced with the soldiers, and Broadway entertainments including celebrity cameos.[19] The Canteen also tapped designers for the design, decoration, and maintenance of its New York home on West Forty-Fourth Street. Two designers, Peggy Clark and Emeline Roche, chaired its scenic design committee. They supervised the construction and upkeep of the Canteen and oversaw the scenic effects and lighting used for performances. These women's civic volunteerism on the home front was another form of design service. Still, persistent gender bias hampered their attempts to turn this service work into something more professionally valuable than the home front labor expected of American women in the forties.

Peggy Clark and Emeline Roche are best known today as lighting and costume designers, respectively, but both began by producing scenery as well. Roche began her career working with Norman Bel Geddes in the twenties and proved herself to be an effective scenic assistant and technical supervisor to a number of New Stagecraft designers, including Aline Bernstein and Robert Edmond Jones. She practiced both scenery and costume design but found that she was more accepted as a costume designer in New York commercial theatre circles. Peggy Clark began her studies at Yale in the mid-thirties, learning from Oenslager, Stanley McCandless, and Frank Bevan. She realized that lighting was a quickly growing area, and her specialization led to Broadway costume work and union membership within a year after her graduation. Clark is one of the earliest examples of someone regularly billed as a lighting designer on Broadway, instead of being credited with "lighting by" or as a "technical supervisor."[20] Roche's and Clark's move away from scenic design, a stereotypically male pursuit, and into emergent "supportive" roles such as costume and lighting design is notable for its strategic engagement with gendered ideologies of service (something addressed in detail later in this chapter).

The American Theatre Wing's Stage Door Canteen was a close alliance between the Wing and the union. Both groups gained significant good press for the Canteen, as the effort was an obvious show of support for Allied soldiers. As the Canteen's technical directors and designers, Roche

4.2. Officer of the Day Emeline Roche and Walter at the Stage Door Canteen. *Carl Van Vechten (1880–1964) / Museum of the City of New York.* ©*VanVechtenTrust.*

and Clark coordinated donations and correspondence between the union and the Canteen's committee, liaised with contracted designers and scene painters, supervised renovations to the space, and tended to the technical needs of the performers. Other work included renting curtains and other production materials, planning for renovations and upkeep, and, when technical needs were slow, helping to write policies for the hostesses and servicemen.[21] They made use of their talents for logistical planning, spatial design, and managing labor, and they placed scenic design near the center of the professional theatre's war effort.

The most conspicuous contributions from scenic designers were a series of paintings mounted in the hallways and the main dancing room. Commissioned specially for the Canteen, twenty-five paintings depicted backstage work and life from famous designers and respected scenic painters. Oenslager, Mielziner, Howard Bay, Peggy Clark, Aline Bernstein, and others contributed a panel.[22] Roche herself did not contribute a panel, but she designed and painted images of theatre union seals, which flanked the stage, and a painting of Allied national and military flags, which hung upstage of the performance area. Although infrequently remarked on in histories of the Canteen, and often obscured in photographs behind servicemen, hostesses, and performers, these images placed theatre labor in front of Canteen attendees.

After the Canteen closed, these paintings were either returned to designers or destroyed, and little photographic evidence exists of them.[23] From fragments, though, it is possible to reconstruct the range of subjects. The paintings depicted dance rehearsals, renderings of Broadway lights at night, scenes of backstage carpentry and painting, lighting rehearsals, and performers onstage in costume. As designers of the space, Clark and Roche thought it important that theatre labor be featured. The glitz of Broadway was possible only through the hard work of performers, technicians, designers, and others; backstage subjects were equally represented alongside glamorous scenes onstage or on the street. The work of then-known designers such as Mielziner and Bernstein, each signed in a lower corner in white paint, marked the space as participating in the social networks of professional Broadway theatre. Military servicemen were likely drawn to the Canteen by the promised performances or to glimpse celebrities, but the depiction of design and painting labor on the walls would have foregrounded theatrical work for at least some attendees.

Although Clark and Roche were responsible for the design of the space, and they oversaw renovations and conceptualized the Canteen's design,

4.3. Private First Class Herbert Hoburn, Officer of the
Day Emeline Roche, and Private Alan Hewitt at the
Stage Door Canteen. *Carl Van Vechten (1880–1964) /
Museum of the City of New York.* ©*VanVechtenTrust.*

they were not able to maintain intellectual property rights to it. In 1943
Roche and Clark sued Sol Lesser, producer of the film *Stage Door Canteen*,
seeking damages for alleged copyright infringement. Their design for the
Canteen was reproduced in Lesser's film, but only Harry Horner, the art
director hired by Lesser, appeared in the film's credits. In court documents
Roche and Clark alleged that Horner and his team photographed and
measured the Canteen and then rebuilt it for the film. Horner appears
to have done this with the approval of the American Theatre Wing, but
Clark and Roche took exception, stating that the renovations to Lee Shubert's donated basement, and to the physical arrangement of art, seating,
and performance space, were their design. Clark and Roche first sought
payment—as Lesser had paid other Canteen volunteers appearing in and

working on the film—but they were not paid, nor did Lesser acquiesce to their request for screen credit. When the film was complete, Roche and Clark realized that they had not been credited, so they sought payment for damages.

Because their work was not explicitly design for the theatre, Roche and Clark had difficulty accessing the institutional support that had defended a designer's right to copyright and fair payment. They first appealed to the union, which had held de facto copyrights for designers since the twenties. Because their work was not, strictly speaking, a stage design, however, and since the film had already been completed, the union would not intercede. The American Theatre Wing was conflicted about the suit, as well. Some on the Wing's board (including Roche's close friend Jane Cowl, an actress) privately sympathized, but when the board discussed it formally, they decided it was too risky to defend Roche and Clark against Lesser. The suit was finally settled with the payment of one dollar to Clark and Roche, and with the Wing and Lesser paying for the legal fees incurred in the suit, for a total of approximately $2,000.[24] Roche and Clark were not financially straitened by the litigation, yet their design rights were not upheld, either. Some peers viewed them as difficult collaborators. The extra-theatrical location and ethic of war service as volunteerism (and therefore not worthy of usual designers' rights) were what had permitted Lesser to exploit their work. This intellectual property dispute provides an example of the value that Roche and Clarke brought to the Canteen, while also illustrating the difficulties faced by women designers who contributed to the field through service.

After the forties, the war service of scenic designers ended, but scenic design's wider applicability endured. Both Oenslager and Mielziner frequently reported on theatre and design in publications in the fifties. Their works envisioned new theatres and described theatre cultures that would have been unfamiliar to American readers. Oenslager's travel led to a small set of articles on theatre in Asia and the Americas, while Mielziner wrote several opinion pieces that advocated for an expanded landscape of American theatres. Both of these interests were conceived by designers as types of service to ideals they had served in the war: American expansion and national pride through newer and better theatre arts. Women continued in service and leadership after World War II, having broken through in wartime, yet their service was most often in sex-stereotyped institutional roles. For instance, Emeline Roche succeeded Aline Bernstein as union committee chair for education, and costume designer Emile Stoner served as chair of the union's costume design associate group. Stoner's position allowed her access to executive board meetings, but she could only speak when costume matters were discussed.[25] Other women rose to union leadership as secretary or treasurer. Even then, women's access to leadership remained in similar roles until 1968, when Clark was elected union president.[26]

For the most part, as the next section elaborates, women's wartime service was framed within the context of volunteer, institution-sustaining work. Their volunteerism reflected a widespread ethic in the early forties. In the United States, magazines, women's fiction, and print and radio advertisements constructed women into what Maureen Honey has called a "symbol of the ideal home-front spirit, standing for national unity, dedication to the cause, and stoic pursuit of victory."[27] This ideology tended to render the wartime service of professional men as heroic, exceptional, and innovative, while women's service was seen as patriotic but expected. Moreover, men's service allowed them to capitalize on the application of design to real-world problems as a form of consulting, while women were discouraged from transforming their designing experience into paid consultancy outside the theatre.

The Service Ideal, Consulting, and Volunteerism

Within scenic design, appeals to service occurring inside and outside the theatre helped solidify the field's claims to professional standing. A more general overview of the link between service and the professions is useful, however. Classically, professions such as medicine, law, and the clergy served socially useful ends that could not be easily served by market solutions: for instance, health, justice, and morality.[28] Professionalism ideology suggests that such work can and should operate outside traditional business arrangements because these ideals would be better met by ostensibly disinterested, independent actors. Newer professions joined existing ones, and similar claims of service to ideals smoothed the road for social closure—for instance, professional architecture promised lasting, safe construction of buildings. To preserve such an orientation, sociologist Eliot Freidson notes, professions reinforce pro-service ideologies. By identifying a value around which a profession can coalesce, a profession can "claim to be a secular priesthood" by focusing on higher purposes.[29]

Allegiance to a service value does more than justify professional monopolies, however. Service underpins professional judgments, ethical standards, and practitioners' independence. The claim to be serving the client's greater interest is especially relevant in practices such as medicine and law, where personal profit-based motivations might be at odds with client needs. As theorist Howard Wilensky has pointed out, "devotion to the client's interests more than personal or commercial profit should guide decisions when the two are in conflict," and "the service ideal is the pivot around which the moral claim to professional status revolved."[30] Independence is necessary for a functioning profession; it underpins claims that professional groups prize: self-determination of standards, election of membership by peers, and a shared code of ethics. In fact, the very claim to professional status depends on a service ideal. Freidson explains that even though "the assertion of such independence is more ritual than not in ordinary times . . . the ideological claim of collective devotion to that transcendent value and, more importantly, the right to serve it independently when the practical demands of patrons and clients stifle it" remain central today.[31] Among applied artists, the need for beautiful (and safe) environments, products, and experiences justified the professionalizing claims of architecture and, later, industrial and scenic design.

Professionals, once they achieve monopoly over their practice, may sell their expertise or knowledge to businesses or other professionals, rather than selling their services directly to clients. Such professionals may be formally framed as a consultant or their advice may be informally described as a professional "engagement," such as a lecture, a symposium, or simply a conversation. In the early twentieth century, as US corporations began to hire independent research and management consulting firms, the concept of the consultant as an independent contractor became more common. Professionals may be able to diagnose and solve difficult problems within a business organization, just as they would for a client visiting their practice.

Consulting—the sale of expert advice—became a lucrative pursuit for scenic designers, too, particularly those who had publicly demonstrated their expertise by the middle of the century. The skills of analysis, conceptualization, communication, and execution inherent in theatre design could benefit businesses, governments, and nonprofits when creating performance venues and events. Such work upheld service claims, even though much of this work was not strictly pro bono.[32] This was especially the case for Jo Mielziner and Donald Oenslager, as well as consultants in engineering and lighting such as Stanley McCandless, George Izenour, and Jean Rosenthal.

Gender ideology and sexism complicated women's abilities to claim professional standing, including the ability to sell advice as a consultant.[33] Professional women were still rare in many fields in the early and mid-twentieth century United States, and those professions that did have large numbers of women practitioners had not attained a high degree of closure and self-determination. The "separate spheres" gender ideology of the nineteenth century held strong. Women were permitted professional standing only in their appropriate sphere: those occupations closely associated with private, moral, family, and care-centered work such as nursing, primary and secondary education, libraries, social work, and clothing and fashion.[34] Even within these fields, it should be noted, the highest authority often remained with male members: doctors, school administrators, directors, and organization leaders.[35] So, women faced a double bind. "Female" professions were of a secondary status and led by men, and women were excluded from the more powerful and autonomous "male" professions.

Gender also intersected with the idea of service in professions. The ideology of separate spheres discouraged women from pursuing paid work outside the home, and whenever a woman would perform labor outside the home, it was most acceptable when done on a volunteer basis. Historically, the separate spheres ideology permitted women to participate in civic life through volunteerism, through service on committees and in associations committed to the public good, including the arts. As social historians Joan Jacobs Brumberg and Nancy Tomes note, "Within the nineteenth-century woman's sphere, unpaid work outside the home became a route to self-respect and power oftentimes involving a lifetime commitment to a single organization or cause."[36] This route was open mostly to middle- and upper-class white women who were not financially obligated to work outside the home. Such gendered expectations, though, obtained beyond this particular racial and economic group.

As a result, professional women in theatre occupied service roles as a matter of course, and rarely were their service roles seen as a crucial part of a woman's professional development. When women scenic designers contributed to the field through service, by working within the union, by volunteering their labor to charitable events, or by advising peers on how to approach a problem, their service was conventional and normalized, not noteworthy. Women were simply expected to serve where they could.

As Helen Krich Chinoy has observed, narratives of women's theatre work "reinforc[e] Miss [Eva] Le Gallienne's suggestion that, counter to [Edward Gordon] Craig's perverse admonition, serving the art of theatre has in many ways been the special function of women."[37] Chinoy's emphasis on contribution through service, not revolution or innovation, underscores the ways in which service functioned as an ideological trap for some women, instead of as a springboard for greater professional success, as it was for many men.

In the context of service, the clearest division can be seen in the ways in which men leveraged their expertise through consulting, while women were more often conceived as volunteers. This division had ideological roots and material results. In the late nineteenth and early twentieth century, philanthropic and volunteer groups contributed greatly to the Little Theatre movement, art theatres, and social reform projects such as Chicago's Hull House.[38] The location of these theatres outside the (elitist, limited, yet influential) domain of commercial theatre production cast women's theatre work as subordinate. Chiefly their work was devalued by assertions of its being amateurism or volunteerism, sometimes both. Women scenic designers had to overcome Victorian-era expectations that their labor should be provided freely or at reduced cost and that their service should serve existing (male-designed) institutions. When they did provide service, it was seen as amateur or was limited to sex-stereotypical areas of design. Their service was less easily parlayed into more lucrative endeavors of professional expertise, such as lecturing or consulting. Women did achieve professional standing in scenic design, eventually, even taking positions as architectural and lighting consultants by the 1960s, but it happened less frequently and took more time than similar advancement made by male scenic designers.

Counterpoint: Service Expectations and Women's Design Careers

Because their contributions in scenery were often overlooked, many women designers shifted their careers into areas where their work could be more easily accepted by commercial theatre. This section turns to the full careers of Roche, Clark, and other women scenic designers whose work included scenic design but also included costume or lighting design as well. Many of these women gained influence through service-based volunteerism. This mirrored the way in which their design work, too, was seen as a service, their designs being secondary to and supportive of the scenic designer's primary visual idea. Some designers, such as Roche, felt pushed into the more "feminine" world of costume, despite her attempts to remain a designer of scenery as well. Other women, such as Peggy Clark and Aline Bernstein, embraced the once-secondary status of their design fields—lighting for Clark, costume for Bernstein—and eventually helped elevate the standing of costume and lighting design. Despite their original intentions to become designers in many fields, including scenery, most women designers working in the theatre before 1960 adjusted their aspirations to fit into a patriarchal system. From their point of view, working in supportive design fields was the most strategic way to gain recognition in the commercial, professional theatre. And so the story of women's scenic design professionalization needs to consider costumes and lighting.

Emeline Clark Roche was a scenic and costume designer, technical director, and art director who worked steadily from the mid-twenties until the fifties, after which she retired from Broadway and most of her professional engagements. She began her career as a design assistant and technical supervisor for Robert Edmond Jones, Aline Bernstein, and Norman Bel Geddes. Her expertise ranged from scenic design and costume design to technical direction and stage management, and she moved among these pursuits throughout her career. Most of her scenic design work was for non-Broadway productions, notably in association with Helen Arthur's Actor-Managers, Inc., a women-owned and -run company that produced in Newport, Rhode Island, and Ann Arbor, Michigan, from the late 1920s until 1939. In addition to her work with the Stage Door Canteen, she designed for many Broadway productions, mostly costumes, throughout the forties and early fifties, including several seasons as a costume designer at New York's Civic Center. The 1952 revival of Eugene O'Neill's *Anna Christie*, featuring Celeste Holm, was Roche's most elaborate, well-received production; critics especially praised its costume design.[39]

As for her extra-theatrical work, Roche taught classes through the union, and in 1935–36 she taught three scenic design courses—beginner, advanced, and history—at the Florence Cane School of Art.[40] She organized and designed commercial exhibitions and special dramatic presentations such as the American National Theatre and Academy Album (a year-end revue of Broadway snippets) from 1948 to 1951.[41] In 1950 her close friend Jane Cowl died, leaving her the executor of an estate, and by 1954 she became frustrated with the limitations she perceived in her career, particularly with the sexism she experienced. Roche's correspondence with Cowl evinces her frustration with the lack of progress and of her displeasure with the gendered expectations of design professionalism for women.[42] Writing about the Stage Door Canteen lawsuit, she felt she had spent most of life, it seemed, "turning the other cheek. . . . [G]oodwill just doesn't seem to be enough."[43] Roche remained active in the union until her death in 1995 and provided oral histories to historians of costume and scenic design.[44] She did not design professionally after the mid-fifties.

In many ways Roche's career replicated a path that set up many men for high-profile Broadway careers. In the thirties and forties, her career looked much like that of Mielziner or Oenslager. She began with education and assistantships, broke into off-Broadway productions, and established long-standing relationships with influential producers and directors, such as Helen Arthur and Jean Dalrymple at the City Center. She engaged in union service after the war, probably spurred on by her work on the Stage Door Canteen in the early forties. She had a professional network, too; she was a close friend of Aline Bernstein, who mentored her throughout her early career, and her union service and apprenticeships connected her closely with Lee Simonson, Robert Edmond Jones, and many other influential figures. And yet, Roche's career remained modest, not without its successes, but only achieving sustained commercial employment in costume design for a decade, from 1944 until 1953.

No one can be assured professional success based on a résumé alone, of course, but Roche's career raises questions about the intersection of gender and service: Who is permitted to access professional networks? What types of work qualify one as a "professional" designer and in which venues? In what ways are those terms partially defined by gender, race, ethnicity, and sexuality? Roche's career combined mainstream professional service and volunteer pursuits (USA 829 and American Theatre Wing) with many off-Broadway productions, special events, and shows outside New York City. This likely made it difficult for her to break into the male-dominated theatre design circle. Male designers and producers hired her as a technical director or costume supervisor, but her lack of quality credits prevented them from seeing her as a full-fledged peer in the field. As Peggy Clark recalled of her own career, commercial theatre producers might be willing to hire women in costume design, or even as a scenic designer for a short-term project like a revue by the American National Theatre and Academy, but not to hire a woman scenic designer on a full-scale project: "all things being equal—equal experience, equal background—most producers would take a man ahead of a woman just because they think they are probably less trouble."[45] World War II opened opportunities for Roche to advance, yet after the war, she found herself back in the same gendered box she had previously occupied: costumer, secretary, supervisor.

Roche's career suggests that those areas in which she was more accepted (and rehired) were those in which a woman could more easily fit into a theatrical patriarchy. Costume design, lighting design, and technical direction all began as roles that were not historically conceived of as design but rather as associate positions that supported the vision of the scenic designer. Acknowledging technical skill in such areas was more permissible than giving women coequal status as a designer, doubly so for gendered skills such as sewing and draping. Yet many women designers who originally trained as scenic designers turned resistance into an opportunity to develop new design areas. From their positions as expert drafters, lighting designers, and costumers, women raised the status of subordinate design areas within the union and the profession at large. Although there is still a long way to go to gender parity in the American professional theater, the persistence of women designers in the twentieth century should not be overlooked.

In that spirit, it is worth noting how labor outside the commercial theatre template helped women position themselves in the male field. In some cases they did so by working in partnerships and collectives. Design professionalism was built on the assumption of a single lead designer—a capitalist hierarchy based in the ownership of intellectual property—yet some women's careers challenged the idea of the designer as one person. The British costume design trio known as Motley (consisting of sisters Margaret and Sophie Harris, and Elizabeth Montgomery Wilmot) produced in New York during and after World War II. When one member chose to stay in the United States, and still used the collective's name in credits, this thoroughly confused the designers' union. It was also a needed reminder that the individual model was not the only way to design.[46] A similar anti-individualist approach characterized the work of William and Jean Eckart, a married multidisciplinary design team most noted for their work on musicals, including *Damn Yankees, Fiorello!, She Loves Me*, and *Mame*.[47] Another strategy women employed was to work where women's contributions were valued in all areas. Helen Arthur's Actor-Managers, Inc., was one such venture, as was Eva Le Gallienne's Civic Repertory Theatre, originally founded with an all-women staff, including several productions with Aline Bernstein as lead designer.[48] For some designers, especially of lighting, dance (especially modern concert dance) provided crucial early-career experience—perhaps because scenery was less prominent in modern dance performances, while costumes and lighting remained imperative. The power of women choreographers in the early twentieth century also made dance a favorable venue for emerging women designers. One iconic example is the early partnership between Martha Graham and Jean Rosenthal, whose lighting work inspired her graduate study at Yale and helped sustain her career afterwards as well.[49]

The most common strategy women used to work in the male-dominated world of design was to move from initial work in scenery toward a concentration in either costumes or lighting. Aline Bernstein produced more costume work on Broadway than scenic design, a departure from her integrated scenic-costume work at the Neighborhood Playhouse and other art theatres. Peggy Clark began her studies in both scenery and lighting at Yale. She found that lighting design was more amenable to women and chose to specialize early in her postgraduate career. She developed favorable, long-lasting collaborations with male scenic designers, especially Oliver Smith.[50] Other women specialized in costumes at the beginning of their careers and established robust design careers within that field, before joining the union en masse in 1936. Such influential designers included Millia Davenport, Lucinda Ballard, Rose Bogdanoff, and Irene Sharaff.[51] These women operated professionally in costume design, although some also worked in scenic design in noncommercial theatre. Their service, however, was mostly focused on building costume analogues to the scenic professionalism this book has been detailing. They advocated for social closure and autonomy within USA 829, established costume curricula, and furthered their own expertise through media, lecturing, and other professional engagements. Women whose work was predominantly scenic design, however, came to prominence (at least in New York City) in the next generation, in the seventies and eighties.[52]

Black women employed similar strategies and charted successful careers outside the commercial field. They joined the union first in costume and lighting, not in scenic design. Yet overt racism caused some artists to abandon design. Lorraine Hansberry, for instance, was actively discouraged from pursuing stage design by her undergraduate advisor because there would be no jobs for her. After this she left the university altogether and sought education in New York's newspapers and art theatres.[53] Other women, however, remained in the field with strategic navigation. Louise Evans Briggs-Hall, the first Black woman admitted to USA 829, joined as a costume designer, but she practiced outside union jurisdiction in all design areas, including scenery. She worked at the American Negro Theatre and the American Negro Ballet Company, along with summer stock and companies not based in New York.[54] Similarly, Shirley Prendergast, the first Black woman union member in lighting, began in dance, first by studying with the lighting designer for the Alvin Ailey American Dance Theater, then by designing for Alvin Ailey and other dance groups herself. Her work with the Negro Ensemble Company led to a Broadway transfer, several lighting assistantships, and her own lead lighting design work on Broadway and in regional theatres in the 1970s. Unlike Briggs-Hall, Prendergast did not do much scenery work within her lighting career.[55] These women combined strategies for getting professional-level work despite the racism and sexism of the industry. They positioned themselves in those design areas most open to them, but they did not remain constrained by the pathways and jurisdictional rules of the white commercial theatre.

As the book's final counterpoint, this consideration of women's design careers shows how professionalism and gender intersected. Often the value of women's work was reduced by men's expectations of service, care work, or free labor. Emeline Roche's career is but one example of women's professional service having been devalued, amateurized, or excluded from historical consideration because of its location away from Times Square. As Chinoy writes in her abundant anthology *Women in American Theatre*, "If the job is lowly, the organization experimental or community-oriented, or the artistic skill new, women are likely to be found doing the work. Once the job becomes an executive . . . or the skill formalized into a profession, women's role seems to diminish and their original pioneer work [is] often ignored or forgotten."[56]

More attention to these women's careers is necessary, and further histories of work outside New York are also crucial. It is important to acknowledge that the levers of professional power, of contracts and curricula and union regulations, were held by the commercial theatre in the early and mid-twentieth century. Women may have had their own established, lucrative, well-reviewed careers, but they were only permitted access to professional power by ones and twos, and often conditionally or in a subordinate capacity. Women designers made inroads into the male world through gender-stereotyped service roles, at first. American theatre tried to push women (and especially women of color) aside, and women designers responded by planting themselves firmly in the field, in the periphery if necessary, yet nevertheless persisting.

Constructing Expertise through Lectures

In the mid-twentieth century, scenic designers leveraged the idea of service. After developing their expertise in scenic design for the commercial theatre, designers then shared that expertise with the public through invited lectures, publications, and exhibitions of their work. These were mostly individual engagements, not a long-term commitment, yet together they established scenic designers as knowledgeable experts with useful ideas. Later, this expertise—and the awareness of it among nontheatrical businesses and organizations—led to longer-term consulting jobs. Joseph Urban and Norman Bel Geddes had done similar work in the twenties and thirties, as was discussed in chapter 2, but they did so after largely leaving behind a career in scenic design for architectural, interior, or industrial design. Jo Mielziner and Donald Oenslager, on the other hand, used professional engagements to construct public awareness of their theatre design expertise, ultimately leading to a consulting practice alongside their other work. Complete histories of such professional engagements have not yet been written by scenic design historians, despite the increasing importance such engagements played in establishing a designer's legacy.[57] The impact of any one lecture was modest, but taken together they represent an attempt to influence American theatre production and an articulation of professional expertise. Designers were often paid significant fees for their lecture appearances, so although many such lectures were given in the spirit of service, they were not given pro bono.[58]

The use of lectures as a professionalization tool was not unique to scenic design. Jo Mielziner, Donald Oenslager, and Robert Edmond Jones were taking up a tradition of lecturing as a way of gaining recognition as an expert. In the early twentieth-century United States, the lecture circuit transitioned from a major source of cultural and intellectual capital (such as in the lyceum movement or circuit Chautauqua) into a new mode of professional appearance in competition with lectures on radio and television.[59] Still, the older idea that certain professionals claimed authority by performing expertise in a lecture proved useful for scenic designers. It was perhaps especially important for artists whose works were not easily reproduced or preserved. Unlike novelists, for instance, theatre designers' art did not endure past closing night. Therefore, the designer's presence stood in for previously accomplished work, making past designs live again through anecdote. Many designers took on multiple roles in their lectures, presenting themselves as part cultural critic, part oral historian of backstage gossip, and part theatrical prophet. They explicated their own careers and "the business," which suggests they saw themselves as aspirational occupational models.

Robert Edmond Jones, Jo Mielziner, and Donald Oenslager began giving lectures in the late twenties and thirties. Jones published intermittently during this period, mostly in theatre periodicals, and kept a significant file of quotations, notes, and lecture fragments in his personal office.[60] Jones's largest lecture tour began in 1941, the same year that *The Dramatic Imagination* was published. He spoke at many universities, and his talks were published or recorded on reel-to-reel tapes.[61] Donald Oenslager composed his first lectures for his Yale faculty appointment (beginning in 1925) and soon broadened his focus to include lectures at theatre conferences and social clubs as early as 1927.[62] Only later versions of his lectures were kept in full-text copies, but it is likely that Oenslager adapted his Yale lectures for such events. Mielziner also received requests to lecture at universities and social clubs beginning the mid-thirties. Professional appearances continued in earnest after he returned from war service in 1946, but the dates on his notes indicate that he began to prepare lectures as a component of his professional obligation as early as 1938.[63] All three men wrote a few basic lectures that they then adapted for different audiences, keeping the structure, examples, and even lecture titles consistent.[64]

Progressive, forward-looking themes emerged in each of these sets of lectures. Often they called for a specific technical or architectural innovation that would revolutionize American theatre. For instance, Jones, in two separate lectures, called both for a simple, nonrepresentational stage celebrating the scenic qualities of light and for "the simultaneous use of the living actor and the talking picture." These lectures were later published in *The Dramatic Imagination*.[65] Mielziner envisioned a scheme for the closed-circuit broadcast of live theatre events to larger proscenium stages (to increase live theatre attendance) in 1949. He called for the redesign of Broadway stages to accommodate new postwar plays, especially their needs for scenic transitions and lighting, in a lecture to the United States Institute of Theatre Technology in 1948.[66] Mielziner frequently gave a talk titled "The Shapes of Our Theatre," which was an introduction to theatre architecture that both promoted his new ideas about theatre construction and implicitly touted his theatre consulting business. This lecture formed the basis of his book, of the same name, published in 1970.[67] Oenslager's lectures were frequently history-based, befitting his role as a scenic design collector and teacher. He, too, called for updates to the technical specifications of theatres, to match developments in film and television. In his lectures Oenslager also looked to international theatre organizations and experimental theatre groups in the United States (off-Broadway, civic and regional theatres, and, later, the downtown avant-garde) as examples of necessary innovation.[68]

Although they did not abandon design work in the commercial theatre for the lecture circuit, these three men's professional engagements took up more time later in their careers. Mielziner had nine documented speaking engagements in 1968, most involving interstate travel.[69] He also recorded an educational television lecture on stage design careers and training for dissemination among Nebraska schools. Oenslager likewise had a busy schedule of engagements. That same year, Oenslager spoke at art museums in Baltimore and Chicago; lectured at the American Educational Theatre Association, the United States Institute of Theatre Technology, and other theatre educational bodies; and gave a Salzburg Seminar lecture series.[70] All this he did along with many lectures at universities other than Yale.[71] The university may have been the primary venue for scenic design lectures, but the audience for designers was national in scope and not limited to students.

Oenslager, for one, expanded beyond the American theatre and constructed his expertise on world stage design. A traveler, Oenslager went on several long tours of Asia, South America, and Europe, each time lecturing on American theatre design and the industry's economics (chiefly the business of Broadway and, later, educational and regional theatres). He collected personal contacts, photographs, artifacts, and drawings of theatre performances, and his tours led to lectures and publications in the United States. Oenslager published a feature on the theatre of Indo-China in *Theatre Arts* in 1941, and in 1950 he published the results of his State Department–funded survey tour of Central and South America in *The Record*, a magazine of the International Exchange Office.[72] These essays combined detailed descriptions of theatre traditions with images of dance performances from Cambodia and scenic designs from theatres of Mexico and Chile. Publications such as these served as both vehicles for intercultural exchange in their own right and as records of Oenslager's international tours, with his formal lectures and informal exchanges alike.

Mielziner, on the other hand, used his professional engagements to promote new theatre architecture. He participated in a seminar on office design in 1959; Westinghouse borrowed his expertise in 1961 for a lecture on lighting for television; and AT&T sponsored his participation in an "Advanced Communications Center Seminar" in 1969, aimed at the "design of facilities for better human communications."[73] Mielziner represented the United States at an international exposition in Prague in 1971 and attended the second event of what is now known as the Prague Quadrennial, and in 1970 he gave a Salzburg Seminar lecture series as well. As perhaps the most recognizable scenic designer in the country, his embodied presence before students, civic groups, and international scholarly organizations promoted the idea that the established scenic designer was also a knowledgeable applied arts professional.

When the designer could not be present, museum and gallery exhibition was another way of constructing expertise. Such work was a form of occupational promotion and often linked to lectures. There had been an established practice of scenic design exhibition in New York City, including Samuel Hume's 1914 display on international stage design and the show of the Bourgeois Galleries in 1918.[74] Even after the first flowering of New Stagecraft faded in the twenties, gallery exhibitions continued to align scenic art with other types of fine visual and applied arts. Exhibits in galleries and art museums (the Museum of Modern Art, the Whitney, the Detroit Institute of Arts) showcased designers' capacity to create visually pleasing renderings or evocative scenic models. Architecture exhibitions such as the ones developed by Joseph Urban in the twenties for the Architectural League of New York emphasized that scenic designs were projects for certain sites and particular clients.[75] Wherever an exhibit was held, though, it featured designers as artists, not craftspeople; it posited designers as the sole creators of objects, as painters or sculptors would be presented, and it positioned scenic design as a subject of catalog criticism.

A significant part of some designers' working lives was taken up in the curation of scenic designs for exhibition. For them, this was simply a part of the work one did for the profession; it effectively promoted designers and designing, as magazine features and book authorship had done. The period between the late forties and late fifties was the most productive period for exhibitions, as the late portion of many designers' careers—ripe for retrospectives—coincided with a peak of interest in commercial theatre, especially musicals.[76] Interested museum curators and academics wrote letters to designers asking for temporary loans of drawings or models. Mielziner's, Oenslager's, and Jones's offices then negotiated the selection, insurance, and transportation of past designs. When possible, they gave lectures or attended opening-night receptions for their major exhibits, and they constructed expertise through the sale and dissemination of catalogs.[77]

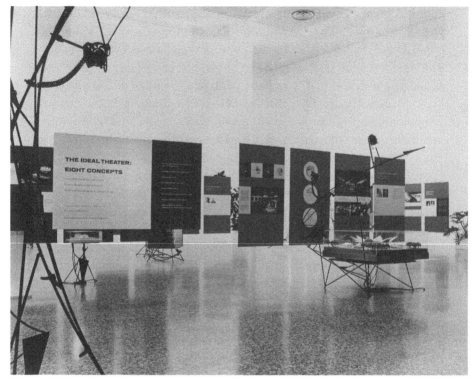

4.4. *The Ideal Theater: Eight Concepts*, an exhibition,
April 1962, unidentified photographer. *American
Federation of Arts Records, 1895–1993, bulk 1909–1969.
Archives of American Art, Smithsonian Institution.*

The link between expertise construction and consulting, though, depended on a new type of exhibit in the sixties: exhibits of proposed theatre
architecture. Rather than celebrating past work or established designers,
these new exhibits looked forward, envisioning new shapes for theatres
and their sites. Two notable theatre architectural exhibitions were the Ford
Foundation's project of 1962, *The Ideal Theater: Eight Concepts*, which
toured until 1965, and the State Department–sponsored Porto Theatre
project for developing a transportable musical theatre venue, active from
1964 until 1968. Both exhibits featured Oenslager's and Mielziner's architectural consulting work prominently. When it became clear that such
projects were more experimental than practical, and funding for their
construction seemed less likely, directors of both projects authorized the
publication and exhibition of the designs. Few of the proposed projects
were built, so exhibitions, lectures, and publications became an alternative,

still-useful end point, if seen as opportunities to construct design expertise and gain public recognition for the scenic design profession.

Architectural Consulting as Service

Jo Mielziner and Donald Oenslager both worked as theatre architectural consultants. Their careers formed a model that later designers—often lighting and sound designers—took up as an adjunct to their professional design pursuits. In the words of Jules Fisher, principal of the theatre architecture consulting firm Fisher Dachs Associates and of architectural lighting firm Fisher Marantz Stone: "the companies I started with Joshua Dachs and Paul Marantz have allowed me to have the freedom to be in a theatre lighting a show for weeks on end. The theatre doesn't pay well, but there are a few of us—and I'm included—who have made a living at it. . . . I have been very fortunate that these parallel companies could help support me financially and artistically because we are all doing related things."[78]

The creation of "parallel companies" whose work could sustain a designer through the ups and downs of Broadway seasons made consulting attractive. After returning from war service, Mielziner began his consulting career in the late forties when he noticed that Broadway theatres were inadequate for the artistic experimentation emerging in American theatre. Theatre facilities outside New York were in even worse technical shape than Broadway. First through his writing, and then through his consulting work, Mielziner imagined many new theatres in New York City and across the country. For Oenslager, on the other hand, consulting grew out of his work as a teacher of design and a researcher of theatre in other countries. Toward the end of his teaching career at Yale, Oenslager began consulting on educational and speculative theatre projects—perhaps inspired by the active theatre consulting career of his Yale colleague George Izenour, a theatre technician known for his innovation in lighting and scenery control systems. Together, Mielziner and Oenslager showed that consulting was a viable later-career pursuit.

At the time that Mielziner began consulting, the role of the consultant was still informal. There had been a brief spurt of architectural consulting in the interwar period, especially for scenic designers who also had credentials as architects (Joseph Urban) or, failing that, worked in a way that approximated architectural work (Norman Bel Geddes).[79] Mielziner's discussion of Broadway theatre architecture drew on a history of modernist experimental innovations. For instance, Bel Geddes had created architectural theatre designs for *The Divine Comedy* and the 1933 Chicago World's Fair, and Urban had designed theatres for Florenz Ziegfeld Jr., Max Reinhardt, and the New School for Social Research.[80] Mielziner wanted to inspire the same amount of modernist innovation in the postwar moment. In 1946, in both the general-interest *New York Times* and in the field-focused *Theatre Arts Monthly*, he argued that architects ought to engage with "the rich reservoir of theatre craftsmen" and not simply theatre real estate owners when planning new construction.[81] It would be some time before Mielziner consulted on a project that was actually built; projects for the Pittsburgh Playhouse and a Los Angeles–based theatre for A&P grocery heir Huntington Hartford foundered in the early fifties. But, with articles, Mielziner called the theatre consultant into existence and quickly stepped into the role.[82]

As envisioned by Mielziner, the theatre consultant would be a specialist in the technical needs of architecture for live performance. In his view, architects rarely provided enough storage space, rigging capacity, or electrical power for contemporary theatre production. When collaborating with an architect, the theatre consultant could point out the needs of the working production early enough for them to be built into the original designs. During the fifties and sixties, Mielziner and other designer-technicians modeled theatre consulting practices by forming regulatory bodies and proposing new projects. In 1955 Mielziner parlayed his relationship with the American National Theatre and Academy into the formation of a new body for establishing architectural standards. Based in New York City, the Board of Standards and Planning for the Living Theatre hosted symposia on new theatre construction, published standards guides, and connected potential theatre consultants with artistic directors and architectural firms. This body, founded by Mielziner and his longtime lighting technical collaborator Eddie Kook, also hosted public talks on new theatre architecture.[83]

The choice of consulting for Mielziner was strategic and timely. American businesses had recently begun to involve management consultants in their planning for operations, and theatre consultants who borrowed the term for their freelance work capitalized on the prestige of the rising management consulting professionals. Just as a business might employ companies such as McKinsey & Company or Booz Allen Hamilton for financial or strategic advice, so too should a theatre company looking to expand its architectural footprint consult a theatre design specialist. Although Mielziner did not explicitly frame it in terms of emulating the

4.5. Jo Mielziner examines power center construction plans, Ann Arbor, MI, 1969. ©1969 MLive Media Group / The Ann Arbor News. All rights reserved. Used with permission.

business world, the sudden appearance of the term *consulting* in *The Ideal Theater* suggests that management consulting firms such as McKinsey offered a useful analogue.[84]

Consulting also may have been popular given the emergence of "knowledge work" as a concept. This term postdates the professionalization of the scene designer, though its emergence has been traced to a shift in American labor culture after World War II. Management consultant Peter Drucker defined the concept of the knowledge worker in his 1959 work *The Landmarks of Tomorrow*: knowledge workers perform "work that applies vision, knowledge and concepts—work that is based on the mind rather than on the hand." In a later work Drucker wrote that knowledge workers were "people with a high degree of formal education who apply knowledge to work, rather than manual skill or brawn."[85] Drucker's categorization of labor by either the results or procedures involved in that labor has been problematized by later labor theorists, most recently in the debate in Marxist studies over immaterial and affective labor.[86] Nonetheless, the concept of knowledge work as a category of labor was popular in business circles, in part because it directed attention to managing and consulting as valuable. Furthermore, Drucker used creative work such as architecture as an example; design involves the manipulation of information and the practice of problem-solving that are characteristic of knowledge work. Many later management books and curricula also used design as an example of the concept. So, at around the time Mielziner started theatre consulting, designers of all disciplines were beginning to view the new knowledge worker as a labor category.

Further Mielziner-inspired developments demonstrated the effectiveness of the consultant-architect blend. In 1959 the Ford Foundation paired consultants and architects and commissioned them to design new conceptual theatre spaces. Mielziner and Oenslager participated, along with American designers Ralph Alswang, Eldon Elder, and George Izenour. The visionary architect Frederick Kiesler also submitted revised designs for his Universal Theater to the project. After a period of development, *The Ideal Theater: Eight Concepts* exhibited the results in 1962, showing off what was imagined to be the next wave of live-performance architecture. The exhibition toured nationally with funding from the American Federation of Arts, and an exhibition catalog published the designs.[87] None of the proposed theatres were actually built, though Mielziner's design in the Ford exhibition was revived in his design for the Vivian Beaumont Theater at Lincoln Center. *The Ideal Theater* coincided with the first wave of large donations to US theatres from the Ford Foundation that encouraged the expansion of nonprofit theatres outside New York City.[88] Around the same time, Mielziner was engaged in one of the most high-profile consulting projects in the country. John D. Rockefeller and New York civic leaders had begun conceptualizing the Lincoln Center for the Performing Arts in 1955, and the American National Theatre and Academy had been involved in planning its theatre spaces. At 1,200 seats, the Vivian Beaumont Theater was to be the largest performance space devoted to staged drama (and the occasional musical) in the complex. Mielziner collaborated with architect Eero Saarinen and a host of other planners on the Beaumont from 1958 until the opening of the building in 1965.

The history of the Lincoln Center project and its ill-fated attempts to bring repertory theater production to New York City have been well documented.[89] So, rather than repeat this history, it is useful to note instead that these tentative projects, some realized but many remaining only conceptual, were successful in promoting Mielziner's vision of the designer as a theatre expert. This is different from deciding the success of a consulting enterprise by whether the theatre was built or not. Mary Henderson writes that the *Ideal Theater* exhibit, for example, was "another exercise in wishful thinking—and futility." Seen from the perspective of labor and occupational history, however, sustained consulting work was important even when the planned buildings were not built. Much more than a futile attempt to remake the theatrical landscape, architectural consulting was a sustained and strategic attempt to remake the designer's job—at a time when Mielziner's Broadway commissions were beginning to wane.

Mielziner's connections allowed the idea of the consultant to blossom. In fact, many consultants picked up on his well-publicized model; they partnered with administrative bodies and para-theatrical organizations like the American National Theatre and Academy and its Board of Standards and Planning. Of the seven theatrical designers who consulted on *The Ideal Theater*, all would go on to consult on or fully design later theatres. Some had been chosen by Ford for previous successes in developing theatre architecture. Both George Izenour and Barrie Greenbie had completed projects by the time the Ford Foundation grant came along: respectively, the Loeb Drama Center at Harvard in 1960 and the Seventy-Fourth Street Theatre, later the Phoenix Theatre, in 1959. Eldon Elder, too, completed his design of the Delacorte Theater in Central Park (opened 1962) while working on the Ford project.[90] For others, though, the speculative architecture project began their consulting careers. After completing the Ford project, Ralph Alswang went on to design two Broadway theatres, the Palace and the Uris (now George Gershwin), and many other venues. David Hays was instrumental in the development of the Mummer's Theater in Oklahoma City in the late sixties, and Oenslager's subsequent consulting projects included the New York State Theater (now David H. Koch Theater) and the Philharmonic Hall (now David Geffen Hall), both at Lincoln Center, and the Kennedy Center in Washington, DC.[91] The Ford Foundation's investment in theatre architecture formed a cohort of proven theatre consultants. Mielziner was foremost in the field, and his influence spilled over to colleagues.

A final example of theatrical consulting applied to service goals was the Porto Theatre, a speculative architectural project from the mid-sixties. In this case the project was international in scope and funded jointly by the US Department of State and the Ford Foundation to solve a problem of Cold War diplomacy. Mielziner and Oenslager partnered with Edward Kook and acoustics expert Cyril Harris to design a portable theatre specifically for the export of American musical theatre. The submitted design was for a structure measuring 112 feet in diameter and seating a thousand, built in the music-circus style.[92] It fit into two military cargo planes and could be assembled in three days by thirty workers. It contained all necessary architecture, equipment, and facilities, from lighting instruments to restrooms. By 1968, however, plans for the Porto Theatre had been scrapped by both funding organizations and were destined for library exhibits and, finally, the archive.[93]

When the Porto project began, the State Department had already been funding foreign tours of performing arts groups, beginning with a production of Robert Breen's *Hamlet* in Norway in 1949 and continuing with productions of *Porgy and Bess*, *Oklahoma!*, and *Medea* at the Berlin Festival.[94] Compared with other performing arts, however, theatre was less frequently represented in US-sponsored cultural diplomacy; this has been attributed to several causes, including the high cost of sending ensembles abroad, the lack of a national theatre to create tour-ready productions, the unwillingness of performers to exchange Broadway for international touring, and language barriers.[95] In the Porto's official narrative, published in a small portfolio book in 1968, the designers described a State Department "faced with the problem of sending examples of American theatre to foreign lands ... where it encountered great difficulty locating and renting appropriate theatre buildings." This narrative goes on to cite both the lack of usable theatre spaces in "certain underdeveloped countries which the State Department considered most important to visit" and the outlay required to send musical theatre on an international tour. Musical theatre was, at once, "the art form in which the American theatre most excels"

4.6. Porto Theatre cutaway model, 1964. *From* Porto Theatre: A New Concept in Totally Integrated Portable Theatre Design, *by Edward F. Kook and KOHM Group. Credit: Lauren K. Gibbs and Kenneth D. Gibbs.*

and "the most costly kind of theatre to export."[96] The funding bodies approached Oenslager and Mielziner with a consulting job, and they enlisted Kook and Harris as well. The Porto Theatre project was the first and only architectural collaboration between Oenslager and Mielziner, and it was also one of only a few projects of its time to stem from a proposal of joint federal and private foundation funding.

McNeil Lowry awarded a small amount of Ford Foundation money to the project in 1964, and the KOHM group began work. (The name was derived from the designers' last-name initials.) The principals agreed to work pro bono so that they could use the full grant on project expenses, indicating the service orientation underlying the project.[97] The design of the theatre attempted to solve as many of the problems of international touring as possible, and it also helped position KOHM as a team of top-flight architectural consultants. The theatre's annular design blended the music-circus style and arena staging, both ascendant in new American theatre construction of the time. Music circus consisted of bare-stage presentation of musicals, light opera, and revues under a semi-permanent tent. The design economized by forcing minimal settings, establishing a permanent lighting plot, and reducing scenic and crew costs.[98] The Porto project justified what might be read as a reduction in spectacle by touting a modern, fresh style: "costumes, lighting, and a few colorful stage properties stimulate theatregoers to work upon their imaginations. . . . [S]ome experts feel that since the unique quality of American musicals lie [sic] in their tempo and vitality, they flourish better when they contrast with the more old-fashioned forms of eye-overwhelming extravaganza."[99] Color renderings of the proposed space emphasized dancing costumed performers over scenery or properties.

The design was modular and made for portability. The structure was to be loaded in sections for transport, and it required no concrete foundation. Most of the structure was to be fiber-reinforced plastic, not steel. The roof inflated, and a lighting truss hung above the stage after the walls were erected. The distributed weight of the seating banks supported the walls, and the whole structure was supported by being in continuous tension. Cramped backstage space fit under the seating. Electricity was generated on-site, water was obtained through a centralized hookup, and lavatories were similar to airline toilets. Finally, the fluted walls were designed for acoustic concentration inside, while externally they resembled the neoclassical architecture of Washington, DC. All this, KOHM proposed, could be built for $1.2 million, with later iterations costing somewhat less.

In their proposed touring schedule, companies would perform several musicals in repertory for multiple-night engagements. A crew arriving ahead of the company and staying behind would set up, tear down, and transport the theatre.[100] In full-scale operation, KOHM proposed building two theatres and working in a "leapfrog operation," in which one Porto would put on shows while the other was being transported to and set up at the next touring stop.

The State Department may have considered such an investment if costs had been lower and shared with other funders. Sadly, the budget of the Cultural Presentations Program (CPP) was halved from its prior level in the 1967 fiscal year, and further reductions followed in 1969 and 1970.[101] The Porto's $1.2 million price tag was slightly less than half of the CPP's total budget in 1965; however, once the costs of hiring a small company

of actors and a skeleton crew and staff, along with minimal transport, producing, and artistic costs, were added to the construction price, the Porto Theatre would have consumed all the CPP's resources. Nonetheless, KOHM attempted to justify the high costs to the State Department in its proposal. They cited the savings in weight and cost over permanent theatres and gestured toward a future when "its price will be so reasonable that many cities will install a Porto Theatre permanently rather than go to the greater expense of building its own new and unproven theatre building." A map of "hypothetical remote locations" in the Porto booklet suggests the nature of KOHM's pitch to the State Department by proposing travel to areas where the United States would have sought strategic cultural influence.[102] Though the cities are unlabeled on the map, they seem to mark places in the Soviet Union, in far-flung Cold War ally nations

4.7. Porto Theatre exterior model, 1964. *From* Porto Theatre: A New Concept in Totally Integrated Portable Theatre Design, *by Edward F. Kook and KOHM Group. Credit: Lauren K. Gibbs and Kenneth D. Gibbs.*

(Saudi Arabia, Japan, Australia), and in countries where the United States would have wanted more cultural influence in the mid-sixties (Vietnam, Indonesia, Argentina, Chile). The outlay would be high, KOHM admitted, but returns in goodwill would justify the multimillion-dollar price tag. The State Department disagreed.

After the federal government declined the proposal, KOHM pivoted from selling the State Department on the program to winning the hearts and minds of the American public. Following the approach it had employed for the *Ideal Theater* project, the Ford Foundation encouraged the KOHM group to send their drawings, photographs, and models on a tour of libraries and universities.[103] The United States Institute for Theatre Technology published an exhibition booklet, which was reprinted almost entirely by the sympathetic editors of *Theatre Crafts* magazine in May 1969. Designs for the Porto Theatre sit alongside a number of other projects for theatre buildings created between 1960 and 1970, as Arnold Aronson has explained.[104] Aronson does not include the Porto in his list of futuristic theatres, though he does note that the explosion of innovative, unbuilt projects in theatre architecture in the sixties represents a high-water mark of innovative theatre designs, rivaled perhaps only by the 1920s. Where architectural modeling was most influential, however, in both the twenties and the sixties, was in developing the career of the artist. As projects circulated in exhibits and magazine spreads, the value of the theatre designer or the designer-architect collaboration increased. The notion of the theatre consultant spread more quickly through the exhibition and publication of attractive models and drawings than it would have were it only visible in fully realized architecture. By aligning their work and expertise with larger cultural priorities, designers made the claim that their work served the public.

Consulting fully caught on by the mid-sixties. In 1966 *Theatre Design and Technology*, the journal of the United States Institute of Theatre Technology, featured a series of interviews titled "Consulting in the Theatre," in which working theatre consultants both explained their field and advocated for hiring consultants as a regular practice. Jean Rosenthal spoke of her consulting work as a process of sharing expert knowledge: "It seems to me that most of us operating as consultants are really not consultants in the architectural use of the word at all. We are advisors. We are experts because of our passion for the theatre, and in terms of our own experience. And we will do anything to communicate this information to anybody who asks us for it."[105] In this interview, which primarily focused on best practices in theatre architectural consulting, Rosenthal and other consultants sketched out the breadth of the field and considered ethical concerns that arose in their work. Rosenthal spoke up in favor of "good manners" and the benefits of hiring a consultant who can "offer creative solutions to problems, and can warn [the client] of unfavorable consequences as a result of unfunctional design." In trade-focused magazines such as *Lighting Design* and *Stage Directions*, later articles and interviews with working consultants both explained their role and advertised them to potential clients.

Like lighting and costume design, theatre consulting underwent its own professionalization process. Theatre consultants' principal professional organization, the American Society of Theatre Consultants, was founded in 1983. Since then, consulting firms branched off from theatrical design. In today's business environment, consulting firms hire a mix of architects and theatrically trained designers in all fields—lighting, sound, acoustics— yet remain largely separate from the working lives of commercial theatre designers. (Jules Fisher is a notable exception.) So, although midcentury designers found an opportunity for extra-theatrical service work in architectural consulting, it remained the purview of that generation—Mielziner, Oenslager, Izenour, McCandless, Rosenthal—and includes only a few scenic designers today who have their feet planted firmly in both fields.

Conclusion

Having established robust Broadway careers, practitioners such as Mielziner and Oenslager turned to projects that allowed them to "give back." This chapter has suggested that such service, whether or not it was truly uncompensated pro bono work, helped expand the idea of the designer as a professional. Consulting professionalized in its own way and became less of a side pursuit for working scenic designers around midcentury.

Yet as theatre occupied less of the American popular-culture imagination in the later twentieth century, the type of broad consulting role that Mielziner had enjoyed became less viable. Changing attitudes toward American military power in the seventies and the end of large-scale public investments in the arts meant that designers felt less personally or politically compelled to participate in governmental service. Lighting designers, particularly those with a background in architectural lighting, and acoustics experts and sound designers still made the leap into consulting, but fewer scenic designers developed the same dual expertise that Mielziner had. Theatre consulting firms organized themselves to look more like architectural firms than freelance theatre design studios. Many of these firms hired specialists full-time, so employees did not need to combine freelance design work with consulting. The service that did endure in scenic designers' careers, however, was the extra-theatrical work discussed in previous chapters. Today's designers regularly teach in training programs and some provide volunteer service with the union and other professional groups as well. The existence of conferences for designers working in professional and educational capacities (United States Institute of Theatre Technology, Live Design International, Prague Quadrennial, World Stage Design) provides opportunities for service through administration, speaking, and teaching.

Having surveyed much of the careers of the first generation of professional scenic designers, from their first actions in the teens and twenties through their final projects in the sixties, this study of the freelance professional scenic designer comes to a close. The heavy lifting of professionalization was mostly complete; scenic designers were professionals, working on a freelance basis, and had attained a creative authority over their work. They were seen as distinct artists, separate from scenic painters, and many institutions and practices supported their new identity. Up-and-coming designers studied in schools, took the union exam, and found mentors through union connections. They sought to build portfolios of work that blended commercial and nonprofit theatre design with teaching, consulting, or other types of nontheatrical design. Once integrated in union structures, media coverage paradigms, and university departments, design labor became much more resistant to structural change than it had been at the beginning of the century.

Today's theatre market exists within the long shadow of modernist theatre labor organization, a model that valued the independent knowledge work of the head designer and instituted a hierarchy of associates, assistants, and students. Designers and theatre artists are still wrestling with the contemporary meaning of terms such as *freelancer, independent contractor, consultant,* and *professional*. Each term was shaped by the labor paradigms of the mid-twentieth century. The service projects profiled in this chapter fill out a more complete picture of design labor. Designers worked on productions and also outside them, and speculative, service-oriented, and institutional projects are worth studying as expressions of ideology and desire, even if, like Oenslager's camouflage, they disappeared, or if, like the Porto Theatre, they were never realized.

CONCLUSION: LEGACIES OF PROFESSIONALISM

This book has attempted to reorient theatre design history toward institutions. Foregrounding institutional work, rather than exceptional individuals and their designs, brings into focus foundational assumptions and ideologies of American scenic design. This may seem an unorthodox approach. However, for those working in design areas, and those interested in US theatre writ large, the shapes of institutions such as unions, schools, and federal tax and labor law have significant ramifications. The question of freelance labor is one such shaping factor. It emerged from twentieth-century designers' advocacy of contract labor and was sustained as designers gained more independence and authority in commercial productions. The idea of design as freelance labor endures as a dominant paradigm in the twenty-first century.

In a 2016 episode of *in 1: the podcast*, a theatre design interview series, host Cory Pattak, a lighting designer and writer, spoke with guest Carl Mulert, United Scenic Artists business representative and a member of USA Local 829, IATSE. Their discussion brought up one important relationship between labor law and the profession of scenic design. Specifically, Mulert was careful to explain the conflict between freelance labor and unionism when the subject of taxes came up:

> MULERT: Any member of a union has to be an employee. By law, a union cannot represent independent contractors. That is the way the federal labor law is established. If you are represented by a union, you are an employee. As an employee, you should only be being paid on W-2. Now, there are certain unions and disciplines, who shall remain nameless . . .
>
> PATTAK: This tightrope walk you're doing is exemplary.
>
> MULERT: . . . . A lot of people have heard the phrase *misclassification of employees*. It's a big phrase in government right now, in the labor movement right now, and it's very common. An employer tries to misclassify an employee as an independent contractor. And there's a whole list of, you know, when is somebody an independent contractor and when are they an employee? Are they working at the direction of the employer? Is the employer setting a budget and a timeline and parameters of the job?

Do they have their own workplace or are they working at the employer's workplace? Lots of things. Our members—designers, which we are talking about right now—are employees. Adamantly, they are employees who happen to be paid many times on 1099, on a fee basis, simply for the benefit of the employer, the employee, and because historically, a long time ago, that's what happened. But they are fee-basis employees, nothing more. There is a movement, within state governments primarily, to stop this practice. Many small employers, theatre companies, have started paying designers on W-2 because they are being cracked down on. You can't collect workmen's comp unless you're paid on W-2.

PATTAK: And the union likes that, the union's stance is, we love when you're paid on a W-2, right?

MULERT: Of course we do.... We do not want anyone to try to say you are an independent contractor. And if you're paid on 1099, there's a little bit of a risk that somebody could try to say, some group of employers could try to say [to the union] that you don't have the right to bargain for these people; they're independent contractors.[1]

Mulert's "tightrope walk" continued with a discussion of workers' compensation payments, the hiring of assistants and associates, and estimated tax contributions by freelancers. The conversation may be technical, yet peeking through are glimmers of the endurance of tradition in scenic design labor ("a long time ago, that's what happened"). Mulert did not mention it, but in the fifties and sixties, several lawsuits directed at USA 829 challenged the tax status of union designers, precisely because they met some criteria of independent contractor status. If these suits had determined that designers were contractors and not employees, the union would have lost its bargaining ability, and designers would have lost union-guaranteed pay minimums and intellectual property rights. The union's insistence that designers are employees, paid on a fee basis "simply for the benefit of the employer [and] the employee," is fundamental to its continued representation of theatre designers.[2]

US federal law regarding the tax status of employees and contractors has had significant effects on scenic design. Much of the union's official position is meant to defend against current independent contractor guidelines, by keeping designers employees of the producer or contracting theatre and protecting designers' studios from being treated as employing businesses. For instance, both the union and working designers recommend that all design assistants be paid directly by a producer, not by the designer, since direct hiring of assistants by designers is an indicator of

independent contractor status. Furthermore, the language "for the convenience of the employer" is frequently used to justify the existence of a
designer's studio space, as the presence of an off-site personal studio also
favors contractor status. Because of these and several other criteria, the
union has carved out a tradition of viewing designers more like employees so as to preserve their right to union representation. This tradition
is passed along nowadays through social networks and systems similar
to those that were used to promote professionalism in the 1920s. Today,
designers have word of mouth, guidance given in classes and books (such
as James Moody's *The Business of Theatrical Design*), and advice provided
in sessions held by the union—or embedded in an industry-insider podcast. These are not always the most public of vehicles, but as this book has
attempted to show, those vehicles shaped the field.

The tax status challenges of the fifties and sixties are only one of the
ways in which the scenic design profession continued to change in the later
twentieth century. Discussion of these changes could merit its own book,
but the most significant shifts can be summarized in a few observations.
(Much on these developments can be found in portfolio-interview books
written or inspired by Arnold Aronson's writing on designers and in other
projects published by the United States Institute for Theatre Technology,
or USITT.)[3] In the generation following Robert Edmond Jones, Lee Simonson, Norman Bel Geddes, Jo Mielziner, and Aline Bernstein, designers
tended to follow career trajectories that were more alike. Many younger
designers studied drama at Yale or elsewhere and pursued the new MFA
course of study in which they learned a defined set of skills. Many went
on to became teachers: Howard Bay, Ralph Alswang, John Ezell, and Ming
Cho Lee all took up teaching in their middle or later careers. Others advocated for the designer as a worker by volunteering through USA Local
829 or by writing books on design. At some point in their careers, many
designers turned to nontheatrical freelance work, whether in film, exhibition design, or products and interiors. Many still maintained (and taught)
the skills of design execution as well, especially scenic painting.

With time, these pathways became accessible to men and women designers of different cultural backgrounds. The work of Aline Bernstein,
Perry Watkins, Emeline Roche, Peggy Clark, Jean Rosenthal, and Shirley
Prendergast, among others, showed that success was achievable for women
and Black designers—although designers continued to face bias and discrimination. Documentation of this bias can be found in surveys from
American Theatre, in initiatives based in the union or USITT to encourage

career development by those in underrepresented groups, and in historical research on Black designers, such as the criticism and curatorial work of Kathy Perkins.[4] Getting commercial theatre work remains difficult for women in scenery, sound, and lighting, and for African American, Latinx, Native American, and Asian American designers in all areas. On Broadway, designers of color are underrepresented, and few are nominated for Tony Awards and other prizes. Theatre organizations have begun initiatives to change this, but many such efforts are still nascent. Regarding these efforts, I hope that this volume encourages scholars and artists to consider the ways in which discrimination was foundational to professionalism. Forward progress means changing the way professional standing is assessed, precisely because it has been and still is so heavily dependent on exclusion.

Another major shift in the careers of scenic designers in the sixties and seventies was in the range of venues hiring them. Unlike the forties and fifties, in which design was concentrated in New York City and Broadway contracts, the near-simultaneous emergence of off-Broadway and regional theatre meant that designers could build careers somewhere other than New York City. Some maintained residences outside the metropolis. For others, their careers began in summer festivals and regional theatres, and then they transitioned to higher-profile theatres, some of which (but not all) were in New York. In an interview Ming Cho Lee recalled, "When I started working for Jo and Boris the theatre was very different. . . . Broadway had that whole group of designers—Jo, Boris, Oliver Smith, David Hays, Peter Larkin, Will Steven Armstrong—and it was a little hard to break into. I found that I had to start working somewhere else because it felt like I'd just be an assistant all my life."[5] Lee is perhaps best known for his work at the New York Shakespeare Festival, but he also designed for regional operas, including productions at the San Francisco Opera and Baltimore's Peabody Institute. Through these other venues, lines of influence and recommendation began to be established. Broadway producers were (and still are) loath to sign design contracts with untested assistants and associates, but regional theatres were more willing, especially when a newer designer was already known to the company from previous work as an assistant or associate.

Working Broadway designers in the fifties and sixties included, as Lee noted above, Oliver Smith, Boris Aronson, Ben Edwards, Ralph Alswang, Peter Larkin, and William and Jean Eckart. Most of these designers either had informal training through assistantships or had attended Yale or Carnegie Tech in the early years of their drama departments. These designers' entrance into the field came when a producer was willing to take a chance on a relatively green designer, and soon many of them landed Broadway contracts. The subsequent generation, which included Ming Cho Lee, John Lee Beatty, John Conklin, Marjorie Bradley Kellogg, David Mitchell, Tony Walton, and Robin Wagner, largely followed the mainstream professionalizing path laid down previously. This path began with some type of general theatre work, then developed into a preprofessional phase at the graduate level—Yale was a popular option but New York University or Lester Polakov's classes also sufficed—and was quickly followed by a period of assistant work. Then, through off-Broadway, regional, or other work, these designers began to build reputations. For some, their way led toward nonprofit theatre; for others, commercial and Broadway theatre was the path; for others still, work in opera, ballet, or even film and television established their careers.

A generation of designers working steadily in the eighties and nineties included Tony Straiges, Santo Loquasto, Michael Yeargan, Heidi Ettinger (previously Landesman), George Tsypin, and Adrianne Lobel. This later generation was more diverse in gender and also in the type of work they produced. Sculptural, metaphorical, and abstract approaches challenged the American domestic, "suggestive" realism that had been dominant. This was in part due to European scenographic influences, particularly interest in Czech designer Josef Svoboda's work, and a larger number of European-trained artists working in the United States. Also, increased reliance on noncommercial theatre and more substantive links between theatre design and film and television art direction changed designers' aesthetics. A rough path to a professional career still existed, and it continued to rely on a combination of formal education in schools and a series of assistantship positions, after which designers began to lead their own projects. Networks helped develop one's early career—particularly for those individuals who attended the Yale School of Drama—especially after the assistantship period. Yet, as Ronn Smith's interviews with Charles McClennahan and Loy Arcenas made clear, the entrenched bias of producers and theatrical unions made it more difficult for designers of color to get a foothold. Designers who were not white men found themselves seeking other career paths, either through combined work in theatre and television or film, or through the creation of their own relationships and networks from working with non-white designers.[6]

Public-facing media coverage and service manifested through "public good" projects became less important later in the century. Fewer designers were publishing articles and books, and there were fewer design projects bankrolled by corporate or Ford Foundation funds, which may be attributable to the waning importance of theatre in American public life. Articles about designers continued apace, but the need to publicize the work of the designer to the public was no longer as important as it had been. Articles endured in specialized journals and magazines, though fewer appeared in general-interest periodicals. Presses published books of interviews and retrospectives, but they were not the joint acts of public presentation completed by Mielziner, Oenslager, Bel Geddes, Gorelik, or Simonson. Monographs and retrospectives on designers were now written by scholars, not by the designers themselves. The justification of designers' expertise through extra-theatrical projects for the public good was no longer as necessary and so faded away.

A decrease in works of service and in wide-ranging professional appearances may be a result of successful professionalization, however. Younger designers saw a career path, and their efforts shifted from convincing the general public of their freelance status toward working within tighter networks of producers, artist colleagues, and theatre-interested audiences. The celebrity status some designers had enjoyed in the twenties and thirties was no longer as available to most designers—especially those whose work remained strictly in live theatre—but there were also more opportunities and a larger field in which to work. A period of popularity in the public eye, first in journalists' features and profiles and then through designers' publications and exhibits, had accelerated professionalization. But once it was achieved, working designers pulled back on the public-facing work, lecture tours, and retrospective exhibitions. There was simply more designing to do.

As scenic design matured in the last decades of the twentieth century and as production expenses and business costs grew while contract fees failed to keep pace, designers continued to turn to a mixed model of professional practice. They blended teaching or art direction or other non-theatrical design work with their scenic design. In 2011 Richard Isackes wrote of the American theatre, "while no one likes to admit it, the profession of designing for live theatre is virtually conflated with that of design teacher. . . . [M]ost design training, and by extension most design, in this country is done by designer/academics."[7] Designers have done as they always did, making do with the materials and resources at hand, while the profession has tended to rehearse and retrace the career trajectories of those who earlier established the structures of professional life. A mix of theatrical work, freelance occupation outside the theatre, temporary or permanent teaching appointments, and the management of a studio may well continue to be the dominant model of scenic design professionalism for many more decades. Institutions, after all, tend to conserve their own models of working, though at the time of writing, the lasting results of the COVID-19 pandemic on theatre and live events remain to be seen.

In a recent seminar of mine on scenic design, a student asked about the history of the "professional assistant." Assistantship is not quite its own career as yet, but it is a job category in which designers seem to be spending more time than they did in previous decades. The history of assistantship predates the emergence of the professional scenic designer, and many of the figures who later came to define professional practice worked as assistants and associates. Emeline Roche, for example, assisted Aline Bernstein for many years. Donald Oenslager began as a shopper and assistant for Robert Edmond Jones and Millia Davenport, and the relationship between Jo Mielziner and Eddie Kook began as something like that between a designer and an assistant or lighting technical supervisor, out of which emerged a strong lifelong collaboration. Such assistant jobs, however, lasted months or perhaps a season or two. Today, scenic designers may choose to work with the same assistants and associates for years, emulating the model of principals and associates in architecture or graphic design firms.[8] The expansion of Broadway and other commercial theatre production has formalized the roles and hierarchy of assistants and associates, due to increased technical complexity and a design's longer projected life span from initial workshops to multiple touring productions. For some assistants, sustained employment under another designer may be a viable career path, especially for those working on Broadway and other large high-profile venues.[9] So, although saying that a new occupation of professional assistant has emerged may well overstate matters, it is true that some designers make a good living by working with or for another designer and, at times, may make more than the lead designer does on contract fee payments after studio expenses are deducted.[10]

As the ecosystem of design for live performance changes, the balance of work that is typical or even ideal will also change. A version of what developed in the United States in the twentieth century—the modernist, creative, freelance professional designer—will likely evolve in the twenty-first. Given increased demand for applied design expertise, new developments of the "gig economy," and the effects of new media and social media, I cannot help but wonder whether the union-represented labor model will remain dominant. Could it be that the field sheds its individualized freelance orientation? How might the field change if the cognitive tasks of designing were packaged in some container other than in professional expertise? Design could become standardized, perhaps through artificially intelligent software that builds designs semi-autonomously. There could be corporations of salaried designers who operate sizable firms, as many architects do today. There could even be the elimination, casualization, or nonpayment of design expertise altogether. The employment of assistants, associates, programmers, and designer-technicians is already testing the single-artist, freelance contract labor model of design. Automation, algorithms and artificial intelligence, and collective creation and devised performance methods all challenge older models of design expertise and authority. The field is being further transformed by new specification and fabrication technologies, democratized access to design software, globalized competition for design and construction, and a crisis of expertise that may reduce the perceived need for professional, trained designers. To think beyond the current labor model in scenic design, the field ought to take a close look at how and why the current systems were built. Taking one such look was a purpose behind this book.

To name the institutions of professionalism helps us understand how design labor paradigms emerged. Institutional history has been inadequately researched, especially given institutions' power to direct flows of labor and capital. Institutions' policies are translucent barriers like scrims: visible in the right light but just as easily looked through or past. They may well obscure other potential methods of doing (or paying for) live performance. In light of theatre's current-day crises—of automation and live-streamed performance, of fights for working conditions free of bias and racism, of economic recovery from prolonged shutdown—theatre design will need to refashion itself again. Let us not ignore history's subtleties and precedents, especially those ideas that the powerful may want workers to accept as the show business status quo. A deeper understanding of scenic design's past will position theatre artists to imagine a better, fairer, and more creative labor model—in the studio, in rehearsals, and at the negotiating table.

NOTES

BIBLIOGRAPHY

INDEX

NOTES

Introduction

1. Kenneth Macgowan, "The New Stagecraft in America," *Century Magazine*, January 1914; Kenneth Macgowan, "The New Path of the Theatre," in *American Stage Designs: An Illustrated Catalogue* (New York: Bourgeois Galleries, 1919).

2. Norman Bel Geddes, *Miracle in the Evening, an Autobiography* (Garden City, NY: Doubleday, 1960), 208–9.

3. The "Bergman bath" was a favorite technique for adding visual depth to flat-colored drops and walls, making the simplified New Stagecraft–designed sets shimmer under stage lighting. This technique is still often used today and is best described in Claude Fayette Bragdon, *More Lives than One* (New York: Cosimo Classics, 2006), 205. See also the unpublished scene-painting manual of Bradford Ashworth, a longtime Bergman's studio painter: "Notes on Scene Painting," box 28, folder 5, Donald Oenslager Papers and Designs, *T-Mss 1996–015, Billy Rose Theatre Division, The New York Public Library for the Performing Arts.

4. Bel Geddes, *Miracle in the Evening*, 209.

5. Bel Geddes, 211.

6. Bragdon, *More Lives than One*, 203.

7. James Fisher and Felicia Hardison Londré, "Bergman's Studio," in *Historical Dictionary of American Theater: Modernism* (Lanham, MD.: Scarecrow Press, 2008), 59.

8. Bel Geddes, *Miracle in the Evening*, 211.

9. Norris Houghton, "Credits," *Theatre Arts* 30, no. 11 (November 1946): 658.

10. Aline Bernstein also supervised work at Bergman's but does not appear in Bel Geddes's or Bragdon's memoirs, both of which enclose a circle of white male designers at the studio.

11. Robert Edmond Jones, *The Dramatic Imagination: Reflections and Speculations on the Art of the Theatre* (New York: Duell, Sloan and Pearce, 1941), 28, 77–78.

12. Houghton, "Credits," 658.

13. Arnold Abramson, partner and chargeman at Nolan Scenic Studios, recalled in 1975: "Well, many years ago, before there were designers as such—

this was way before my time—the shop supplied a service, building, designing, and painting. Designers worked for the shop. There were no such things as a designer. The shop supplied the scenery. There was a model room, and people built models and painted. I believe one of the first designers as an individual was Robert Edmund [sic] Jones. And Lee Simonson." Jeffrey Collom, "The Role of Contemporary Scene Building Houses for Broadway Theatre" (PhD diss., Michigan State University, 1975), 171.

14. Orville K. Larson, *Scene Design in the American Theatre from 1915 to 1960* (Fayetteville: University of Arkansas Press, 1989), 84.

15. Ralph Pendleton, *The Theatre of Robert Edmond Jones* (Middletown, CT: Wesleyan University Press, 1958); Mary C. Henderson, *Mielziner: Master of Modern Stage Design* (New York: Back Stage Books, 2001); Arnold Aronson, Derek E. Ostergard, Joseph Urban, Matthew Wilson Smith, and Wallach Art Gallery, *Architect of Dreams: The Theatrical Vision of Joseph Urban* (New York: Miriam and Ira D. Wallach Art Gallery / Columbia University, 2000); Anne Fletcher, *Rediscovering Mordecai Gorelik: Scene Design and the American Theatre* (Carbondale: Southern Illinois University Press, 2009). See also Lee Simonson, *Part of a Lifetime: Drawings and Designs, 1919–1940* (New York: Duell, Sloan and Pearce, 1943); Bel Geddes, *Miracle in the Evening*; Jo Mielziner, *Designing for the Theatre: A Memoir and a Portfolio* (New York: Atheneum, 1965); Howard Bay, *Stage Design* (New York: Drama Book Specialists, 1974); Mordecai Gorelik, *New Theatres for Old* (New York: Octagon Books, 1975).

16. Christin Essin, *Stage Designers in Early Twentieth-Century America: Artists, Activists, Cultural Critics* (Basingstoke, UK: Palgrave Macmillan, 2012); Marlis Schweitzer, *When Broadway Was the Runway: Theater, Fashion, and American Culture* (Philadephia: University of Pennsylvania Press, 2011); Timothy R. White, *Blue-Collar Broadway: The Craft and Industry of American Theater* (Philadelphia: University of Pennsylvania Press, 2014); Christopher Innes, *Designing Modern America: Broadway to Main Street* (New Haven, CT: Yale University Press, 2008).

17. This duality structures his book, allowing for a history that identifies the intentional political actions taken by artists in the thirties and discusses the content of works that inspired more self-consciously political actions. Michael Denning, *The Cultural Front: The Laboring of American Culture in the Twentieth Century* (London: Verso, 2010), xix–xx.

18. Denning, xix.

19. OED Online, s.v. "freelance (*n.*)," def. 2, http://www.oed.com/view dictionaryentry/Entry/74409.

20. "In practice the term industrial designers is limited to those who set up as free lances in all fields of design for mass production, who are ready to

tackle anything from automobiles to zoological gardens." Daniel Schwarz, "Art for Industry's Sake," *New York Times*, April 2, 1939.

21. See Lee Simonson, *The Stage Is Set*, 6th ed. (New York: Theatre Arts Books, 1963); Lee Simonson, "The Scene Designer and the Theatre," *New York Times*, October 16, 1932, sec. 10; Elihu Winer, "Stage Designers Seeking New Illusions," *New York Herald Tribune*, August 12, 1934, sec. D; Lucius Beebe, "Donald Oenslager and the Technique of Sets," *New York Herald Tribune*, April 28, 1935, sec. D; Donald Oenslager, "The Fine Art of Variation," in *Almanac and Classified Directory* (New York: USA Local 829, 1940), 8, 29.

22. Steven Brint, "Eliot Freidson's Contribution to the Sociology of Professions," *Work and Occupations: An International Sociological Journal* 20, no. 3 (1993): 259–78; Steven Brint, *In an Age of Experts: The Changing Role of Professionals in Politics and Public Life* (Princeton, NJ: Princeton University Press, 1994); Eliot Freidson, *Professional Powers: A Study of the Institutionalization of Formal Knowledge* (Chicago: University of Chicago Press, 1986); Eliot Freidson, *Professionalism: The Third Logic* (Chicago: University of Chicago Press, 2001); Julia Evetts, "The Concept of Professionalism: Professional Work, Professional Practice and Learning," in *International Handbook of Research in Professional and Practice-Based Learning*, Springer International Handbooks of Education (Dordrecht, NL: Springer, 2014), 29–56.

23. Brint, "Eliot Freidson's Contribution," 261.

24. Literature on the professions has debated definitions and challenged the desire for definitions itself. Yet, as Andrew Abbott has written, the centrality of the term seems clear in everyday speech. *Profession* "means at once a form of organization, a level of social deference, an association with knowledge, a way of organizing personal careers. Our ambivalent concept holds them all together and, I believe, acquires its power precisely from the yoking of these often-disparate realities." Andrew Abbott, *The System of Professions: An Essay on the Division of Expert Labor* (Chicago: University of Chicago Press, 1988), 318.

25. Richard L. Florida, *The Rise of the Creative Class: And How It's Transforming Work, Leisure, Community and Everyday Life* (New York: Basic Books, 2002); Barbara Ehrenreich and John Ehrenreich, "The Professional-Managerial Class," in *Between Labor and Capital*, ed. Pat Walker (Boston: South End Press, 1979), 5–45; Peter F. Drucker, *Landmarks of Tomorrow* (New York: Harper & Row, 1959). For further discussion of the role Broadway played in developing middle-class identities through onstage representations, see Michael Schwartz, *Broadway and Corporate Capitalism: The Rise of the Professional-Managerial Class, 1900–1920* (New York: Palgrave Macmillan, 2009).

26. Magali Sarfatti Larson, *The Rise of Professionalism: A Sociological Analysis* (Berkeley: University of California Press, 1977), 6; Abbott, *System of Professions*, 2, 59–85.

27. Harold L. Wilensky, "The Professionalization of Everyone?," *American Journal of Sociology* 70, no. 2 (1964): 137–58.

28. Julia Evetts, "Professionalism: Value and Ideology," *Current Sociology* 61, nos. 5–6 (September 1, 2013): 34.

29. Debate over the definition of the term has endured since at least the middle of the twentieth century. See Barrett H. Clark, "Professionalism in the American Theatre," *Educational Theatre Journal* 3, no. 2 (May 1951): 99–104.

30. Such usage of the term in acting, referring to everything from behavior in rehearsals and backstage to respecting the requests of director and producer, was already in print by midcentury. See the Code of Ethics at the Circle Theatre, founded in 1945 by actress Kathleen Freeman. The code was found in her estate after her death in 2001. See https://backstage.blogs.com/blogstage/2009/09/taking-the-profession-seriously-.html and https://www.broadwayworld.com/board/readmessage.php?thread=1003383.

31. Benjamin McArthur, *Actors and American Culture, 1880–1920* (Iowa City: University of Iowa Press, 2000), 86.

32. Sean P. Holmes, *Weavers of Dreams, Unite! Actors' Unionism in Early Twentieth-Century America* (Champaign: University of Illinois Press, 2013), 40.

33. Letter to Actors' Equity Association, April 11, 1922, and USA 829 Working Rules of 1926, box 3, folders 1 and 5, United Scenic Artists Records WAG.065, Tamiment Library / Robert F. Wagner Labor Archives, New York University. Similar language about the professional was not used to describe waged painting work.

34. "In any case, the plays produced by the Department of the Drama of Yale University are essentially a by-product. The machine is intended—like all college machinery—to turn out men, not material. The output at which its energies are aimed is the professional man—or woman—of the theatre, just as the output of the law school is the professional man of law." H. I. Brock, "Yale's Theatre Makes Its Bow with First Play," *New York Times*, December 5, 1926, sec. SM.

35. Herb Lager and Fred Jacoby, from Abramson and Variety Scenic Studios, as interviewed by Jeffrey Collom. Collom, "Role of Contemporary Scene Building Houses," 31, 189, 263, 268.

36. "According to Webster, 'project' means 'a planned undertaking.' As the term is currently used in sociological analysis, it does not mean that the goals and strategies pursued by a given group are entirely clear or deliberate for all members, nor even for the most determined and articulate among them. Applied to the historical results of a given course of action, the term 'project' emphasizes the coherence and consistency that can be discovered

ex post facto in a variety of apparently unconnected acts." Larson, *Rise of Professionalism*, 6n.

37. Evetts, "Professionalism"; Brint, *In an Age of Experts*; Freidson, *Professionalism*.

38. While professional ideology was also disseminated hegemonically through American print and entertainment culture, and designers of course claimed cultural capital and status through their work on influential productions, these mechanisms of coercive cultural power were not the most immediate ways that designers built their profession.

39. The United Scenic Artists Local 829 reaffiliated with IATSE in 1999, making USA 829 a nationwide autonomous Local of IATSE. In the historical period discussed in this book, USA 829 and IATSE were different unions, and they often conflicted.

40. These elements are clearly enumerated in Evetts, "Professionalism," 788–89.

41. "As one AIA [American Institute of Architects] bureaucrat ruefully stated, 'It would appear that architects have hesitated to follow the lead of the doctors and the lawyers who have so thoroughly convinced the public—first, that their services were indispensable and, second, that in the public interest the armor of legislation should protect the furnishing of their services and exclude from practice the quacks and shysters.'" Andrew M. Shanken, "Breaking the Taboo: Architects and Advertising in Depression and War," *Journal of the Society of Architectural Historians* 69, no. 3 (September 2010): 411.

42. The most commonly cited dates of origin for the New Stagecraft were the hiring of Joseph Urban at the Boston Opera in 1911 or Robert Edmond Jones's production of *The Man Who Married a Dumb Wife* in New York in 1915. William Leigh Sowers, "The Progress of the New Stagecraft in America," *The Drama*, November 1917.

43. The *Washington Post* heralded "the first American woman scene painter" in 1909. Inez Kendrick, "one of Richmond's fairest daughters," studied composition and art at her father's engraving plant. Despite her mentor's anxiety about her climbing the paint bridge, her "persistency and talent won." "First American Woman Scene Painter," *Washington Post*, July 11, 1909.

44. Oscar G. Brockett, Margaret Mitchell, and Linda Hardberger, *Making the Scene: A History of Stage Design and Technology in Europe and the United States* (San Antonio: Tobin Theatre Arts Fund, 2010), 163–64.

45. Larson, *Scene Design in the American Theatre*, 12–30; Brockett, Mitchell, and Hardberger, *Making the Scene*, 205–8, 215–16.

46. C. Sadakichi Hartmann praises the work of the Bruckner Brothers, a European house that built scenery for the duke of Saxe-Meiningen, among

others: "as the spectators can look in all directions the concentration of the subject in one point is not necessary; there must be several points which excite the attention anew." C. Sadakichi Hartmann, "Scene Painters at Work," *Washington Post*, September 1892, 9.

47. See John P. Ritter, "Scene-Painting as Fine Art," *Cosmopolitan*, November 1889; "A Scene Painter's Work," *New York Times*, June 15, 1884; Hartmann, "Scene Painters at Work"; Alexandra Ramsay and John Rettig, "The Art of a Scene-Painter," *Monthly Illustrator*, 1895; Stanhope Sams, "How a Play Is Staged," *New York Times*, August 21, 1898.

48. "That art today exacts not only imagination and ideality, but a wide knowledge of history and architecture. The public of the present time, which is a traveled public, and familiar with things as they should be, requires that every detail of theatrical scenes, interior as well as exterior, shall be presented in a state as nearly approaching perfection as the exigencies of the stage will permit." Ramsay and Rettig, "Art of a Scene-Painter," 329.

49. Robert Suddards Joyce, "A History of the Armbruster Scenic Studio of Columbus, Ohio" (PhD diss., The Ohio State University, 1970), 31.

50. The Armbruster Studio, founded in 1875, and the Lee Lash Studio in New York City, founded in 1898, were two prominent mail-order houses. For detailed descriptions of working conditions in scenic studios, see Joyce, "History of the Armbruster Scenic Studio"; Wendell Cole, "Scenery on the New York Stage, 1900–1920" (PhD diss., Stanford University, 1951). Lee Lash produced for local productions as well as mail-order sets. A complete Lee Lash studio scenery catalog from 1912 can be found online at https://catalog .hathitrust.org/api/volumes/oclc/857917213.html.

51. W. J. Lawrence, "Scenery and Scenic Artists," *Gentleman's Magazine*, June 1889, 614.

52. Joyce, "History of the Armbruster Scenic Studio," 71–76.

53. Unitt quoted in Mary Gay Humphreys, "Stage Scenery and the Men Who Paint It," *Theatre Magazine*, August 1908, 203–4.

54. Quoted in Larson, *Scene Design in the American Theatre*, 17.

55. Hoyt worked regularly for Daly, though he also maintained some freelance employment, working with other managers as well in the 1890s. Hoyt was unusual among his peers in this arrangement, as noted in Ritter, "Scene-Painting as Fine Art," 43. Physioc regularly worked with Mansfield until his death in 1907, after which Physioc founded his own scenic equipment and construction studio in 1916. "Vaudeville: New Production Co.," *Variety*, July 14, 1916.

56. "Some New Stage Effects: Old-Time 'Wings' Have Been Superseded by Box Setting," *Washington Post*, January 8, 1899. *Problem play* refers to an

issue-based domestic drama in which an interior location and minimal scene changes made the box setting possible.

57. Physioc began working for fellow designer Ernest Gros after Mansfield's death in 1907.

58. Scenic artists had initially affiliated with IATSE around 1897 but were separated from IATSE by the American Federation of Labor (AFL) and required to join the BPDPA owing to a jurisdictional dispute. The scenic artists' union (then United Scenic Artists of America, USAA) rejected this and chose to remain an independent union for two decades. In 1918 the AFL forced USAA to affiliate with the BPDPA, though with an agreement to recognize the scenic artists as an "autonomous local," which meant that USAA would be nominally affiliated with the BPDPA but granted significant authority to set its own policies, wage scales, and standard contracts. That autonomous local became United Scenic Artists Local 829. In 1999 the union voted to reaffiliate with IATSE, ending its relationship with the Brotherhood (then the International Brotherhood of Painters and Allied Trades). Today the scenic artists' and designers' union is known as United Scenic Artists, Local USA 829, IATSE. Lawrence Robinson, Local USA 829 historian, phone conversation with author, September 27, 2021; "History," United Scenic Artists, https://www.usa829.org/About-Our-Union/History.

59. There are of course many other instances of othering and exclusion that this book does not address. As an example, some "star" designers here discussed were Jewish and may have been read as non-white by some peers because of their ethnicity. Jewish identity was somewhat less of a professional liability in the theatre communities of New York City than elsewhere in the United States. Jo Mielziner is an interesting case, as he was born into a Jewish family and in 1936 converted to Catholicism at age thirty-five. In his early career, he was mostly able to detach any religious or ethnic prejudice from his work. See Milton Lomask, "Return to Orthodoxy," *The Sign* (January 1955): 31–33.

1. The Unionized Artist

1. Larson, *Scene Design in the American Theatre*, 295–96.

2. "Urban Plans Guild of Scene Painters; Would Reorganize Union on the Lines of Art Craft in the Middle Ages," *New York Times*, August 9, 1923.

3. "Urban Plans Guild," *New York Times*. The Wiener Werkstätte (Werkstetter) was a cooperative of architects, artists, and designers in Vienna, Austria, active from 1903 until the early 1930s. Their linkage of modern design and high-quality artisanship inspired later modernist groups in Germany (Bauhaus), the United States (Art Deco), and Denmark (Scandinavian Modernism).

4. "Scene Painters Planning a Guild; Joseph Urban's Idea of Creating an Artcraft Organization Approved by Union," *New York Times*, August 12, 1923, sec. E.

5. Elliott A. Krause, *The Sociology of Occupations* (Boston: Little, Brown, 1971), 77.

6. Right-to-work laws and national skepticism toward unions have weakened many manufacturing and extractive industries that dominated the labor movement of the early twentieth century. More recent unionization efforts in education (secondary and higher education), protective services (police, firefighting), and in health care have blurred the previously stark differences between professionalism and unionism.

7. "The union perspective approaches the determination of the price of labor as a conflict between antagonistic and opposing class interests; this indeed is one of the dimensions of class consciousness. . . . [G]oals and strategies focus exclusively on collective benefits, even if the union members may translate economic incentives into purely individualistic terms." Larson, *Rise of Professionalism*, 156–57.

8. Larson further muses that while union organization in the twentieth century and its sometimes-socialist politics advocated for revolution through the awakening of class consciousness, professionalism attaches itself to an individualized ideology more aligned with capitalist thinking. An "ideology of neutrality" appeases capitalists, one which "implicitly stresses the classlessness of professionals and, explicitly, the service of the public as a whole." Larson, 157.

9. "Monopolization is directed against competitors who share some positive or negative characteristics; its purpose is always the closure of social and economic opportunities to *outsiders*." Max Weber, *Economy and Society*, ed. Guenther Roth and Claus Wittich (Berkeley: University of California Press, 1978), 342, http://archive.org/details/MaxWeberEconomyAndSociety.

10. In addition to Weber and Marx, Georg Simmel and Émile Durkheim imply some degree of closure in their theorization of social class and the conflicts among classes and groups. See Juergen Mackert, "Social Closure," in *Oxford Bibliographies*, ed. Lynette Spillman, Sociology, September 15, 2014, doi:10.1093/OBO/9780199756384-0084.

11. Weber, *Economy and Society*, 128.

12. Frank Parkin, *Marxism and Class Theory: A Bourgeois Critique* (New York: Columbia University Press, 1979), 47–54.

13. Parkin, 58.

14. Such actions often include "solidaristic" actions, such as strikes, sit-ins, or other demonstrations, and as they are not sanctioned by the state, they are often met with state-sponsored discouragement or violence. Parkin, 74–77.

15. Architecture is famously a non-unionized profession in the United States. Jessica Myers, "Why Don't Architects Have Unions?," *Architect's Newspaper*, October 28, 2019, https://www.archpaper.com/2019/10/why-dont -architects-have-unions/. Other US design professions have followed similar paths, creating professional organizations like the American Institute of Architects rather than labor unions. This is true of industrial design (IDSA), graphic design (AIGA), interior design (ASID), and landscape design (APLA). Newer fields seem to follow the same path: video game design has a professional organization (IGDA) and is considering unionization, interaction design has organized (IxDA), and internet content creators have attempted a professional organization (ICG) without success. See chapter 2 for these cross-disciplinary links in the early twentieth century.

16. "For many independent professionals and creative class workers traditional labor unions are anathema. . . . [F]reelancers generally have high levels of mobility, satisfactory working conditions, and a strong culture of individualism, all of which tend to make union mobilization unlikely." Martha W. King, "Protecting and Representing Workers in the New Gig Economy: The Case of the Freelancers Union," in *New Labor in New York: Precarious Workers and the Future of the Labor Movement*, ed. Ruth Milkman and Ed Ott (Ithaca, NY: ILR Press of Cornell University Press, 2014), 161–62.

17. Some theorists argue that capital and management have conquered labor and induced it to accept the same conditions of competition and maximal profit that govern postmodern capitalism, effectively eliminating limits on exploitation by embracing, and then selectively ignoring, the advice of professional organizations. David Graeber, *The Utopia of Rules: On Technology, Stupidity, and the Secret Joys of Bureaucracy* (Brooklyn, NY: Melville House, 2015), 20; Michael Hardt and Antonio Negri, *Multitude: War and Democracy in the Age of Empire* (New York: Penguin Books, 2005), 136.

18. Designers in charge of their own design and production houses included H. Robert Law (who did Shubert productions between 1906 and 1921), Frank Dodge, Lee Lash, E. J. Unitt, Homer Emens, and Joseph Physioc. Larson, *Scene Design in the American Theatre*, 17–18.

19. The Internet Broadway Database lists 440 productions opening between 1895 and 1920 with design credits for the six designer-operators named in the previous note: Law, Dodge, Lash, Unitt, Emens, and Physioc. Frequently the company was credited, as in "Lee Lash & Co," but in other cases, the head of the firm was listed as the designer. This is an incomplete listing and rough count, given simply for illustration.

20. Larson, *Scene Design in the American Theatre*, 72.

21. Essin, *Stage Designers in Early Twentieth-Century America*, 139.

22. "Minimum Rate Set for Stage Designs," *Billboard*, July 18, 1925, 11.

23. The Theatrical Syndicate was a monopoly operation of Broadway producers who had commanding control over New York theatres and touring theatre circuits across the United States, from 1896 until about 1910. They were challenged by the Shuberts, three brothers who grew a competing producing network in New York City. The Shubert Organization is still a major owner of Broadway theatres.

24. One such example was Margaret Anglin's ongoing employment of Livingston Platt at the Toy Theatre in Boston from 1913–1915. Edwin Carty Ranck, "An American Stage Wizard," *Theatre Magazine*, August 1915, 83.

25. Primary strikes are strikes waged by a union against an employer with which it has contracted labor. Secondary/solidarity strikes are strikes undertaken by sympathetic unions that are not under contract with the targeted employer. Secondary strikes are illegal in the United States under the 1947 Taft-Hartley Act. Melvyn Dubofsky and Foster Rhea Dulles, *Labor in America: A History* (Wheeling, IL: Harlan Davidson, 2004), 213, 224.

26. Holmes, *Weavers of Dreams, Unite!*, 82; Paul F. Gemmill, "Equity: The Actor's Trade Union," *Quarterly Journal of Economics* 41, no. 1 (November 1926): 135–40.

27. Philip A. Alexander, "Staging Business: A History of the United Scenic Artists, 1895–1995" (PhD diss., City University of New York, 1999), 39. In the case of Actors' Equity, it "leans toward the settlement of differences through negotiation rather than through direct action. . . . [W]arlike measures are not likely to be adopted by any of its branches, despite their strength, unless in the face of grievous managerial abuses which clearly will not yield to milder treatment." Paul F. Gemmill, "Types of Actors' Trade Unions," *Journal of Political Economy* 35, no. 2 (April 1927): 303.

28. "Scenic Artists Arbitrate," *Variety*, August 16, 1918, 12.

29. Here *jurisdiction* is applied as a term of unionism, referring specifically to the set of tasks over which a union has regulatory authority. However, the term can also be applied to professional domains protected through licensure or organizational membership. Professional "jurisdictional boundaries are perpetually in dispute, both in local practice and in national claims." Abbott, *System of Professions*, 2.

30. Here *architect* was used as a term for artists who drew plans for three-dimensional forms for the stage or screen without overt pictorial "design." Minutes, General Meetings, April 2 and July 7, 1922, reel 1, United Scenic Artists Records WAG.065, Tamiment Library / Robert F. Wagner Labor Archives, New York University. This archive is hereafter cited as USA Records in this chapter's notes.

31. "Scenic Artists' Union Makes Amazing Demand," *Variety*, May 30, 1923, 11.

32. Larson, *Scene Design in the American Theatre*, 72.

33. At least some owner-operators paid their workers weekly and managed hiring in response to the need for labor by day or by week. These transactions communicated the labor needs of Broadway production on a weekly basis to the union, which kept track of the number of men working in a given period. It also was accepted that owner-operators would casualize labor arrangements, hiring and firing as necessary for a given week's work. Painters appeared to be a quite flexible lot, moving from shop to shop in some cases. See interview with Leo Meyers in appendix A-6 of Collom, "Role of Contemporary Scene Building Houses," 185–296.

34. The United Managers and Producers Association, with whom Actors' Equity negotiated initial standard contracts in 1917, re-formed as the Producing Managers' Association in 1919. For more on the strike that followed, see Holmes, *Weavers of Dreams, Unite!*; Robert Simonson, *Performance of the Century: 100 Years of Actors' Equity Association and the Rise of Professional American Theater* (Milwaukee: Applause, 2012).

35. "Scenic designers should be grateful to the union for taking them in, as they will thus be protected from the free-lancers and the growing army of novice artists now developed in various schools. He [Volz] said that the present contract, however, would not throttle worth-while innovations in stage designing which may be introduced by new comers in the field." "Scenic Artists' New Contract," *Billboard*, June 9, 1923, 123.

36. General Meeting Minutes, April 6, 1923, reel 2, USA Records; "Scene Painters Planning a Guild," *New York Times*. For reference, $25 in 1924 is equivalent to $427 in 2022, and the journeyman rate of $77 per week would equal about $1,316 weekly in 2022.

37. General Meeting Minutes, January 4, 1924, reel 2, USA Records.

38. Executive Meeting Minutes, September 24, 1924, and General Meeting Minutes, November 6, 1925, reel 2, USA Records.

39. Jack Poggi, *Theater in America: The Impact of Economic Forces, 1870–1967* (Ithaca, NY: Cornell University Press, 1968), 46–55.

40. General Meeting Minutes, January 21, 1927, reel 3, USA Records.

41. General Meeting Minutes, March 18, 1927, reel 3, USA Records.

42. General Meeting Minutes, April 1, 1927, reel 3, USA Records.

43. "Standard Form of Contract Adopted by Scenic Designers," *Billboard*, April 2, 1927, 9.

44. Of the standard contract Orville Larson writes, "Although many of the problems pertaining to the appearance and acceptance of scene designers were resolved during the twenties, it wasn't until the thirties that scene designing as a profession truly settled in on Broadway. Threats of blacklisting by the theatrical unions eliminated many of the producers' sharp practices,

and designers were no longer at their mercy." Larson, *Scene Design in the American Theatre*, 89.

45. General Meeting Minutes, September 20, 1929, reel 3, USA Records.

46. Poggi, *Theater in America*, 56–57.

47. General Meeting Minutes, September 20, 1929, reel 3, USA Records.

48. Pushback from the studios resulted in concessions, such as the designation of "key" men who could work overtime, but doing so penalized the studio with fees. "Artists' 4-Day Week Aid to Jobless," *Variety*, February 4, 1931.

49. Sean P. Holmes has noted that younger actors raised on Popular Front politics, who identified as artists and workers far more easily than their forebears of a generation before, nearly splintered Actors' Equity with the formation of the Actors' Forum in 1934, which agitated for more aggressive relief and protection policies. Holmes, *Weavers of Dreams, Unite!*, 176–77.

50. "Union Status Irks Designers," *Variety*, February 25, 1931.

51. *Dual organization*, or dual unionism, refers here to the creation of potentially competing groups in an established union. This is seen to be harmful to solidarity, as it may jeopardize a union's jurisdictional claims. Dual organization was forbidden by the constitution of the United Scenic Artists at this time. Dual unionism was also the charge leveled against the Committee for Industrial Organization (CIO, now the Congress for Industrial Organizations) during the split between the AFL and the CIO in 1936, resulting in CIO-affiliated unions being suspended from AFL membership.

52. Norman Bel Geddes, "Ten Years from Now," *Ladies' Home Journal*, January 1931, 3.

53. Executive Board Meeting Minutes, January 26, 1931, reel 4, USA Records.

54. General Meeting Minutes, September 8, 1932, reel 4, USA Records.

55. General Meeting Minutes, January 16, March 6, and June 30, 1933, and August 13, 1934, reel 4, USA Records.

56. The basic rate was $0.15 per square foot; $0.10 for plain drops, borders, and ceilings; and $0.20 for sets that were "secondhand," or built from stock.

57. The fine for violating any one of these new regulations was an amount, paid to the union, "EQUAL TO THE ENTIRE PRICE [caps in original] of the work calculated at basic minimum rates." The capital letters speak to the tone of the Ways and Means Committee. General Meeting Minutes, March 6, 1933, reel 4, USA Records.

58. Report of Ways and Means Committee, General Meeting Minutes, February 21, 1933, reel 4, USA Records.

59. General Meeting Minutes, June 19, July 7, and July 17, 1933, reel 4, USA Records. A minimum labor budget for scene painters based on the square footage measurement of the set was enforced by the union in the 1940s. However,

this minimum only pertained to waged painting labor and not to designers' payments.

60. "Scene Designers Make a Must of Authentic Replica Models," *Variety*, July 17, 1934, 46.

61. Executive Board Meeting Minutes, December 21, 1934, reel 5, USA Records.

62. Executive Board Meeting Minutes, January 7, 1935, reel 5, USA Records.

63. "For a long while the designers felt that the organization did not understand their problems and some were not taken up in the proper way." Jo Mielziner quoted in Executive Board Meeting Minutes, January [?], 1935, reel 5, USA Records.

64. Untitled legal brief, box 3, folder 3, United Scenic Artists Records WAG.065, Tamiment Library / Robert F. Wagner Labor Archives, New York University.

65. General Meeting Minutes, October 21, 1935, reel 5, USA Records.

66. General Meeting Minutes, October 21, 1935.

67. General Meeting Minutes, March 15, 1937, reel 6, USA Records.

68. Costume painting, a now-obsolete category in USA 829, referred to those artisans who painted, dyed, and aged fabrics.

69. See General Meeting Minutes, May 16, October 3, and October 17, 1938, and June 11, 1939, reel 6, USA Records.

70. Alexander, "Staging Business," 180–81.

71. United Scenic Artists Local 829, *Almanac and Classified Directory*, 1941, box 28, folder 2, Donald Oenslager Papers and Designs, *T-Mss 1996-015, Billy Rose Theater Division, The New York Library for the Performing Arts.

72. Bay also had notable Broadway and World's Fair projects by 1942: on Broadway, *The Little Foxes* (1939) and *Morning Star* (1940); for the World's Fair, puppets and settings in the film *Pete Roleum and His Cousins* (dir. Joseph Losey, 1939) for the Petroleum Industries Exhibition. See Bay, *Stage Design*; Jerry Leon Davis, "Howard Bay, Scene Designer" (PhD diss., University of Kansas, 1968).

73. In September 1936 Bay proposed a union grievance committee to address members' concerns about FTP pay and layoffs, and in May 1938 Bay initiated union action to protest cuts to the FTP and other programs of the Works Progress Administration. Special Meeting Minutes, September 15, 1936, reel 5, USA Records; General Meeting Minutes, May 2, 1938, reel 6, USA Records.

74. Comically, scenic and lighting designer Peggy Clark wrote the minutes of this meeting, in which she included her own opinion on Morange's long-standing complaints with a struck-through word: "Bro. Morange continued

his time-honored ~~insulting~~ statements that Designers were contractors and therefore it was illegal in holding positions on Executive Boards." General Meeting Minutes, May 1, 1944, reel 8, USA Records.

75. Bay's 1974 book *Stage Design* described the realities of American theatre. On the union: "The various contracts set modest fees and wage scales, humane working conditions, and are free of muscle for hiring minimum crews or other feather-bedding devices. A demerit must be handed the union for its failure to hammer out an apprentice system. Speaking from the tired vantage point of seventeen years as president of the quixotic, talent-packed club, I would say that we have been too ladylike to the sharks that infest the entertainment waters; too conscious of being artists about it all." Bay, *Stage Design*, 155.

76. General Meeting Minutes, May 16, 1946, reel 9, USA Records.

77. Larson, *Scene Design in the American Theatre*, 126; Essin, *Stage Designers in Early Twentieth-Century America*, 73–78, 116–18; Davis, "Howard Bay, Scene Designer."

78. Several attempts to sustain California locals of USA failed, as Local 235 and Local 631, both based in Los Angeles, went defunct by the later 1940s. The remaining BPDPA union was Motion Picture Painters Local 644. See General Meeting Minutes, March 1, 1948, reel 9, USA Records; Untitled legal brief, box 3, folder 3, United Scenic Artists Records WAG.065, Tamiment Library / Robert F. Wagner Labor Archives, New York University.

79. General Meeting Minutes, October 15, 1945, reel 9, USA Records.

80. This affidavit demand, later declared unconstitutional by the US Supreme Court in 1965, was a source of leadership turnover in USA 829. Walter Walden, scene painter and president of the union elected in 1947, refused to sign this affidavit, ostensibly out of support for Truman's veto and for finding it "to be an infringement of personal right" as well as "a form of censorship of private citizenship." He resigned the presidency in October 1947. Charles Lessing, who had served as president in the twenties, took the position. General Meeting Minutes, October 6, 1947, reel 9, USA Records.

81. United Scenic Artists Designing Artists Contract for Death of a Salesman, September 22, 1948, box 31, folder 1, Jo Mielziner Papers, *T-Mss 1993-002, Billy Rose Theatre Division, The New York Public Library for the Performing Arts.

82. Kathy A. Perkins, "Their Place in History: African-Americans behind the Scenes of American Theatre," *Theatre Design and Technology* 31, no. 3 (Summer 1995): 31. In this book I use the term Black, capitalized, to refer to the racial classification and cultural group also known as African American, following shifts in journalistic practice by the *New York Times* and the Associated Press beginning in 2020. Watkins was racially categorized using the

antiquated term Negro, and Perkins's scholarship uses the terms African-American and Black.

83. Carole Klein, *Aline* (New York: Warner Books, 1980), 172–74; Kyle Rex, "Perry Robert Watkins (1907–1974)," *Blackpast* (blog), December 28, 2012, https://www.blackpast.org/african-american-history/watkins-perry-robert -1907–1974/.

84. Don Stowell Jr., "Unionization of the Stage Designer, Male and Female," *Theatre Design and Technology* 38 (October 1974): 8–9.

85. Alexander, "Staging Business," 35; "Women Much on the Job," *Washington Post*, March 12, 1922, 53.

86. Further research into Bernstein's activist work at the Henry Street Settlement and Neighborhood Playhouse can be found in Essin, *Stage Designers in Early Twentieth-Century America*, 107–15.

87. Finding Aid for Emeline Roche Collection, *T-Mss 1996-016, Billy Rose Theatre Division, The New York Public Library for the Performing Arts; General Meeting Minutes, December 10, 1937, reel 6, USA Records; Wendy Waszut-Barrett, "Historical Excerpt—'Women in Scenic Art,' Lillian Gaerstner," *Drypigment* (blog), February 6, 2017, http://drypigment.net/2017/02/06 /historical-excerpt-women-in-scenic-art-part-2/.

88. "The rank and file, who come to meetings, all had prostate trouble. If they had a female member they'd have to move headquarters to a place with two toilets. . . . [I]t was more practical just to let me work." Stowell, "Unionization of the Stage Designer," 9. The claim is repeated in Millia Davenport, unpublished notes labeled "Lincoln Center," box 1, folder "Millia Davenport," Orville K. Larson Papers, 2006MT-50r, Houghton Library, Harvard University.

89. Peggy Clark Kelley, "Peggy Clark Kelley: Remembrances of a 'Designing' Woman," in *Women in American Theatre*, 3rd ed., ed. Helen Krich Chinoy and Linda Walsh Jenkins (New York: Theatre Communications Group, 2006), 213–14.

90. "The shocked doorman, confronted with her indisputable credentials, took one look at the pretty blue-eyed, pink cheeked little woman whose gown of cloth-of-gold shimmered in the flickering gaslight. Then calling on the toughness that had been his lifelong pride, he threw wide the door, 'Brother Bernstein!' he shouted." Stowell, "Unionization of the Stage Designer," 9.

91. Frederika D. Brochard, "Full Life of Costume and Scene Designing Follows Early Struggle to Join Scenic Art Labor Union," *Christian Science Monitor*, March 30, 1951, 6; Klein, *Aline*, 172.

92. Klein, 174.

93. Perkins, "Their Place in History."

94. Edward Lawson, "He Crashed the Color Line," *Opportunity: Journal of Negro Life* 17, no. 2 (February 1939): 52–53.

95. Kathy A. Perkins, "Black Backstage Workers, 1900–1969," *Black American Literature Forum* 16, no. 4 (Winter 1982): 160–63.

96. Executive and General Meeting Minutes, December 20, 1937, and August 1, 8 and December 5, 6, and 10, 1938, reel 6, USA Records.

97. General Meeting Minutes, March 20 and August 7, 1939, reel 6, USA Records.

98. Jonathan Dewberry, "Black Actors United: The Negro Actors' Guild," *Black Scholar* 21, no. 2 (May 1990): 6.

99. Dewberry, "Black Actors United."

100. Executive Board Minutes, September 19, 1939, reel 6, USA Records.

101. Lillian Scott, "Perry Watkins Is Proof Hard Work Will Bring Success in New Fields," *Chicago Defender*, August 9, 1947, 10.

102. "Beggar's Holiday Producer Believed Race Pioneer," *New Journal and Guide*, 5 April 1947, 11.

103. Oenslager paraphrased in Mike Alan Barton, "Aline Bernstein: A History and Evaluation" (PhD diss., Indiana University, 1971).

104. Alexander, "Staging Business," 147–51, 163.

2. The Celebrity Artist

1. Joseph Roach, *It* (Ann Arbor: University of Michigan Press, 2007), 44.

2. Anthony Slide, *Inside the Hollywood Fan Magazine: A History of Star Makers, Fabricators, and Gossip Mongers* (Jackson: University Press of Mississippi, 2010), 12.

3. Julian Johnson, "Marietta Serves Coffee," *Photoplay* 18, no. 25 (October 1920): 31–33, 132–33. Box 34, folder 34.1, Joseph Urban Papers, 1893–1933, Rare Book & Manuscript Library, Columbia University.

4. "Geddes Provides 'War' as a Game for Guests," *New York Times*, March 6, 1929; "Indoor War Game Demands Skill of a General," *Popular Science Monthly*, July 1929, 71; "Artist Geddes Works 10 Years on 'War Game,'" *Denver Post*, March 26, 1929; "A New Yorker at Large," *Seminole Oklahoma News*, November 15, 1929. UNCAT 1.10, box 194, job 937, Norman Bel Geddes Theater and Industrial Design Papers, Harry Ransom Center, University of Texas at Austin. Hereafter cited as NBG Papers in this chapter's notes.

5. John Loring, *Joseph Urban* (New York: Harry N. Abrams, 2010); Essin, *Stage Designers in Early Twentieth-Century America*; Innes, *Designing Modern America*; Schweitzer, *When Broadway Was the Runway*; Aronson et al., *Architect of Dreams*; B. Alexandra Szerlip, *The Man Who Designed the Future: Norman Bel Geddes and the Invention of Twentieth-Century America* (Brooklyn, NY: Melville House, 2017).

6. Emily Carman, *Independent Stardom: Freelance Women in the Holly-wood Studio System* (Austin: University of Texas Press, 2016), 8, 10.

7. David Remnick, *Life Stories: Profiles from* The New Yorker (New York: Modern Library, 2001), x.

8. Neal Gabler, *Winchell: Gossip, Power and the Culture of Celebrity* (New York: Vintage Books, 1994); Lindsay Starck, "Janet Flanner's 'High-Class Gossip' and American Nationalism between the Wars," *Journal of Modern Periodical Studies* 7, no. 1 (2016): 11–13.

9. Kenneth Macgowan, "Profiles: Caprice Viennois—Profile of Joseph Urban," *New Yorker,* June 25, 1927; Gilbert Seldes, "Profiles: The Emperor Jones—Profile of Robert Edmond Jones," *New Yorker,* May 9, 1931; Gilbert Seldes, "Profiles: Artist in a Factory—Profile of Henry Dreyfuss," *New Yorker,* August 29, 1931.

10. Susman further argues that "every American was to become a performing self," and this was especially true of nonperforming artists, who were induced to "become performers so that they may become celebrities so that in turn they may exert genuine influence on the public." Warren Susman, "'Personality' and the Making of Twentieth Century Culture," in *Culture as History: The Transformation of American Society in the Twentieth Century* (New York: Pantheon Books, 1973), 277–83.

11. Michael Denning, "Class and Culture: Reflections on the Work of Warren Susman," *Radical History Review* 36 (1986): 110.

12. Charles L. Ponce de Leon, *Self-Exposure: Human-Interest Journalism and the Emergence of Celebrity in America, 1890–1940* (Chapel Hill: University of North Carolina Press, 2002); Richard Schickel, *Intimate Strangers: The Culture of Celebrity* (New York: Fromm International, 1986); Leo Braudy, *The Frenzy of Renown: Fame & Its History* (New York: Vintage, 1997).

13. See Innes, *Designing Modern America*; Essin, *Stage Designers in Early Twentieth-Century America*, 131–66; Jeffrey Meikle, *Twentieth Century Limited: Industrial Design in America, 1925–1939* (Philadelphia: Temple University Press, 2010); Aronson et al., *Architect of Dreams*.

14. "Ironically, Urban may also have been harmed by his prodigious creativity in such a wide area of endeavor. . . . Many of the leading theater practitioners at the beginning of the twentieth century were attempting to establish theater as an art, as opposed to an entertainment. . . . Norman Bel Geddes, it is true, actually made his mark as an industrial designer . . . but had less impact as a stage designer." Aronson et al., *Architect of Dreams*, 36.

15. H. T. Parker, "At the Opera House," *Boston Evening Transcript*, October 19, 1912, pt. 3, p. 2.

16. Randolph Edgar, "The Vanished Garden of Paradise: A Glimpse at

the Scenic Obstacles Surmounted by Joseph Urban," *Vanity Fair,* January 1915.

17. "Innovations at Opera House," uncited newspaper clipping ca. 1915; "The Art of Joseph Urban, *The Theatre* 23, no. 175 (January 1915): 124; "Urban at Work on Stage Settings," *Dramatic Mirror,* ca. 1915. Clipping Scrapbooks, vol. 1, reel 1, Joseph Urban Papers, 1893–1933, Rare Book & Manuscript Library, Columbia University.

18. Blanding Sloan, "With Stage Settings By:," *Shadowland,* June 1923, 41. Clipping Scrapbooks, vol. 3, reel 1, Joseph Urban Papers, 1893–1933, Rare Book & Manuscript Library, Columbia University.

19. "Viennese Art Wrought on the Shores of Boston Bay," *New York Times,* November 7, 1915; "Urban, the Ambidextrous," *New York Times,* June 17, 1917; Kenneth Macgowan, "The Myth of Urban," *Theatre Arts Magazine* 1, no. 3 (May 1917): 99–109.

20. Loring, *Joseph Urban,* 147, 169–246.

21. The Hagenbund refers to a breakaway movement in Austrian art, founded in 1898 along similar lines to the better-known Vienna Secession. Both groups were organizations for artists pushed out of mainstream Viennese art circles for reasons of style, ethnicity, or class, and both competed at the turn of the century in their exhibitions of Art Nouveau and Jugendstil-inspired works. The Hagenbund exhibited and sold visual arts of various media, and Urban was instrumental in maintaining the organization until his brother-in-law and Hagenbund cofounder, Heinrich Lefler, began to experience a decline in health around 1911 and Urban left for Boston. Loring, 30–34, 42. On Urban's early career, see Dean Howd, "Joseph Urban and American Scene Design," *Theatre Survey* 32, no. 2 (November 1991): 173–86.

22. "Urban, the Ambidextrous," *New York Times.*

23. "Our Scenic Art Leads the World," *Sunday World,* January 18, 1920; Oliver M. Saylor, "Urban, of the Opera, the 'Follies,' and the Films," *Shadowland,* November 1921, 39, 72, 74; Monroe Lathrop, "Scenic Wizard in Los Angeles—Joseph Urban Speaks," *Evening Express,* July 17, 1920. Box 34, folder 34.3, Joseph Urban Papers, 1893–1933, Rare Book & Manuscript Library, Columbia University.

24. Mary Beth Betts, "The American Architecture of Joseph Urban" (PhD diss., City University of New York, 1999), 380.

25. Betts, 380–92, 409–12.

26. Frank Cadie, "Excels Because He Does Not Specialize," *Brooklyn Eagle Magazine,* March 30, 1930.

27. Joseph Urban, "Wedding Theatre Beauty to Ballyhoo," *New York Times,* August 19, 1928.

28. Joseph Urban, "Says Joseph Urban: Modern Art Is a Force—Not a Fad: Catch Up with It," *Sales Management and Advertisers' Weekly* 16, no. 13, (December 22, 1928): 715–17, 746; Joseph Urban, "The Spirit of the Roof Garden," *National Hotel Review*, [December?], 1928, 70–71; "Unusual Conservatory," *Mosaic Messenger* 5 (May 1929): 1–3; Thomas A. Pilkey, "The New School for Social Research in New York—a Gem of Modern Lighting," *Lighting*, March 1931, 18–20. Clipping Scrapbooks, vol. 5, reels 3–5, Joseph Urban Papers, 1893–1933, Rare Book & Manuscript Library, Columbia University.

29. Deems Taylor, "The Scenic Art of Joseph Urban: His Protean Work in the Theatre," *Architecture*, July 1934, 286, 289.

30. Innes, *Designing Modern America*, 25.

31. Szerlip, *Man Who Designed the Future*; Essin, *Stage Designers in Early Twentieth-Century America*, 66–73, 149–65; Innes, *Designing Modern America*.

32. Kenneth Macgowan, "Introducing Mr. Geddes," *New York Herald Tribune*, February 17, 1924; Geraldine Fitch, "Artist's Settings for 'The Miracle' Were the Fruit of His Dreams," [publication unknown], 1924; Bruce Bliven, "Norman Bel Geddes: His Art and Ideas," *Theatre Arts Magazine*, July 1919. UNCAT 1.2, 1.3, and 1.4, box 194, job 937, NBG Papers.

33. Norman Bel Geddes, "Traffic Towers," *Vanity Fair*, July 1921, 62; Norman Bel Geddes, "1922—the Beginning of the 'Age of Masks,'" *Vanity Fair*, January 1922, 54–57. UNCAT 1.2 and 1.3, box 194, job 937, NBG Papers.

34. "Norman Bel-Geddes to Speak Here Twice," *Richmond Times-Dispatch*, March 1, 1925; "Geddes Believes Art Should Be Untrammeled," *Brooklyn Eagle*, July 11, 1926; "Behind the Screens," *The World*, June 6, 1926; Ralph Barton, Caricature of Norman Bel Geddes, *New Yorker*, November 7, 1925; Norman Bel Geddes, "The New Magic of the Stage," *New York Magazine Program*, Broadhurst Theatre, July 4, 1927. UNCAT 1.5 and 1.6, box 194, job 937, NBG Papers.

35. Only one portrait of Jones from that decade exists in a non-theatre press archive, and that by theatre photographer Francis Bruguière. Lee Simonson also had only one published photograph, a "Who's Who" article dating from 1924. Simonson's formal, staid portrait is elegant, but he was clearly not selling his image to the extent that Bel Geddes did. John Kimberly Mumford, "Who's Who in New York—No. 29, Lee Simonson, Whose Success in a Field Not Included in His Ambitions, Has Been Unique," *New York Herald Tribune*, September 7, 1924, sec. A.

36. H. I. Brock, "Theatres for the Age of the Machine," *New York Times Magazine*, November 16, 1930, 12, 23; "Bel Geddes," *Fortune*, July 1930, 51–57; Arthur Strawn, "Norman Bel Geddes, Jack of All Arts, Deserves Name of Genius,"

Kansas City (MO) Journal-Post, March 8, 1931. UNCAT 1.11 and 1.13, box 194, job 937, NBG Papers.

37. Donald John Bush, *The Streamlined Decade* (New York: Braziller, 1988), 17.

38. "The selling of industrial design to corporate clients was difficult at first, but some designers were better at it than others. One of the first to standardize a system for publicity, Norman Bel Geddes included the sales procedure in an employee manual. . . . The design profession was wide open for anyone willing to call themselves a designer, thanks in no small part to the publicity generated by Loewy, Bel Geddes, Teague, and Dreyfuss." John Wall, *Streamliner: Raymond Loewy and Image-Making in the Age of American Industrial Design* (Baltimore: Johns Hopkins University Press, 2018), 63–64.

39. Edited copy of R. L. Duffus, "A Designer's 'Brave New World'; Norman Bel Geddes Lets the Function of Machine Age Objects Dictate Their Form," *New York Times*, December 18, 1932, sec. BR. Box 195, folder UNCAT 2.2, job 937, NBG Papers. Lucius Beebe, "From Hamlet to the World's Fair," *New York Herald Tribune*, May 28, 1939, sec. F. Box 196, folder UNCAT 3.2, job 937, NBG Papers. "Edited" articles from earlier years include "Bel Geddes," *Fortune*, July 1930; Arthur Strawn, "Norman Bel Geddes Starts Another Revolution," *St. Louis Post-Dispatch*, May 12, 1929. Box 194, folder UNCAT 1.11, job 937, NBG Papers.

40. Harold L. Van Doren and Walter Dorwin Teague also released books in 1940. Walter Dorwin Teague, *Design This Day: The Technique of Order in the Machine Age* (New York: Harcourt, Brace, 1940); Harold L. Van Doren, *Industrial Design; A Practical Guide* (New York: McGraw-Hill, 1940).

41. Geddes & Company, Standard Practice Manual, chap. 19, "Books and Articles," box 90, job 940, folder 940.37 Publicity, NBG Papers.

42. A 1944 revision of Geddes & Company's standard practices reads, "Within two weeks either side of the initial solicitation date a leading trade journal, of the field under solicitation, will publish an article by an authoritative writer. This article establishes Geddes & Company authoritatively in this and allied fields. Trade magazine publicity regarding special phases of our work, in specialized magazines such as: *Architectural Form, Tide, Creative Design, Variety, Product Engineering, Advertising and Selling, Packaging, Theatre Arts, Business Week*. This type of publicity is secured through contacts with writers and editors." Geddes & Company, Standard Practice Manual, chap. 32.7, "Trade Journal Article," box 88, job 940, folder 940.6 Office Procedure, NBG Papers.

43. Such articles were most common in 1933 and 1934, "when industrial design was changing from a suspect fad to a common practice." Meikle, *Twentieth Century Limited*, 77.

44. Clippings of these articles can be found in folders UNCAT 1.8, 1.11, 1.13, box 184, and UNCAT 2.3, box 195, job 937, NBG Papers.

45. Stuart Ewen, *PR! A Social History of Spin* (New York: Basic Books, 1996); Ponce de Leon, *Self-Exposure*, 11–42, 76–105; Irving J. Rein, Philip Kotler, Michael Hamlin, and Martin R. Stoller, *High Visibility: Transforming Your Personal and Professional Brand*, 3rd ed. (New York: McGraw-Hill, 2006), 274–98.

46. Lee Simonson, "Lee Simonson Discloses Secrets of Scene Design," *New York Herald Tribune*, June 12, 1927, sec. E; "Says Home Planning Is Half of Comfort," *New York Times*, May 16, 1928; Lee Simonson, "The Problems of the Scenic Designer," *New York Times*, November 17, 1929.

47. Christin Essin has connected a rise in "public relations" to the development of "scenographic entrepreneurship" among theatrical designers in this period, especially Urban and Bel Geddes. "The 1930s, according to historian Stuart Ewen, was a period of significant growth in the burgeoning profession of public relations. Industry leaders needed to combat Depression-era perceptions of corporate America as greedy and arrogant and offer a counter argument to the Roosevelt administration's promotion of New Deal social programs. . . . With the help of industrial designers like Bel Geddes, business leaders assumed the role of social advocates and cast Americans as consumers whose purchase of new products would pave the road to economic recovery." Essin, *Stage Designers in Early Twentieth-Century America*, 144.

48. Dana Cuff, *Architecture: The Story of Practice* (Cambridge, MA: MIT Press, 1991), 24.

49. The American Institute of Graphic Arts was founded in 1914. The American Institute of Architects consolidated its power from a network of state licensing boards into an interstate organization in the 1910s and 1920s. Precursor organizations to the Industrial Designers Society of America emerged in the 1930s. See Gregory Votolato, *American Design in the Twentieth Century: Personality and Performance* (Manchester: Manchester University Press, 1998), 6–7; Stanley Abercrombie, *George Nelson: The Design of Modern Design* (Cambridge, MA: MIT Press, 1995), 310; Dana Cuff, "Historical License: Architectural History in the Architectural Profession," *Journal of the Society of Architectural Historians* 76, no. 1 (March 1, 2017): 5–6.

50. "The exclusivity of AIA membership meant not only standing in high society . . . but also knowledge in architectural history that distinguished those with an education from workingmen, those in the building trades, and artisans." Cuff, "Historical License," 5.

51. Architecture "depends on implicit appeals to the telos, the culturally significant, and the noble tradition of architecture. Not merely adequate building but culturally significant building is the lasting confirmation of

architecture's professional claims." Magali Sarfatti Larson, *Behind the Post-modern Facade: Architectural Change in Late Twentieth-Century America* (Berkeley: University of California Press, 1995), 8.

52. Even this status would be tenuous in relationship to other, established professions such as medicine, law, and the clergy. Architecture's association with fine art practices resulted in a weaker professional claim. Cuff, *Architecture*, 31–33.

53. Cuff, 24.

54. Roger K. Lewis, *Architect? A Candid Guide to the Profession* (Cambridge, MA: MIT Press, 1985), 193.

55. In 1895 the AIA banned members from "association with any publication containing advertisements," though the production of promotional "souvenir" sketchbooks continued longer into the twentieth century. Mary N. Woods, *From Craft to Profession: The Practice of Architecture in Nineteenth-Century America* (Berkeley: University of California Press, 1999), 49–50.

56. "The best way to get new commissions and clients is to design an outstanding building, have it admired and possibly published, and let that be what they say honey is to the errant bee." Morris Lapidus, *Architecture: A Profession and a Business* (New York: Reinhold, 1967), 54.

57. Shanken, "Breaking the Taboo," 406, 411–21.

58. "The use of persona, the use of lay (and not just architectural) media to attract business ... are still seen as ethically suspect in a discipline that views itself as both artistically too creative and professionally too aristocratic to succumb to such tactics." Peggy Deamer, "Branding the Architectural Author," *Perspecta* 37 (2005): 43.

59. This term, now most commonly applied to high-profile postmodern architects such as Frank Gehry or Daniel Libeskind, might also be applied in spirit to modernist celebrity architects such as Frank Lloyd Wright, Ludwig Mies van der Rohe, or Le Corbusier. Most working architects did not seek out such stardom.

60. For instance, in Italy: Sebastiano Serlio, Andrea Palladio, the Galli-Bibiena family; in Germany: Joseph Furttenbach; and in England: Inigo Jones.

61. John Morris Dixon, "A White Gentleman's Profession?," *Progressive Architecture* 75, no. 11 (November 1994): 55; Reed Kroloff, "'Gentleman's Profession' No More," *New York Times*, September 16, 2018.

62. Roland Marchand, *Advertising the American Dream: Making Way for Modernity, 1920–1940* (Berkeley: University of California Press, 2008), 25–28.

63. Marchand, 49.

64. Poggi, *Theater in America*, 46–64.

65. "Mielziner Went from Oils to Stage Settings," *New York Herald Tribune*, July 10, 1932, sec. F.

66. Journalist champions of scenic designer features included Lucius Beebe at the *New York Herald Tribune* and Bosley Crowther at the *New York Times*. Among editors, Edith J. R. Isaacs included writings on designers and photographs of their work in *Theatre Arts Monthly*, while Harold Ross included a number of designers (for the stage and otherwise) in his string of *New Yorker* profiles, beginning with Joseph Urban in 1927.

67. Elihu Winer, "Stage Designers Seeking New Illusions."

68. Norris Houghton, "The Designer Sets the Stage: III, Lee Simonson; IV, Donald Oenslager," *Theatre Arts Monthly*, November 1936, 891.

69. School of Fine Arts Bulletin, Department of Drama, 1941, Draft, p. 7, box 31, folder 2, Yale School of Drama Records (RU 728), Manuscripts and Archives, Yale University Library; Jones, *Dramatic Imagination*, 68.

70. See the Norris Houghton series "The Designer Sets the Stage." Robert Edmond Jones wrote that design is "not the problem of an architect or a painter or a sculptor or even a musician, but of a poet." Jones, *Dramatic Imagination*, 77–78.

71. Donald Schön, *Educating the Reflective Practitioner: Toward a New Design for Teaching and Learning in the Professions* (San Francisco: Jossey-Bass, 1987).

72. See also Gabriela Goldschmidt, "The Dialectics of Sketching," *Creativity Research Journal* 4, no. 2 (January 1, 1991): 123–43; Donald Schön, "Designing as a Reflective Conversation with the Materials of a Design Situation," *Knowledge-Based Systems* 5, no. 1 (1992): 3–14.

73. Larson, *Scene Design in the American Theatre*, 160–63.

74. Simonson, *Stage Is Set*, 10. Jones: "It is to the credit of our designers that they have made almost a fetish of abnegation." Jones, *Dramatic Imagination*, 71–72.

75. Norris Houghton, "The Designer Sets the Stage V, Robert Edmond Jones; VI, Mordecai Gorelik," *Theatre Arts Monthly*, December 1936, 966–75; Jo Mielziner, "Practical Dreams," in *The Theatre of Robert Edmond Jones*, ed. Ralph Pendleton (Middletown, CT: Wesleyan University Press, 1958), 20–27; Lee Simonson, "Tale of a Scene Designer's Misery: Lee Simonson Takes Issue with Mr. Pemberton regarding the Cost of Sets and Other Matters," *New York Times*, January 22, 1933, sec. 10; Jo Mielziner, "So Little Time," *New York Times*, October 12, 1945, sec. 2; Donald Oenslager, "Passing Scenes," *Theatre Arts* 33 (November 1949): 16–25, 93–94.

76. Such an image may have been crafted by earlier iterations of scenic artistry, such as Ernest Gros, Joseph Physioc, or other salaried designers hired by producers before the New Stagecraft era.

77. Shanken argues that architecture was less stable than other professions, such as law and medicine, especially with regard to effective state

licensing and public recognition of expertise. Shanken, "Breaking the Taboo," 411.

78. Ruth Woodbury Sedgwick, "Biography of a Decorator," *Scene*, March 1937, 66.

79. Oliver M. Sayler, "Robert Edmond Jones, Artist of the Theatre," *New Republic*, June 20, 1930; Kenneth Macgowan, "Robert Edmond Jones," *Theatre Arts Monthly*, November 1925, 720–30; Seldes, "Profiles: The Emperor Jones—Profile of Robert Edmond Jones."

80. Young Boswell, "Young Boswell Interviews Lee Simonson," *New York Tribune*, May 11, 1923.

81. Lee Simonson, "Men as Stage Scenery Walking," *New York Times*, May 25, 1924; Simonson, "Problems of the Scenic Designer."

82. William H. Baldwin, "Modern Art and the Machine Age," *The Independent*, July 1927; "Mr. Simonson and His Scenic Art," *New York Times*, November 30, 1930, sec. 10; Kenneth Macgowan, "Five Little Productions and How They Grew," *New York Times*, January 3, 1932.

83. Lee Simonson, "The New 'Road': One Way to Revive the American Theatre," *Forum and Century*, August 1932; Lee Simonson, "The Theatre: Gambler's Paradise," *New Republic* 72 (September 7, 1932): 93–96; Lee Simonson, "On the Place of the Designer in the Theatre," *New York Times*, January 14, 1934.

84. Brock Pemberton, "A Dissertation on the Liabilities, and the Few Blessings, of the Depression," *New York Times*, January 15, 1933.

85. Simonson, "Tale of a Scene Designer's Misery."

86. Simonson detailed designers' problems with obtaining the final third of payments from managers, who "have learned the trick of incorporating each show" to avoid liability, and he called for a revitalization of theatrical production to redistribute wages and contract fees more fairly among actors and designers.

87. Robert Edmond Jones, "The Decorator," *New York Times*, December 10, 1916; Robert Edmond Jones, "A Plea for Make-Believe Scenery," *New York Times*, August 31, 1924.

88. Seldes, "Profiles: The Emperor Jones—Profile of Robert Edmond Jones," 25–26.

89. Houghton, "The Designer Sets the Stage V, Robert Edmond Jones; VI, Mordecai Gorelik."

90. Jones quoted in Houghton, 969.

91. "Bobby was younger than Margaret, who continued to call herself Mrs. Carrington. Since he was a homosexual, she sent him to Vienna to see Sigmund Freud and later claimed the father of psychoanalysis had cured her husband.... Bobby and Mrs. Carrington were to remain devoted to each other to

the end of their lives." Axel Madsen, *John Huston: A Biography* (Garden City, NY: Doubleday, 1978), 21. Readings of Jones's marriage as one of convenience are explored by Martin Green, *New York, 1913: The Armory Show and the Paterson Strike Pageant* (New York: Collier Books, 1989); Jane T. Peterson, "'Not as Other Boys': Robert Edmond Jones and Designs of Desire," in *Staging Desire: Queer Readings of American Theater History*, ed. Kim Marra and Robert A. Schanke (Ann Arbor: University of Michigan Press, 2002), 338–64; Christin Essin Yannacci, "Landscapes of American Modernity: A Cultural History of Theatrical Design, 1912–1951" (PhD diss., University of Texas at Austin, 2006), 70–71.

92. John Peale Bishop, "Youngest among the Moderns: James Reynolds as an Artist in Settings and Costumes," *Theatre Arts Magazine* 5, no. 1 (January 1921): 75, 79.

93. Ziegfeld paid for nine months of Reynolds's travel in Europe in 1921–1922 as he gathered source material for his extravagant designs. "James Reynolds Back," *Billboard*, April 1, 1922, 7; "Reynolds with Ziegfeld," *Billboard*, July 9, 1921, 30.

94. "The Brooks Costume Company to Sell thru Dept. Stores," *Billboard*, January 16, 1926, 6.

95. Millia Davenport, "Wits & Fingers Revised," 4–5, box 1, folder "Millia Davenport," Orville K. Larson Papers, 2006MT-50r, Houghton Library, Harvard University.

96. "James Reynolds, Author, Artist," *New York Times*, July 24, 1957, 25.

97. Reynolds quoted in Lawrence Sullivan, "Arthur Schnitzler's 'The Bridal Veil' at the American Laboratory Theatre," *Dance Research Journal* 25, no. 1 (1993): 15.

98. Millia Davenport, "Wits & Fingers," 5.

99. In addition to this chapter's many citations of features in the *Times*, *Herald Tribune*, *New Yorker*, and *Vanity Fair*, see "Theatre Delays Shortened," *Scientific American*, March 1928; Kate Sproehnle, "The Curtain Calls," *Mademoiselle*, March 1937; Kate Sproehnle, "Dreamlining Tomorrow," *Mademoiselle*, July 1944.

100. See Howard Bay, "From Shubert Alley to Play Production 304B," *Educational Theatre Journal* 17, no. 1 (1965): 46–48; Norman Bel Geddes, Edward C. Cole, Arch Lauterer, Serge Chermayeff, and Stanley McCandless, "Theatre Planning: A Symposium," *Educational Theatre Journal* 2, no. 1 (1950): 1–7. For *Theatre Arts* examples, see Aline Bernstein, "The Craftsmen," *Theatre Arts* 29, no. 4 (April 1945): 208–14; Howard Bay, "Design for the Musical Stage," *Theatre Arts* 29, no. 11 (November 1945): 650–55; Boris Aronson, "Designing Sweet Bye and Bye," *Theatre Arts* 30, no. 10 (October 1946): 573–75; Jo Mielziner, "Make the Theatre Building Pay," *Theatre Arts* 30, no. 6 (June 1946):

363–66; Donald Oenslager, "Let There Be Light," *Theatre Arts* 31, no. 9 (September 1947): 46–52; Oenslager, "Passing Scenes."

101. Simonson, *Part of a Lifetime*; Donald Oenslager, *The Theatre of Donald Oenslager* (Middletown, CT: Wesleyan University Press, 1978); Mielziner, *Designing for the Theatre*. Christin Essin cites Simonson as the innovator of the profile-memoir trend. Essin, *Stage Designers in Early Twentieth-Century America*, 39–42.

102. Brooks Atkinson, "Value of an Idea: Five Set Designers at Work on Incoming Broadway Productions," *New York Times*, August 25, 1957, sec. Arts & Leisure; "Three Designers Set the Stage for Broadway's New Season," *New York Times*, August 24, 1958.

103. Leo Sullivan, "A Designing Duo Sets for a Spell," *Washington Post and Times-Herald*, September 4, 1957; Murray Schumach, "Broadway's Busy Jeremiah: Oliver Smith, Scenic Designer, Laments State of Stage Active Schedule," *New York Times*, April 28, 1957; Richard L. Coe, "Lee: Setting the Stage for an Exhibit," *Washington Post*, May 25, 1975.

3. The Teaching Artist

1. Five of these productions opened within a month of one another, leading Brooks Atkinson to quip, "Donald Oenslager, who has not done a setting since the night before last." Brooks Atkinson, "The Play: 200 Were Chosen,' *New York Times*, November 21, 1936; George Rose, "So This Is Broadway," *New York World-Telegram*, December 11, 1936; Rowland Field, "Both Sides of the Curtain," *Brooklyn Times Union*, November 8, 1936. See Donald Oenslager Scrapbooks, box 55 (1936–1937), Donald Oenslager Papers and Designs, *T-Mss 1996-015, Billy Rose Theatre Division, The New York Public Library for the Performing Arts. Hereafter cited as Oenslager Papers and Designs in this chapter's notes.

2. Donald Oenslager, "Drama 112—Orientation," Lecture Notes Revised, September 30, 1937, box 10, folder 6, Oenslager Papers and Designs.

3. Variations on the idea that "the scene designer is not a decorator, painter, or an architect ... [but] a craftsman possessing knowledge of all these arts" can be found in the Scene Design section of the Yale Department of Drama catalog from 1925 through the 1950s, as well as in many of Oenslager's publications. Yale School of Fine Arts Bulletin, 1930–1931, box 34, folder 46, Yale School of Drama Records (RU 728), Manuscripts and Archives, Yale University Library; Donald Oenslager, "Stage Design and the Repertory Theatre," *Education: A Monthly Magazine* 67, no. 5 (January 1947): 273–77; Donald Oenslager, "Fine Art of Variation," USA 829 *Almanac*, 1940–1941, box 3, folder 9, United Scenic Artists Records, WAG.065, Tamiment Library / Robert F. Wagner Labor

Archives, New York University. These two archives are hereafter cited as Yale School of Drama Records and USA 829 Records in this chapter's notes.

4. Donald Oenslager, "Passing Scenes," *Theatre Arts*, November 1949, 16–25, 93–94.

5. Oenslager, "Passing Scenes."

6. Shannon Jackson, *Professing Performance: Theatre in the Academy from Philology to Performativity* (Cambridge: Cambridge University Press, 2004), 69–72.

7. "History of the Department," 1–5, box 32, folder 31, Yale School of Drama Records. This history is unsigned but contains revision notes by A. M. Nagler and is dated 1965. In that year Robert Brustein assumed leadership as dean of the Drama School, and the Yale Repertory Theatre was founded. The history contains individual profiles of teachers in each department, often with direct quotations from them or recollections from their students.

8. Robert A. M. Stern and Jimmy Stamp, *Pedagogy and Place: 100 Years of Architecture Education at Yale* (New Haven, CT: Yale University Press, 2016), 37, 42.

9. Many of these observations have been asserted in passing and linked to later changes in the academy, such as the rise of performance studies, the prevalence of the MFA among university faculty—a trend to which Yale directly contributed—and the general "crisis in the humanities." Jackson, *Professing Performance*; Susan Harris Smith, *American Drama: The Bastard Art* (Cambridge: Cambridge University Press, 2006); Joseph Roach, "Reconstructing Theatre/History," *Theatre Topics* 9, no. 1 (1999): 3–10; Marvin Carlson, "Theatre and Performance at a Time of Shifting Disciplines," *Theatre Research International*, no. 2 (July 2001): 137–44; Julia A. Walker, "Why Performance? Why Now? Textuality and the Rearticulation of Human Presence," *Yale Journal of Criticism* 16, no. 1 (2003): 149–75; Anne Berkeley, "Changing Theories of College Theatrical Curricula, 1900–1945," *Journal of Aesthetic Education* 31, no. 4 (August 1997): 77–90.

10. Paul E. Leitner, "The Scene Designs of J. Woodman Thompson" (PhD diss., University of Nebraska, 1990), 30–35.

11. Donald K. Smith, "Origin and Development of Departments of Speech," in *History of Speech Education in America: Background Studies*, ed. Karl Richards Wallace and the Speech Association of America (New York: Appleton-Century-Crofts, 1954), 589.

12. "History of the Department," 50.

13. "History of the Department," 9. Yale was the first school to award an MFA in theatre. Before 1930 the MFA was extremely rare and was awarded by select schools for graduate coursework in arts fields for which professionalizing experience was necessary. Princeton offered an MFA in architecture as

early as 1921, and one (unspecified) American university awarded an MFA in music before 1930. Frank Eugene Kidder, *The Architects' and Builders' Handbook: Data for Architects, Structural Engineers, Contractors, and Draughtsmen* (John Wiley & Sons, 1921), 1785; Peter W. Dykema, *Survey of College Entrance Credits and College Courses in Music* (New York: National Bureau for the Advancement of Music, 1930), 6.

14. Yale School of Fine Arts Bulletin, 1930–1931, D9, box 34, folder 46, Yale School of Drama Records.

15. "In order to make the transition from school to professional work as smooth as possible for his students, Mr. Oenslager lays great stress on the teaching of 'problems' which are as similar as possible to those encountered by professionals in the field." "History of the Department," 54.

16. Courses changed titles regularly, but the progression of full-year courses in three successive years remained the same. Yale School of Fine Arts Bulletin, 1930–1931, D12, box 34, folder 46, and Yale School of Fine Arts Bulletin, 1942–43, 54, box 31, folder 2, Yale School of Drama Records.

17. "History of the Department," 55.

18. Slide Lists and Outline for Drama 112, box 1, folder: Drama 112, Donald Oenslager Papers (MS 1416), Manuscripts and Archives, Yale University Library.

19. "The 'O,' or 'Uncle Don' as his students affectionately call him, believes that the school must focus on the students and on their creativity." "History of the Department," 57.

20. Book list, "Drama 112, Mr. Oenslager and Mr. Bevan," September 27, 1949, box 31, folder 1, Yale School of Drama Records.

21. "History of the Department," 57.

22. "History of the Department," 57.

23. "Often the best criticism may be the student's comparison of his own work with that of his fellow students. In the beginning they are side by side at the post ready for their arduous three years' race. Competition is healthy and essential to their development." Oenslager, *Theatre of Donald Oenslager*, 7.

24. Oenslager, 8.

25. Memo from Frank McMullen to Boyd Smith, December 30, 1945, box 34, folder 49, Yale School of Drama Records.

26. Stanford attempted an artist-in-residence program in drama in the late 1940s, which met with some success even though Stanford was unable to attract senior working artists to teach for any extended period of time. See F. Cowles Strickland, "Artists-in-Residence as an Aid to Better Teaching," box 34, folder 49, Yale School of Drama Records.

27. After one busy year at Yale establishing curriculum, Oenslager reasoned that he needed to live in New York City to maintain his professional status. "History of the Department," 50.

28. Bevan and McCandless have a handful of Broadway credits listed on the Internet Broadway Database, while Oenslager is credited with over 140. Bevan focused on teaching and designing for Yale's theatres, while McCandless developed a significant career in consulting, architectural lighting, and the development of lighting instruments and technology while living in New Haven.

29. Susan Harris Smith, "Did She Jump or Was She Pushed? American Drama in the University Curriculum," *American Drama*, 114–58.

30. "Two 'Baker Maps,'" *Theatre Arts Monthly* 17, no. 7 (1933): 552–54, 553.

31. The Yale Drama Alumni Association tracked and publicized alumni successes in its newsletter and other publications. Drama Alumni Records, boxes 36–39, Yale School of Drama Records.

32. "YALE ALUMNI IN DRAMA," box 34, folder 41, Yale School of Drama Records.

33. In a 1940 communique to alumni, the following designers were cited as "outstanding scene designers" who had "designed one or more New York" shows: Stewart Chaney, Sam Leve, Isaac Benesch, Peggy Clark, Johannes Larson, Larry Goldwasser, and John Koenig. Later versions of this list would add, among others, John Conklin, William and Jean Eckart, Peter Larkin, Tharon Musser, and Jean Rosenthal. "Statistics of What the Department of Drama at Yale Is Doing in the Theatre Today," February 21, 1940, and "From E.C.C. List, 1965–66," box 39, folders 25 and 45, Yale School of Drama Records.

34. Donald Oenslager, "U.S. Stage Design, Past and Present," in *Contemporary Stage Design! USA*, ed. Elisabeth B. Burdick, Peggy C. Hansen, and Brenda Zanger (Middletown, CT: International Theatre Institute of the United States, 1974), 13–15.

35. "While in fact professional education by no means required university affiliation—witness dozens of night law schools and so prestigious a medical school as the Jefferson Medical College—profession after profession turned to the university for help in seizing control of its own educational apparatus." Abbott, *System of Professions*, 207.

36. Magali Sarfatti Larson, "In the Matter of Experts and Professionals, or How Impossible It Is to Leave Nothing Unsaid," in *The Formation of Professions: Knowledge, State, and Strategy*, ed. Michael Burrage and Rolf Torstendahl (London: Sage, 1990), 30.

37. Of course, many careers require formal postsecondary education, whether or not they are considered to be a profession or within "the professions." (See this book's introduction.) There is quite a bit of complexity in the relationships among professions, trades, and universities. In the United States, certain research universities (also called institutes of technology or polytechnic institutes) and technical colleges (sometimes called technical institutes) specialize in training students for work in trades, vocations, or

technological careers. In this chapter, the Carnegie Institute of Technology is one such technical institute that later became a research university.

38. Abbott, *System of Professions*, 184–85.

39. "Medicine, law, and optometry, for instance, were licensed either before they established a university connection or before they formed a national professional association. Legal protection is apparently not an integral part of any 'natural history' of professionalism." Wilensky, "Professionalization of Everyone?," 145.

40. Evetts, "Concept of Professionalism," 39.

41. "In the ideal-typical occupational labor market the credential is a labor market signal based on a formal system of training that is controlled directly or indirectly by representatives of the occupation and sustained by force of law or strong custom." Freidson, *Professionalism*, 78.

42. Arthur Efland, *A History of Art Education: Intellectual and Social Currents in Teaching the Visual Arts* (New York: Teachers College Press, 1990), 1–4; Timothy Allen Jackson, "Ontological Shifts in Studio Art Education: Emergent Pedagogical Models," *Art Journal* 58, no. 1 (March 1, 1999): 68; Stuart Macdonald, *The History and Philosophy of Art Education* (Cambridge: James Clarke, 2004), 16–40.

43. Lois Hetland, Ellen Winner, Shirley Veenema, and Kimberly M. Sheridan, *Studio Thinking: The Real Benefits of Visual Arts Education* (New York: Teachers College Press, 2007).

44. See Mark Hodin, "'It Did Not Sound like a Professor's Speech': George Pierce Baker and the Market for Academic Rhetoric," *Theatre Survey* 46, no. 2 (November 2005): 225–46.

45. Hetland et al., *Studio Thinking*, 6.

46. Hetland et al., 21–29.

47. Michael Yeargan remembered being in Oenslager's last scenic design class in 1969: "Donald was a great gentleman of the theatre, and he ran his classes like an old school. The classes were two hours long, on Thursday, and were all critique-based. He would assign a project one week, and you were expected to bring it in the next week. The project consisted of a matted, color sketch and, on the back, in 1/8″ scale on graph paper, the ground plan. You put it on the table in the front of the room when you entered and then took your seat. If you were late, you couldn't put it on the table. . . . He would say only one or two things about the design, but you never forgot it." Yeargan in Ronn Smith, *American Set Design 2* (New York: Theatre Communications Group, 1995), 177–79.

48. "History of the Department," 50.

49. Collection Overview, Papers of Arthur Pope, 1907–1979, Harvard Library, https://hollisarchives.lib.harvard.edu/repositories/9/resources/388.

50. "The most important addition, in many years, to the teaching staff of the School of Architecture was Professor J. J. Haffner, who came in the winters of 1921–1922 to teach advanced courses in Design. Professor Haffner completed the work for the diplôme at the Ecole des Beaux-Arts in 1909, and in 1919 was awarded the Grand Prix de Rome. He is one of two men so distinguished ever to come to this country to teach in an American school. . . . [F]or some time, the Boston Architectural Club, the Massachusetts Institute of Technology, and the Harvard School of Architecture have maintained a system of conjunctive problems by which the same projects are undertaken in all three schools, and are judged by a jury composed of delegates from the schools. . . . [A] system of this sort requires the closest sympathetic collaboration, and this is best safeguarded by the continual presence on the jury of men like Professors Haffner and Ferran." G. H. Edgell, "The School of Architecture and the Department of Fine Arts," *Harvard Alumni Bulletin* 25, no. 14 (1922): 383, 385–86.

51. Woods, *From Craft to Profession*, 81.

52. Joan Draper, "The Ecole des Beaux-Arts and the Architectural Profession in the United States: The Case of John Galen Howard," chap. 8 in *The Architect: Chapters in the History of the Profession*, ed. Spiro Kostof and Dana Cuff (Berkeley: University of California Press, 2008), 224.

53. "The final push before a project deadline, it begins with the student dedicating all waking hours to the production of project drawings and ends with the addition of sleeping hours as well. The test is to see how many consecutive nights one can work without sleep. It is not uncommon to be 'on charrette' (the American bastardization of 'en charrette') for a week, culminating in two or even three all-nighters. This is a competitive arena, for not only is one racing against the clock, but students compete with each other: for the most complete set of drawings, the most precise model, the most elegant presentation." Cuff, *Architecture*, 126–28.

54. For a summary of this history of education, see Woods, *From Craft to Profession*, 53–81.

55. "Arbiter of the Arts: A Beaux Arts Dean Has Reigned," *Architectural Forum* 86, no. 6 (June 1947): 76.

56. Because architecture was "traditionally one of the most expensive subjects to teach," wrote Meeks's successor, Charles Sawyer, in 1948, the department found it advantageous to use "part-time teaching personnel from the architectural profession at a comparatively low salary scale." Yale's architecture courses cost "approximately forty percent of the cost per student in the School of Design at Harvard." Charles H. Sawyer, "President's Committee on Clearance of Projects," January 8, 1948, box 34, folder 49, Yale School of Drama Records.

57. "The principal social relation in school—that between studio instructor and student—is cast as a relation between unique individuals. The primacy of the individual is then carried into practice.... [I]n other words, the structural conditions within which individuals must operate in practice are exempted from careful consideration by schools and from inclusion within belief systems." Cuff, *Architecture*, 45.

58. "History of the Department," 54.

59. "He ... explained that, any way, scenic designing and stage settings are the field of a craftsman not an artist. 'And by craftsman I mean a person who combines original and imaginative endeavor with practical utilitarian facility,' he said." Lucius Beebe, "Donald Oenslager and the Technique of Sets," *New York Herald Tribune*, April 28, 1935, D2.

60. Donald Oenslager, "Fine Art of Variation," USA 829 *Almanac*, 1940–1941, box 3, folder 9, USA 829 Records; Catalog of the Yale School of Drama, Yale School of Fine Arts Bulletin, 1930–1931, box 34, folder 46, Yale School of Drama Records.

61. Oenslager, *Theatre of Donald Oenslager*, 7.

62. Abbott, *System of Professions*, 40–52.

63. Schön, *Educating the Reflective Practitioner*, 13.

64. Schön, 31.

65. Cheri Logan, "Metaphor and Pedagogy in the Design Practicum," *International Journal of Technology and Design Education* 18, no. 1 (January 1, 2008): 1–17; Philippa Lyon, *Design Education: Learning, Teaching and Researching through Design* (Surrey, UK: Gower, 2011).

66. Jon Drtina, "A Conversation with John Ezell," *Theatre Design and Technology* 43, no. 1 (Winter 2007): 43; Daniel Robinson, "The Innovations and Legacy of Frank Poole Bevan," *Theatre Design & Technology* 49, no. 4 (Fall 2013): 62.

67. Robinson, "Innovations and Legacy of Frank Poole Bevan," 62.

68. Robinson, 70.

69. B. Iden Payne recalled that "the first small group which formed the drama department consisted of students who were interested solely, or at any rate primarily, in acting." Both Payne and McCarthy quoted in B. Iden Payne et al., "Recollections and Impressions of 'T.W.,'" *Educational Theatre Journal* 3, no. 4 (1951): 294–317.

70. "The emphasis on acting was automatic; in any theatre, ours included, the employment load works out about twelve to one against scene designers, directors, and playwrights. . . . [T]he inference is plain that the theatre needs trained actors." In this 1939 article extolling Carnegie Tech's achievements, acting and direction received top billing; the only design achievements Stevens mentioned were those of the faculty. Thomas Wood Stevens, "The

Background: The First Plan and the Goal," *Theatre Arts Monthly* 23, no. 7 (July 1939): 494.

71. Jackson, *Professing Performance*, 74.

72. Henry Hornbostel, architect of many Carnegie Institute buildings and the first dean of the College of Fine Arts, trained at the École des Beaux-Arts and taught its methods. Stevens wrote, "For thoroughness in preparing the curriculum we based many things on the parallel problems in the school of architecture." Quoted in Stevens, "Background," 494. However, Carnegie Tech instructor Alexander Wyckoff recalled that the department followed "a Beaux Arts system" but only "at first." Payne et al., "Recollections and Impressions of 'T.W.,'" 297.

73. "Stevens saw no need for courses in the theory of theatre or stagecraft, unless a history of dramatic literature could be so construed. All such information was acquired under practical working conditions." Alexander Wyckoff in Payne et al., "Recollections and Impressions of 'T.W.,'" 297.

74. Stevens, "Background," 491.

75. An example of this integration: "As he picked up a chair to use in rehearsal, it was the natural thing for Stevens to comment on its design, function, and history; and it became the natural thing for the student to heed such information. No matter what his special field in the theatre, such information was a necessary tool of the student's trade." Alexander Wyckoff in Payne et al., "Recollections and Impressions of 'T.W.,'" 297.

76. Elizabeth Schrader Kimberly, *A History of the Drama Department of Carnegie-Mellon University, Formerly Carnegie Institute of Technology, 1914–1981* (Pittsburgh: Carnegie-Mellon University, 1981), 4.

77. Bay attended Carnegie Tech for one year but did not earn a degree. Perhaps Bay's pragmatic Carnegie Tech education contributed to his ease with scene painters as president of the union in the forties. Bobbi Owen and United States Institute for Theatre Technology, *Late & Great: American Designers, 1960–2010* (Syracuse, NY: United States Institute for Theatre Technology, 2010), 53.

78. "The Carnegie Map," *Theatre Arts Monthly* 23, no. 7 (July 1939): 510–11.

79. Henry C. Zabierek, "Interests Transcended: The Early History of Carnegie Tech," *Western Pennsylvania Historical Magazine* 53, no. 4 (October 1970): 352.

80. Kimberly, *History of the Drama Department of Carnegie-Mellon University*, 9.

81. Kimberly, 11, 21.

82. Walker, "Why Performance?," 154–55; Berkeley, "Changing Theories of College Theatrical Curricula," 79.

83. "Efforts to establish courses and programs in drama met opposition in

institutions throughout the country, but whereas the newer state and private schools outside of the east yielded either to the persuasion of a determined instructor or to the popularity of his productions, the older eastern colleges and universities resisted more firmly. Yale was the exception to the rule set by Harvard and emulated by the remaining schools of the Ivy League until quite recently." Bernard Beckerman, "The University Accepts the Theatre: 1800–1925," in *The American Theatre: A Sum of Its Parts* (New York: Samuel French, 1971), 351–52. See also Smith, "Origin and Development of Departments of Speech," 462.

84. Beckerman, "University Accepts the Theatre," 352; Berkeley, "Changing Theories of College Theatrical Curricula," 86.

85. Brochures from these programs, with dates of foundation, box 17, folder 216, Yale School of Drama Records.

86. "Our History," Goodman Theatre, www.goodmantheatre.org; "Goodman Drama School Forced to Close Doors," *Los Angeles Times*, September 15, 1975, E10.

87. Course Catalog, Dramatic Workshop of the New School for Social Research, New School Archives and Special Collections Digital Archive, http://digitalarchives.library.newschool.edu.

88. "Our History," Department of Theatre Arts, University of Iowa, https://theatre.uiowa.edu/about-us/mission-history; "From E.C.C. List, 1965–66," box 39, folder 45, Yale School of Drama Records.

89. "Reflecting on 75 Years of Theatre and Dance," Theatre and Dance, University of Texas at Austin, https://theatredance.utexas.edu/news/reflecting-75-years-theatre-dance; Lucy Barton in Payne et al., "Recollections and Impressions of 'T.W.'"

90. Leitner, "Scene Designs of J. Woodman Thompson," 69–70.

91. "Stage Design Course and Book," job 79, boxes 149–54, Norman Bel Geddes Theatre and Industrial Design Papers, Harry Ransom Center, University of Texas at Austin.

92. Brochure, "Lester Polakov Studio of Stage Design," ca. 1960, box 17, folder 216, Yale School of Drama Records.

93. Fletcher, *Rediscovering Mordecai Gorelik*, 186–88. Brandeis University bulletin, May 1965, 10, https://archive.org/details/brandeisuniversi6167bran; Abram Leon Sachar, *Brandeis University: A Host at Last* (Hanover, NH: University Press of New England, 1995), 162–65.

94. General Meeting Minutes, February 18, 1927, measure approved March 18, 1927, reel 3, USA 829 Records.

95. Minnelli was a designer and director better known for his work in film and musical revues (*Gigi, Meet Me in St. Louis*). He married Judy Garland and was Liza Minnelli's father. "Vincente Minnelli," folder 30, box 1, United

Scenic Artists Exam Designs, *T-VIM 2011-256, Billy Rose Theatre Division, The New York Public Library.

96. Undated exams, folder 4, box 40, USA 829 Records. Cross-referencing the wording of instructions, typesetting, and pagination with exams from the New York Public Library suggests that the undated exams likely were printed sometime between the late thirties and the very early fifties. Other material in this collection also dates from Thompson's tenure as chair of the examining committee.

97. Untitled grading sheets, "Thompson the Teacher I," box 107, James Woodman Thompson Collection, Rare Book & Manuscript Library, Columbia University.

98. Union membership applications from the 1940s required a report from the chair of the examining committee and three signatures of endorsement before the names could be presented to the full membership for election. "Application for Membership," folder 4, box 40, USA 829 Records.

99. "Thompson the Teacher II," box 107, James Woodman Thompson Collection, Rare Book & Manuscript Library, Columbia University.

100. Leitner, "Scene Designs of J. Woodman Thompson," 74–81.

101. Howard Bay, for instance, challenged his denial by arguing that applicants with lower scores had joined, and he won membership on that appeal in 1934. General Meeting Minutes, October 1, 1934, reel 5, USA 829 Records.

102. Memo, March 11, 1943, in "Educational Committee," folder 42, box 4, USA 829 Records.

103. Memo, March 11, 1943.

4. The Consulting Artist

1. Simonson, *Part of a Lifetime*, 68.

2. Simonson, 67, 69.

3. Oenslager, *Theatre of Donald Oenslager*, 15.

4. The term *service* or *faculty service* is a common one among academics, although a similar sense of service to one's field can also be found in many professions (law, architecture, scientific subfields, engineering, etc.).

5. These are likely coded references to the younger, out, gay James Reynolds and to the famous marriage of Robert Edmond Jones to the wealthy and much older Margaret Carrington.

6. See Larson, *Scene Design in the American Theatre*, 130–31; Roy R. Behrens, *Camoupedia: A Compendium of Research on Art, Architecture and Camouflage* (Dysart, IA: Bobolink Books, 2009), 82–83, 249, 253, 276.

7. Otis L. Guernsey, "The Playbill: Jo Mielziner, Stage Designer in Reverse," *New York Herald Tribune*, October 29, 1944.

8. Design historian Victor Margolin notes that a "collective understanding" marked the war enterprise as different from competitive, corporate work. As a result, "the professional boundaries and attitudes that normally divide scientists, engineers, and designers and that frequently inhibit their working together did not apply during wartime." Victor Margolin, "The United States in World War II: Scientists, Engineers, Designers," *Design Issues* 29, no. 1 (Winter 2013): 15.

9. "Organize 'Screening' Corps: Artists, Sculptors and Architects Enroll in Camouflage Association," *Washington Post*, April 18, 1917.

10. Excellent discussions of Bel Geddes's models can be found in Essin, *Stage Designers in Early Twentieth-Century America*, 167–80; Szerlip, *Man Who Designed the Future*, 296–315.

11. Behrens, *Camoupedia*, 119, 258.

12. Behrens, 83.

13. "A Statement of Aims and Policy from the Camouflage Society of Professional Stage Designers," box 9, folder 2, Donald Oenslager Papers and Designs, 1922–1982, *T-Mss 1996-015, Billy Rose Theatre Division, The New York Public Library for the Performing Arts. Hereafter cited as Donald Oenslager Papers in this chapter's notes.

14. "Fooling the Spy in the Sky," *Popular Mechanics*, December 1942, 66–70, 174.

15. Oenslager, *Theatre of Donald Oenslager*, 12.

16. Greer Crawley, "The Scenographer as Camoufleur," in *War and Theatrical Innovation*, ed. Victor Emeljanow (London: Palgrave Macmillan, 2017), 49.

17. Guernsey, "Playbill: Jo Mielziner."

18. "Mielziner Marks 150th Setting by Scoring One More Success," *New York Herald Tribune*, March 24, 1946.

19. Of the Canteen, the *New York Daily News* wrote, "All the work will be done by theatre folk. . . . The necessary redecorating will be done by collaboration of every craft and union in the theatrical industry. Lee Shubert has waived rent and will also provide heat maintenance." "Theatre Canteen for Service Men," *Daily News*, February 7, 1942. See Andrea Nouryeh, "The Stage Door Canteen: The American Theatre Wing's Experiment in Integration (1942–1945)," in *Experiments in Democracy: Interracial and Cross-Cultural Exchange in American Theatre, 1912–1945*, ed. Jonathan Shandell and Cheryl Black (Carbondale: Southern Illinois University Press, 2016), 257.

20. Walter Zvonchenko, "Peggy Clark, Lighting Up the Stage," *Library of Congress Information Bulletin* 57, no. 4 (April 1998), https://www.loc.gov/loc/lcib/9804/clark.html; Ben Coolik, "Peggy Clark," in Owen and United States Institute for Theatre Technology, *Late & Great*, 66–75.

21. Policies ranged from attendance and food-service rules to etiquette and conversation guidelines for the female hostesses. Box 1, folders 15–25, and box 2, folders 1–12, Emeline Clark Roche Collection, *T-Mss 1996-016, Billy Rose Theatre Division, The New York Public Library for the Performing Arts. Hereafter cited as Emeline Roche Collection in this chapter's notes.

22. The complete list of designers, in display order, is Walter Walden, Arthur Knorr, A. A. Ostrander, Donald Oenslager, Oscar Weidhas, Jo Mielziner, Horace Armistead, Johannes Larsen, Carl Kent, Harry Horner, Wolfgang Roth, Ken Hartwell, Stewart Chaney, Peggy Clark, Boris Aronson, Raoul Pene Du Bois, Howard Bay, Frederick Fox, Eugene Fitsch, Aline Bernstein, Lucinda Ballard, Irene Sharaff, Nicholas Demolas, Eugene Dunkel, and Bradford Ashworth. Cartoons by Abe Birnbaum, Don Freeman, Al Hirschfeld, and Irma Selz decorated the entryway. Box 3, folder 6, Emeline Roche Collection.

23. Roche corresponded with designers to arrange the return or destruction of these paintings in December 1945. Box 2, folder 1, Emeline Roche Collection.

24. Box 2, folders 11–12, Emeline Roche Collection.

25. Emile Stoner joined the union as a costumer in December 1937; she remained chair and spokesperson for the costume associate category for several years afterward. General Meeting Minutes, December 20, 1937, and following, reels 6–7, United Scenic Artists Records, WAG.065, Tamiment Library / Robert F. Wagner Labor Archives, New York University. Hereafter cited as USA Records in this chapter's notes.

26. Peggy Clark was the first woman elected to the executive board of the union, as she became recording secretary in 1943; Roche followed in Clark's position in 1947 and later was treasurer. General Meeting Minutes, November 11, 1942, and January 25, 1946, reels 8–9, USA Records; "Woman Heads Scenic Local," *New York Times*, July 3, 1968.

27. Maureen Honey, *Creating Rosie the Riveter: Class, Gender, and Propaganda during World War II* (Amherst, MA: University of Massachusetts Press, 1984), 6.

28. These professions derived from gentlemanly occupations and thus embraced an "ideal of public service and . . . public trust vested in those who were fortunate enough to have had opportunities of birth and education." Philip Ross Courtney Elliott, *The Sociology of the Professions* (Boston: Little, Brown, 1971), 48.

29. Freidson, *Professionalism*, 122.

30. Wilensky, "Professionalization of Everyone?," 140.

31. Freidson, *Professionalism*, 122–23.

32. Applied art designers in architecture, graphic design, and other areas adopted the practice of pro bono work after lawyers began to adopt the term in earnest in the fifties. Robert Granfield and Lynn M. Mather, *Private Lawyers*

and the Public Interest: The Evolving Role of Pro Bono in the Legal Profession (Oxford: Oxford University Press, 2009), 3. For a history of pro bono work among United States lawyers, see Judith Maute, "Changing Conceptions of Lawyers' Pro Bono Responsibilities: From Chance Noblesse Oblige to Stated Expectations," *Tulane Law Review* 77, no. 1 (2002): 91–162.

33. There were exceptions to this general trend. Lillian Moller Gilbreth, for instance, was a pioneer of management consulting and industrial engineering in the first half of the twentieth century. In theatre design, women did not often open consulting firms, though Jean Rosenthal opened her theatre lighting and architecture consulting firm in 1958.

34. The separate spheres ideology, at its height in the late nineteenth and early twentieth centuries, held that men belonged in public, through politics and business, and women's proper sphere of influence was with the family and in the home. For links between this ideology and professionalism, see Joan Jacobs Brumberg and Nancy Tomes, "Women in the Professions: A Research Agenda for American Historians," *Reviews in American History* 10, no. 2 (1982): 275–96; Mary Kinnear, *In Subordination: Professional Women, 1870–1970* (Montreal: McGill-Queen's University Press, 1995); Francesca Sawaya, *Modern Women, Modern Work: Domesticity, Professionalism, and American Writing, 1890–1950* (Philadelphia: University of Pennsylvania Press, 2004).

35. Brumberg and Tomes, "Women in the Professions," 275–76; Nancy F. Cott, *History of Women in the United States: Historical Articles on Women's Lives and Activities*, vol. 8, pt. 2 (Munich: K. G. Saur, 1993), xi.

36. Brumberg and Tomes continue: "the history of American philanthropy is largely the story of networks of women volunteers who were the mainstay of urban reform and charity as early as 1850. . . . Moreover, in the guise of the volunteer or amateur, women apparently ventured into less traditional female settings." Brumberg and Tomes, "Women in the Professions," 285.

37. Helen Krich Chinoy, "Art versus Business: The Challenge of Women in the American Theatre," introduction to *Women in American Theatre*, 3rd. ed., ed. Chinoy and Jenkins, xxvii–xxxv, xxx.

38. See, for instance, Shannon Jackson, *Lines of Activity: Performance, Historiography, Hull-House Domesticity* (Ann Arbor: University of Michigan Press, 2001); Cheryl Black, *The Women of Provincetown, 1915–1922* (Tuscaloosa: University of Alabama Press, 2002); Dorothy Chansky, *Composing Ourselves: The Little Theatre Movement and the American Audience* (Carbondale: Southern Illinois University Press, 2005); Allan Nathan Davis, "Organizing White Femininity through Amateur Theatre: Pageants, Residential Gardens, Department Stores, and the Drama League of America, 1912–1946" (PhD diss., University of Maryland–College Park, 2017), https://drum.lib.umd.edu/handle/1903/19472.

39. Brooks Atkinson, "Eugene O'Neill: Two of His Dramas from the Twenties are Now Restored to Broadway," *New York Times*, January 20, 1952, X1.

40. Box 2, folder 12, Emeline Roche Collection.

41. Donald Charles Stowell Jr., "The New Costuming in America: The Ideas and Practices of Robert Edmond Jones, Norman Bel Geddes, Lee Simonson and Aline Bernstein, 1915–1935" (PhD diss., University of Texas at Austin, 1972), 436; Finding Aid for Emeline Roche Collection, and Resume for Emeline Clark Roche, box 6, folder 13, Emeline Roche Collection.

42. Emeline Roche, letter to Jane Cowl, undated [likely 1943], box 2, folder 11, Emeline Roche Collection.

43. Emeline Roche, letters to Aline Bernstein, undated (May–June 1941), box 1, folder 9, Emeline Roche Collection.

44. Stowell, "New Costuming in America"; Barton, "Aline Bernstein."

45. Kelley, "Peggy Clark Kelley," 214.

46. Michael Mullin, *Design by Motley* (Newark: University of Delaware Press, 1996).

47. In 1960 Jean Eckart was the first woman nominated for a Tony Award in scenic design for *Fiorello!*. Andrew Bennett Harris, *The Performing Set: The Broadway Designs of William and Jean Eckart* (Denton: University of North Texas Press, 2006).

48. Robert A. Schanke, *Shattered Applause: The Lives of Eva Le Gallienne* (Carbondale: Southern Illinois University Press, 2010), 66–87.

49. Kelley, "Peggy Clark Kelley," 213.

50. Ben Coolik, "Peggy Clark," 67–75. Kelley, "Peggy Clark Kelley," 210–14.

51. See USA Local 829 Meeting Minutes, 1936–1940, reels 6–7, USA Records; Owen and United States Institute for Theatre Technology, *Late & Great*.

52. Among the women of this generation are Marjorie Bradley Kellogg, Adrienne Lobel, and Heidi Ettinger (previously Landesman). See the conclusion of this book for further discussion.

53. Errol Hill and James V. Hatch, *A History of African American Theatre* (Cambridge: Cambridge University Press, 2003), 422; Perkins, "Their Place in History," 32.

54. Perkins, "Their Place in History," 33; Jonathan Shandell, *The American Negro Theatre and the Long Civil Rights Era* (Iowa City: University of Iowa Press, 2018), 7–8.

55. Interview with Prendergast in Kathy A. Perkins, Sandra L. Richards, Renée Alexander Craft, and Thomas F. DeFrantz, eds., *The Routledge Companion to African American Theatre and Performance* (Abingdon, UK: Routledge, 2018), 30–39.

56. Chinoy further remarks that women were directing, producing, and designing in the early twentieth century. Those women were not "'men who

direct the destinies of the stage,' as the new directors of Broadway were hailed, but they were directing in Hull-House, in the Toy Theatre of Boston, in the Neighborhood Playhouse, in the Washington Square Players and in The Provincetown Players." Chinoy and Jenkins, *Women in American Theatre*, 179–80.

57. Much more energy has been spent on publication, notably in Christin Essin's work. Essin, *Stage Designers in Early Twentieth-Century America*, 17–49.

58. In the last decades of his career, Mielziner established a standard speaking fee. In response to one lecture request, Mielziner wrote, "I cannot participate without a minimum fee. . . . [I]t would be nice to offer my time gratis but, I have too many requests on a professional basis to do this." Jo Mielziner, letter to James L. Mitchell, February 15, 1971, box 97, folder 19, Jo Mielziner Papers, *T-Mss 1993-002, Billy Rose Theatre Division, The New York Public Library for the Performing Arts. Hereafter cited as Jo Mielziner Papers in this chapter's notes.

59. Of the lecture circuit in the nineteenth century, scholar Amanda Adams notes that "the lecture system, especially in America, developed outside the realm of literary authorship, and lecturing as a vocation or pursuit for many kinds of professionals—not just authors—had its own life in the nineteenth century." Amanda Adams, *Performing Authorship in the Nineteenth-Century Transatlantic Lecture Tour* (Burlington, VT: Ashgate, 2014), 2. Tom Wright adds that "the growing network of lyceums and halls formed a web of culture through which itinerant speakers could usher into being an open-minded national audience." Tom F. Wright, *The Cosmopolitan Lyceum: Lecture Culture and the Globe in Nineteenth-Century America* (Amherst: University of Massachusetts Press, 2013), 15. For a discussion of lectures and theatricality in Chautauqua, a cultural educational format that succeeded the lyceum, see Charlotte Canning, *The Most American Thing in America: Circuit Chautauqua as Performance* (Iowa City: University of Iowa Press, 2005).

60. Today this portion of his archive consists of undated lecture notes, some with sentences cut out in thin strips that Jones would assemble into talks. Lecture Notes, box 1, folders 37–38, Robert Edmond Jones Papers, Collection #1000-165, Special Collections & Archives, Wesleyan University, Middletown, CT.

61. Pendleton, *Theatre of Robert Edmond Jones*, 178.

62. Among the lectures documented in Oenslager's archive are talks at the Civic Club of Harrisburg (February 15, 1926); Oenslager's secondary school alma mater, Phillips Exeter Academy (October 28, 1931; March 6, 1932); the Cosmopolitan Club of New Jersey (February 24, 1928); and the Metropolitan Museum of Art (January 28, 1928; February 15, 1931). Box 10, folder 6, Donald Oenslager Papers.

63. Box 100, folders 1–2, Jo Mielziner Papers.

64. Oenslager gave multiple versions of lectures titled "Artists in the Theatre," "Contemporary North American Stage Designers," "How the Stage Designer Works," "Light in the Theatre," and "The New York Theatre Today." Boxes 10–11, Donald Oenslager Papers. Mielziner changed lecture titles frequently but had basic lecture structures for speaking on the history of American theatre architecture, on Broadway production, and on educational and community theatres. Boxes 96–100, Jo Mielziner Papers.

65. Jones, *Dramatic Imagination*, 17, 143–45.

66. "General Outline for Proposed Article for *New York Times*," box 95, folder 2, and Lecture for USITT [United States Institute of Theatre Technology] delivered December 7, 1948, box 98, folder 15, Jo Mielziner Papers.

67. Jo Mielziner and C. Ray Smith, *The Shapes of Our Theatre* (New York: Clarkson N. Potter, 1970).

68. Lecture notes and transcripts, box 10, folders 6–8, Donald Oenslager Papers. Versions of his standard talk, "Theatre Today and Tomorrow," were given at (as a sampling) Bowdoin, December 1954; Richmond, February 1955; Amherst, April 1956; and University of Washington, July 1956. Alternates were made for the Baltimore Museum of Art, January 1960, and the Cambridge Drama Festival, June 1962.

69. In that year Mielziner spoke to students at the College Drama Festival of Virginia, Penn State University, Carnegie Mellon, the University of Michigan, and the State University of New York at Oswego. He also spoke before professional and arts organizations, including the Buffalo Festival for the Arts, the American National Theatre Academy Region Seven Conference in Minnesota, and the Asolo Theatre Festival (Sarasota, FL). Boxes 96–99, Jo Mielziner Papers.

70. The Salzburg Seminar in American Studies, today renamed the Salzburg Global Seminar (https://www.salzburgglobal.org/), is a nonprofit educational organization that hosted yearly sessions for an international audience in Salzburg, Austria. Originally these seminars emphasized American intercultural exchange with postwar Europe, and they spanned topics from arts, literature, and culture to economics and humanities. The seminars still convene in the Schloss Leopoldskron, a palace once owned and renovated by Max Reinhardt and donated for use by the seminar by Helene Thimig, Reinhardt's widow.

71. Boxes 10–11, Donald Oenslager Papers.

72. Donald Oenslager, "The Theatre of Indo-China," *Theatre Arts* 25, no. 5 (May 1941): 344–52; Donald Oenslager, "Theatre Horizons of South America," *The Record* 6, no. 5 (September 1950): 12–22.

73. This seminar put Mielziner in conversation with industrial designers, including Henry Dreyfuss and George Nelson, and corporate and academic

psychologists, engineers, and executives from AT&T and the Ford Foundation.

74. The latter exhibition prompted several designers to write short manifestos on the "new path" of stage design in theatre arts. DeAnna M. Toten Beard, "From Artisan into Artist: The Crucial Role of Gallery Exhibitions of New Stagecraft in the US, 1914–1920," *New England Theatre Journal* 18 (2007): 13–25; Macgowan, "New Path of the Theatre."

75. Innes, *Designing Modern America*, 193–94; "Invite Urban to Show His Picture Sets," *New York Tribune*, January 8, 1922. Joseph Urban Clippings File, reel 1, vol. 3, Joseph Urban Papers, 1893–1933, Rare Book & Manuscript Library, Columbia University.

76. A survey of the most high-profile retrospectives might include a 1945 exhibit of Robert Edmond Jones's drawings at the Museum of Modern Art; the 1949 exhibit *Behind American Footlights* at the Costume Institute of the Metropolitan Museum of Art; Harvard's 1950 Fogg Art Museum exhibition of Jones's, Simonson's, and Oenslager's work (all Harvard alumni); Orville Larson's 1955 survey of American theatre design at the University of Connecticut; Oenslager and Mielziner retrospectives mounted, respectively, in 1956 at the Detroit Institute of Arts Museum and in 1957 at the Virginia Museum of Fine Arts; *The American Stage* exhibit at the Corcoran Gallery of Art in 1957; and the posthumous Jones retrospective at the Whitney Museum of American Art in 1958. These exhibits toured, also. Oenslager's Detroit exhibition visited Yale and a number of other locales for two years with funding from the American Federation of Arts. This partial list was compiled from archival research in Jones's, Simonson's, and Oenslager's collections of papers, the Joseph Urban Clippings File, and secondary works on theatre exhibitions.

77. For overviews of major gallery shows of designers' work before 1976, see Orville K. Larson, "Exhibition Catalogues: Critical Resources for Research in Theatre Art," *Educational Theatre Journal* 28, no. 3 (October 1976): 389–97. Finding aids for designers' archived papers often contain lists and records of the many exhibitions. See aids for the Jo Mielziner Papers and Donald Oenslager Papers and Designs from the Billy Rose Division, The New York Public Library for the Performing Arts.

78. Jules Fisher quoted in Delbert Unruh, *The Designs of Jules Fisher* (Syracuse, NY: United States Institute for Theatre Technology, 2009), 60.

79. Despite his attempts to join the ranks of architects, Bel Geddes was denied licensure.

80. Szerlip, *Man Who Designed the Future*, 59–63; Loring, *Joseph Urban*, 201–9, 215–45.

81. Mielziner, "Make the Theatre Building Pay"; Jo Mielziner, "Note to Architects," *New York Times*, July 14, 1946.

82. Henderson, *Mielziner*, 236.

83. Invited speakers included George Izenour, Tyrone Guthrie, Zelda Fichandler, and noted architects Louis Kahn (architect of Yale University Art Gallery) and Hugh Stubbins (architect of Harvard's Loeb Drama Center, current home of American Repertory Theater). Henderson, 237.

84. "The Man Who Put Consultants in Hats," *Business Strategy Review* 14, no. 3 (Autumn 2003): 63–64; John Peet, "The New Witch-Doctors," *Economist* 306, no. 7537 (February 13, 1988): S3+.

85. Drucker, *Landmarks of Tomorrow*, 120; Peter F. Drucker, *Peter Drucker on the Profession of Management* (Boston: Harvard Business School Publishing, 1998), 47.

86. See Maurizio Lazzarato, "Immaterial Labor," in *Radical Thought in Italy: A Potential Politics*, ed. Paolo Virno and Michael Hardt (Minneapolis: University of Minnesota Press, 1996), 133–47; Emma Dowling, Rodrigo Nunes, and Ben Trott, "Immaterial and Affective Labour: Explored," *Ephemera* 7, no. 1 (2007): 1–7; Dave Beech, *Art and Value: Art's Economic Exceptionalism in Classical, Neoclassical and Marxist Economics* (Chicago: Haymarket Books, 2016).

87. *The Ideal Theater: Eight Concepts* (New York: American Federation of Arts, 1962).

88. Julius Novick, *Beyond Broadway: The Quest for Permanent Theatres*. (New York: Hill and Wang, 1968); Joseph Wesley Zeigler, *Regional Theatre: The Revolutionary Stage* (New York: Da Capo, 1973).

89. Henderson, *Mielziner*, 239–47; White, *Blue-Collar Broadway*, 133–40, 156–61; Edgar B. Young, *Lincoln Center: The Building of an Institution* (New York: New York University Press, 1980).

90. Sarah Goldstein and Rebecca Tran, Finding Aid for Barrie B. Greenbie Papers, Call No. FS 142, Special Collections and University Archives, University of Massachusetts, Amherst, http://scua.library.umass.edu/umarmot/greenbie-barrie/; Doris Malkmus, Finding Aid for "Theater Design, by George C. Izenour, Manuscripts and Related Materials," Collection Number 2359, Special Collections Library, Pennsylvania State University, https://libraries.psu.edu/findingaids/2359.htm; Mel Gussow, "Eldon Elder, 79, Set Designer; Created the Delacorte Theater," *New York Times*, December 13, 2000. Elder later penned a theatre renovations handbook: Eldon Elder, Marsha Imhof, and Sharon Lee Ryder, *Will It Make a Theatre: A Guide to Finding, Renovating, Financing, Bringing Up-to-Code, the Non-traditional Performance Space* (New York: Off Off Broadway Alliance, 1979).

91. Alswang's *New York Times* obituary states that he "was at the peak of his profession a decade ago when he virtually abandoned the stage to forge a new career designing theatres." Robert McG. Thomas Jr., "Ralph Alswang,

Designer of Sets and Innovative Theaters, Dead: Native of Chicago Designed for Simon's First," *New York Times*, February 16, 1979; David Hays, *Setting the Stage. Attention to What We Do, How We Do It, and Why.* (Middletown, CT: University Press of New England, 2017), 123–29. See also Theatre Consulting CV, box 4, folder 19, Donald Oenslager Papers.

92. The seating would have been incredibly tight. The Porto Theatre called for steeply raked stadium seating, in twelve rows, with each row thirty inches deep (seat pitch, in airline terms), and each seat nineteen inches wide. The seats were bare-bones, essentially stadium benches with low-profile armrests, similar to the benches in older New York City subway stations. A thousand patrons would have fit, but they might not have wanted to stay for the duration of a two-act musical. Original drafting for the Porto Theatre is held in box 1, folder 5, and box 2, folders 4–6, and Designs t. 2, Edward Kook Papers, *T-Mss 1990-013, Billy Rose Theatre Division, The New York Public Library for the Performing Arts.

93. Edward Kook and KOHM Group, *Porto Theatre: A New Concept in Totally Integrated Portable Theatre Design* (New York: United States Institute of Theatre Technology, 1968). Book held in box 4, folder 16, Donald Oenslager Papers.

94. See Charlotte Canning, *On the Performance Front: US Theatre and Internationalism* (Basingstoke, UK: Palgrave Macmillan, 2015).

95. W. McNeil Lowry and Gertrude S. Hooker, "The Role of Arts and the Humanities," *Cultural Affairs and Foreign Relations*, ed. Robert Blum (Englewood Cliffs: Prentice-Hall, 1963), 122; Canning, *On the Performance Front*, 27–29; Elizabeth Anne Miles, "United States Cultural Relations: Exchanges in the Arts, 1954–1964" (MA thesis, University of Wyoming, 1965), 32–33.

96. Kook and KOHM Group, *Porto Theatre*, 7–9.

97. These consisted of "consulting engineers' fees, preparation of presentations, drafting, and the building of design models." See the reprinted exhibition booklet in Jo Mielziner et al., "Porto Theatre," *Theatre Crafts* 3, no. 3 (May/June 1969): 33.

98. Edward M. Greenberg and Joel E. Rubin, "Production Aspects of the Music Circus," *Educational Theatre Journal* 4, no. 1 (March 1952): 26–32.

99. Kook and KOHM Group, *Porto Theatre*, 10.

100. Kook and KOHM Group, 13–22.

101. Rhetorically, Lyndon B. Johnson framed domestic budget cuts as a necessary response to the escalating costs of the Vietnam War; theatrical production was but a small part of the many cuts Johnson claimed to be forced to propose. See Julian E. Zelizer, "The Nation: Guns and Butter; Government Can Run More Than a War," *New York Times*, December 30, 2001; Julian E.

Zelizer, "The Power of Lyndon Johnson Is a Myth," *Washington Post*, January 11, 2015.

102. Kook and KOHM Group, *Porto Theatre*, 8, 25.

103. The exhibition traveled throughout 1968–1969, from the Lincoln Center library in November 1968 to the University of Utah art museum in November 1969. Zolotow, "Model of Portable 1,000-Seat Theater to Be Shown"; Patricia Elsen, "College Museum Notes," *Art Journal* 29, no. 2 (December 1960): 234.

104. Arnold Aronson, "Theatres of the Future," *Theatre Journal* 33, no. 4 (December 1981): 489–503.

105. Quoted in David W. Weiss, ed., "Consulting in the Theatre," *Theatre Design and Technology* 6 (October 1966): 38.

Conclusion

1. Carl Mulert, interview with Cory Pattak, *in 1: the podcast*, episode 65, September 30, 2016, https://in1podcast.com/65-united-scenic-artists-w-carl-mulert/. In the United States, Form 1099 from the Internal Revenue Service (IRS) is a record of payment made to an independent contractor or other types of income (not a wage, salary, or tip), and Form W-2 documents payment made to an employee. Copies of both forms are given to payees, who then include them in preparing their yearly income tax return for the IRS. Mulert's questions in the interview reflect the IRS's own determination of independent contractor status. A twenty-factor test used by the IRS assesses a worker's degree of autonomy, control over hours spent and materials used, and integration into the hiring company's overall mission. The IRS's test is reproduced in James L. Moody, *The Business of Theatrical Design* (New York: Allworth Press, 2002), 66–67.

2. The union's interest in classifying its members as employees stems from two thirties-era labor laws. First, the National Labor Relations Act of 1935 (a.k.a. the Wagner Act) barred independent contractors from union representation. Second, the 1938 Fair Labor Standards Act made independent contractors and professional ("white collar") workers exempt from some labor protections otherwise awarded to workers, perhaps most notably, overtime pay. With this act as passed and later amended, employers were also released from providing payroll tax deductions, pension/retirement benefits, workers' compensation insurance coverage, and employer-sponsored health care to independent contractors.

3. Arnold Aronson, *American Set Design* (New York: Theatre Communications Group, 1985); Smith, *American Set Design 2*; Owen and United States Institute for Theatre Technology, *Late & Great*.

4. For instance, the "Equity, Diversity, and Inclusion" column of *American Theatre*, edited by Diep Tran; Porsche McGovern's study of gender diversity in LORT (League of Resident Theatres), "Who Designs and Directs in LORT Theatres by Gender," Howlround Theatre Commons, June 25, 2016; USITT's Gateway Program and the Spark Leadership Program of the Theatre Communications Group; Perkins, "Black Backstage Workers, 1900–1969"; Perkins, "Their Place in History."

5. Aronson, *American Set Design*, 98.

6. See McClennahan's discussion of bias faced by people of color in technical theatre and his founding of the now-defunct Minority Designers and Technicians Network. Smith, *American Set Design 2*, 119.

7. Richard Isackes, "A Change of Scene: Expand the Expectations and Assumptions in Theatrical Design Training, and Students, Teachers and the Profession Will Benefit," *American Theatre*, January 11, 2011, 96–100.

8. While each designer defines these terms differently, assistants generally provide creative and labor support in specific areas, such as modeling, drafting, painting, rendering, or research. Associates might help install or transfer a designer's work between venues, handle projects independently, or otherwise "speak for" the head designer when that person is not present. Mike Lawler, "Design Is Not a Private Affair," *American Theatre*, January 1, 2012, https://www.americantheatre.org/2012/01/01/design-is-not-a-private-affair/.

9. For an introduction to these issues, see Moody, *Business of Theatrical Design*, 21–26.

10. Marjorie Bradley Kellogg [with sidebars by Susan Tsu and Dawn Chiang], "Design and the Bottom Line: For Designers, It's Harder than Ever to Make Ends Meet." *American Theatre*, November 2001, 34–37.

BIBLIOGRAPHY

Abbott, Andrew. *The System of Professions: An Essay on the Division of Expert Labor.* Chicago: University of Chicago Press, 1988.

Abercrombie, Stanley. *George Nelson: The Design of Modern Design.* Cambridge, MA: MIT Press, 1995.

Adams, Amanda. *Performing Authorship in the Nineteenth-Century Transatlantic Lecture Tour.* Burlington, VT: Ashgate, 2014.

Alexander, Philip A. "Staging Business: A History of the United Scenic Artists, 1895–1995." PhD diss., City University of New York, 1999. UMI (9917622).

Aronson, Arnold. *American Set Design.* New York: Theatre Communications Group, 1985.

———. "Ideal Theatres: One Roof or Two?" In *Setting the Scene: Perspectives in Twentieth-Century Theatre Architecture*, edited by Alistair Fair, 179–99. London: Routledge, 2015.

———. *Looking into the Abyss: Essays on Scenography.* Ann Arbor: University of Michigan Press, 2005.

Aronson, Arnold, Derek E. Ostergard, Joseph Urban, Matthew Wilson Smith, and Wallach Art Gallery. *Architect of Dreams: The Theatrical Vision of Joseph Urban.* New York: Miriam and Ira D. Wallach Art Gallery / Columbia University, 2000.

Aronson, Boris. "Designing Sweet Bye and Bye." *Theatre Arts* 30, no. 10 (October 1946): 573–75.

Bablet, Denis. *The Revolutions of Stage Design in the 20th Century.* New York: L. Amiel, 1977.

Barley, Stephen R., and Gideon Kunda. *Gurus, Hired Guns, and Warm Bodies: Itinerant Experts in a Knowledge Economy.* Princeton, NJ: Princeton University Press, 2006.

Barton, Mike Alan. "Aline Bernstein: A History and Evaluation." PhD diss., Indiana University, 1971. ProQuest Dissertations & Theses (7206748).

Baugh, Christopher. *Theatre Performance and Technology: The Development of Scenography in the Twentieth Century.* Basingstoke, UK: Palgrave Macmillan, 2005.

Bay, Howard. "Design for the Musical Stage." *Theatre Arts* 29, no. 11 (November 1945): 650–55.

———. "From Shubert Alley to Play Production 304B." *Educational Theatre Journal* 17, no. 1 (1965): 46–48.

———. *Stage Design.* New York: Drama Book Specialists, 1974.

Beard, DeAnna M. Toten. "From Artisan into Artist: The Crucial Role of Gallery Exhibitions of New Stagecraft in the US, 1914–1920." *New England Theatre Journal* 18 (2007): 13–25.

——. *Sheldon Cheney's* Theatre Arts Magazine: *Promoting a Modern American Theatre, 1916–1921*. Scarecrow Press, 2010.

Beckerman, Bernard. "The University Accepts the Theatre: 1800–1925." In *The American Theatre: A Sum of Its Parts*, edited by Henry B. Williams, 339–55. New York: Samuel French, 1971.

Beech, Dave. *Art and Value: Art's Economic Exceptionalism in Classical, Neoclassical and Marxist Economics*. Chicago: Haymarket Books, 2016.

Behrens, Roy R. *Camoupedia: A Compendium of Research on Art, Architecture and Camouflage*. Dysart, IA: Bobolink Books, 2009.

Belasco, David. *The Theatre through Its Stage Door*. New York: Harper & Brothers, 1919.

"Bel Geddes." *Fortune*, July 1930, 51–57.

Bel Geddes, Norman. *Horizons*. Boston: Little, Brown, 1932.

——. *Miracle in the Evening, an Autobiography*. Garden City, NY: Doubleday, 1960.

Bel Geddes, Norman, Edward C. Cole, Arch Lauterer, Serge Chermayeff, and Stanley McCandless. "Theatre Planning: A Symposium." *Educational Theatre Journal* 2, no. 1 (1950): 1–7.

Berkeley, Anne. "Changing Theories of College Theatrical Curricula, 1900–1945." *Journal of Aesthetic Education* 31, no. 4 (August 1997): 77–90.

——. "Changing Theories of Undergraduate Theatre Studies, 1945–1980." *Journal of Aesthetic Education* 42, no. 3 (Fall 2008): 57–70.

Bernheim, Alfred L., and Sara Harding. *The Business of the Theatre*. New York: Actors' Equity Association, 1932.

Bernstein, Aline. "The Craftsmen." *Theatre Arts* 29, no. 4 (April 1945): 208–14.

Betts, Mary Beth. "The American Architecture of Joseph Urban." PhD diss., City University of New York, 1999. UMI (9946142).

Bishop, John Peale. "Youngest among the Moderns: James Reynolds as an Artist in Settings and Costumes." *Theatre Arts Magazine* 5, no. 1 (January 1921): 75, 79.

Black, Cheryl. *The Women of Provincetown, 1915–1922*. Tuscaloosa: University of Alabama Press, 2002.

Bloom, Thomas Alan. *Kenneth Macgowan and the Aesthetic Paradigm for the New Stagecraft in America*. New Studies in Aesthetics. Vol. 20. New York: Peter Lang, 1996.

Bragdon, Claude Fayette. *More Lives than One*. New York: Cosimo Classics, 2006.

Brain, David. "Practical Knowledge and Occupational Control: The Professionalization of Architecture in the United States." *Sociological Forum* 6, no. 2 (June 1, 1991): 239–68.

Brint, Steven. "Eliot Freidson's Contribution to the Sociology of Professions." *Work and Occupations: An International Sociological Journal* 20, no. 3 (1993): 259–78.

———. *In an Age of Experts: The Changing Role of Professionals in Politics and Public Life.* Princeton, NJ: Princeton University Press, 1994.

Brockett, Oscar G., Margaret Mitchell, and Linda Hardberger. *Making the Scene: A History of Stage Design and Technology in Europe and the United States.* San Antonio: Tobin Theatre Arts Fund, 2010.

Brumberg, Joan Jacobs, and Nancy Tomes. "Women in the Professions: A Research Agenda for American Historians." *Reviews in American History* 10, no. 2 (1982): 275–96.

Bush, Donald John. *The Streamlined Decade.* New York: Braziller, 1988.

Canning, Charlotte. *The Most American Thing in America: Circuit Chautauqua as Performance.* Iowa City: University of Iowa Press, 2005.

———. *On the Performance Front: US Theatre and Internationalism.* Basingstoke, UK: Palgrave Macmillan, 2015.

Carlson, Marvin. "Theatre and Performance at a Time of Shifting Disciplines." *Theatre Research International* 26, no. 2 (July 2001): 137–44.

Carman, Emily. *Independent Stardom: Freelance Women in the Hollywood Studio System.* Austin: University of Texas Press, 2016.

"The Carnegie Map." *Theatre Arts Monthly* 23, no. 7 (July 1939): 510–11.

Chansky, Dorothy. *Composing Ourselves: The Little Theatre Movement and the American Audience.* Carbondale: Southern Illinois University Press, 2005.

Chinoy, Helen Krich, and Linda Walsh Jenkins, eds. *Women in American Theatre.* 3rd ed. New York: Theatre Communications Group, 2006.

Clark, Barrett H. "Professionalism in the American Theatre." *Educational Theatre Journal* 3, no. 2 (May 1951): 99–104.

Cole, Wendell. "Scenery on the New York Stage, 1900–1920." PhD diss., Stanford University, 1951. ProQuest Dissertations & Theses (0184486).

Collom, Jeffrey. "The Role of Contemporary Scene Building Houses for Broadway Theatre." PhD diss., Michigan State University, 1975. ProQuest Dissertations & Theses (7612420).

Cott, Nancy F., ed. *History of Women in the United States: Historical Articles on Women's Lives and Activities.* Theory and Method in Women's History. Vol. 1, pt. 2. Munich: K. G. Saur, 1993.

Crawley, Greer. "The Scenographer as Camoufleur." In *War and Theatrical Innovation*, edited by Victor Emeljanow, 41–60. London: Palgrave Macmillan, 2017.

Cross, Nigel. *Designerly Ways of Knowing*. London: Springer Science & Business Media, 2007.

Cuff, Dana. *Architecture: The Story of Practice*. Cambridge, MA: MIT Press, 1991.

———. "Historical License: Architectural History in the Architectural Profession." *Journal of the Society of Architectural Historians* 76, no. 1 (March 1, 2017): 5–9.

Davis, Jerry Leon. "Howard Bay, Scene Designer." PhD diss., University of Kansas, 1968. ProQuest Dissertations & Theses (6817374).

Davis, Tony. *Stage Design*. Crans-près-Céligny, CH: RotoVision, 2001.

Deamer, Peggy. *The Architect as Worker: Immaterial Labor, the Creative Class, and the Politics of Design*. London: Bloomsbury Academic, 2015.

———. "Branding the Architectural Author." *Perspecta* 37 (2005): 42–49.

Denning, Michael. "Class and Culture: Reflections on the Work of Warren Susman." *Radical History Review* 36 (1986): 110–13.

———. *The Cultural Front: The Laboring of American Culture in the Twentieth Century*. London: Verso, 2010.

Dewberry, Jonathan. "Black Actors United: The Negro Actors' Guild." *Black Scholar* 21, no. 2 (May 1990): 2–11.

Dowling, Emma, Rodrigo Nunes, and Ben Trott. "Immaterial and Affective Labour: Explored." *Ephemera* 7, no. 1 (2007): 1–7.

Draper, Joan. "The Ecole Des Beaux-Arts and the Architectural Profession in the United States: The Case of John Galen Howard." In *The Architect: Chapters in the History of the Profession*, edited by Spiro Kostof and Dana Cuff, 209–37. Berkeley: University of California Press, 2008.

Drucker, Peter F. *Landmarks of Tomorrow*. New York: Harper & Row, 1959.

———. *Peter Drucker on the Profession of Management*. Boston: Harvard Business School Publishing, 1998.

Dubofsky, Melvyn, and Foster Rhea Dulles. *Labor in America: A History*. Wheeling, IL: Harlan Davidson, 2004.

Dykema, Peter W. *Survey of College Entrance Credits and College Courses in Music*. New York: National Bureau for the Advancement of Music, 1930.

Ebrahimian, Babak A. *Sculpting Space in the Theater: Conversations with the Top Set, Light and Costume Designers*. Burlington, MA: Focal Press, 2006.

Edgar, Randolph. "The Vanished Garden of Paradise: A Glimpse at the Scenic Obstacles Surmounted by Joseph Urban." *Vanity Fair*, January 1915, 25.

Efland, Arthur. *A History of Art Education: Intellectual and Social Currents in Teaching the Visual Arts*. New York: Teachers College Press, 1990.

Ehrenreich, Barbara, and John Ehrenreich. "The Professional-Managerial Class." In *Between Labor and Capital*, edited by Pat Walker, 5–45. Boston: South End Press, 1979.

Elder, Eldon, Marsha Imhof, and Sharon Lee Ryder. *Will It Make a Theatre: A Guide to Finding, Renovating, Financing, Bringing Up-to-Code, the Nontraditional Performance Space.* New York: Off Off Broadway Alliance, 1979.

Elliott, Philip Ross Courtney. *The Sociology of the Professions.* Boston: Little, Brown, 1971.

Essin, Christin. *Stage Designers in Early Twentieth-Century America: Artists, Activists, Cultural Critics.* Basingstoke, UK: Palgrave Macmillan, 2012.

Evetts, Julia. "The Concept of Professionalism: Professional Work, Professional Practice and Learning." In *International Handbook of Research in Professional and Practice-Based Learning*, 29–56. Springer International Handbooks of Education. Dordrecht, NL: Springer, 2014.

———. "Professionalism: Value and Ideology." *Current Sociology* 61, nos. 5–6 (September 1, 2013): 778–96.

Ewen, Stuart. *PR! A Social History of Spin.* New York: Basic Books, 1996.

Fischer, James, and Felicia Hardison Londré. "Bergman's Studio." In *Historical Dictionary of American Theater: Modernism*, 59. Lanham, MD: Scarecrow Press, 2008.

Fletcher, Anne. *Rediscovering Mordecai Gorelik: Scene Design and the American Theatre.* Carbondale: Southern Illinois University Press, 2009.

Flinchum, Russell, and Cooper-Hewitt Museum. *Henry Dreyfuss, Industrial Designer: The Man in the Brown Suit.* New York: Cooper-Hewitt / National Design Museum, Smithsonian Institution / Rizzoli, 1997.

Florida, Richard L. *The Rise of the Creative Class: And How It's Transforming Work, Leisure, Community, and Everyday Life.* New York: Basic Books, 2002.

Frase, Peter. "The Precariat: A Class or a Condition." *New Labor Forum* 22, no. 2 (Spring 2013): 11–14.

Freidson, Eliot. *Professionalism: The Third Logic.* Chicago: University of Chicago Press, 2001.

———. *Professional Powers: A Study of the Institutionalization of Formal Knowledge.* Chicago: University of Chicago Press, 1986.

Gabler, Neal. *Winchell: Gossip, Power and the Culture of Celebrity.* New York: Vintage Books, 1994.

Gemmill, Paul F. "Equity: The Actor's Trade Union." *Quarterly Journal of Economics* 41, no. 1 (November 1926): 129–45.

———. "Types of Actors' Trade Unions." *Journal of Political Economy* 35, no. 2 (April 1927): 299–303.

Gilder, Rosamund. "You Bet Your Life: Camouflage Show at March Field." *Theatre Arts* 28, no. 9 (September 1944): 521–27.

Goel, Vinod. *Sketches of Thought.* Cambridge, MA: MIT Press, 1995.

Goldschmidt, Gabriela. "The Dialectics of Sketching." *Creativity Research Journal* 4, no. 2 (January 1, 1991): 123–43.

Gorelik, Mordecai. *New Theatres for Old.* New York: Octagon Books, 1975.

Graeber, David. *The Utopia of Rules: On Technology, Stupidity, and the Secret Joys of Bureaucracy.* Brooklyn, NY: Melville House, 2015.

Granfield, Robert, and Lynn M. Mather. *Private Lawyers and the Public Interest: The Evolving Role of Pro Bono in the Legal Profession.* Oxford: Oxford University Press, 2009.

Green, Martin. *New York, 1913: The Armory Show and the Paterson Strike Pageant.* New York: Collier Books, 1989.

Greenberg, Shoshana. "Female Lighting Designers: Past, Present, and Future." *The Interval* (blog), January 16, 2018. http://www.theintervalny.com/features/2018/01/female-lighting-designers-past-present-and-future/.

Haiven, Larry. "Expanding the Union Zone: Union Renewal through Alternative Forms of Worker Organization." *Labor Studies Journal* 31, no. 3 (September 13, 2006): 85–116.

Hardt, Michael, and Antonio Negri. *Multitude: War and Democracy in the Age of Empire.* New York: Penguin Books, 2005.

Harris, Andrew Bennett. *The Performing Set: The Broadway Designs of William and Jean Eckart.* Denton: University of North Texas Press, 2006.

Harvey, David. *A Brief History of Neoliberalism.* Oxford: Oxford University Press, 2011.

Hays, David. *Setting the Stage. Attention to What We Do, How We Do It, and Why.* Middletown, CT: Wesleyan University Press, 2017.

Henderson, Mary C. *Mielziner: Master of Modern Stage Design.* New York: Back Stage Books, 2001.

Hetland, Lois, Ellen Winner, Shirley Veneema, and Kim Sheridan. *Studio Thinking: The Real Benefits of Visual Arts Education.* New York: Teachers College Press, 2007.

Hill, Errol, and James V. Hatch. *A History of African American Theatre.* Cambridge: Cambridge University Press, 2003.

Hobgood, Burnet M. *Master Teachers of Theatre: Observations on Teaching Theatre by Nine American Masters.* Carbondale: Southern Illinois University Press, 1988.

Hodin, Mark. "'It Did Not Sound Like a Professor's Speech': George Pierce Baker and the Market for Academic Rhetoric." *Theatre Survey* 46, no. 2 (November 2005): 225–46.

Holmes, Sean P. *Weavers of Dreams, Unite! Actors' Unionism in Early Twentieth-Century America.* Champaign: University of Illinois Press, 2013.

Honey, Maureen. *Creating Rosie the Riveter: Class, Gender, and Propaganda during World War II.* Amherst: University of Massachusetts Press, 1984.

Horner, Harry. "Winged Victory—Design by Harry Horner." *Theatre Arts* 27, no. 12 (December 1943).

Houghton, Norris. "Credits." *Theatre Arts* 30, no. 11 (November 1946): 657–60.

———. "The Designer Sets the Stage: I, Norman Bel Geddes; II, Vincente Minnelli." *Theatre Arts Monthly*, October 1936, 776–88.

———. "The Designer Sets the Stage: III, Lee Simonson; IV, Donald Oenslager." *Theatre Arts Monthly*, November 1936, 879–91.

———. "The Designer Sets the Stage: V, Robert Edmond Jones; VI, Mordecai Gorelik." *Theatre Arts Monthly*, December 1936, 966–75.

———. "The Designer Sets the Stage: VII, Jo Mielziner; VIII, Aline Bernstein." *Theatre Arts Monthly*, February 1937, 115–25.

Howd, Dean. "Joseph Urban and American Scene Design." *Theatre Survey* 32, no. 2 (November 1991): 173–86.

The Ideal Theater: Eight Concepts. New York: American Federation of Arts, 1962.

Innes, Christopher. *Designing Modern America: Broadway to Main Street.* New Haven, CT: Yale University Press, 2008.

Isackes, Richard. "A Change of Scene: Expand the Expectations and Assumptions in Theatrical Design Training, and Students, Teachers and the Profession Will Benefit." *American Theatre* 28, no. 1 (January 2011): 96–100.

Izenour, George C. *Theater Technology.* New Haven, CT: Yale University Press, 1996.

Jackson, Shannon. *Lines of Activity: Performance, Historiography, Hull-House Domesticity.* Ann Arbor: University of Michigan Press, 2001.

———. *Professing Performance: Theatre in the Academy from Philology to Performativity.* Cambridge: Cambridge University Press, 2004.

Jackson, Timothy Allen. "Ontological Shifts in Studio Art Education: Emergent Pedagogical Models." *Art Journal* 58, no. 1 (March 1, 1999): 68–73.

Jaffe, Aaron. *Modernism and the Culture of Celebrity.* Cambridge: Cambridge University Press, 2005.

Jones, Robert Edmond. *The Dramatic Imagination: Reflections and Speculations on the Art of the Theatre.* New York: Duell, Sloan and Pearce, 1941.

Jones, Robert Edmond, and George P. Crepeau. "Robert Edmond Jones on the Creative Process: An Interview with a Group of High School Students." *Educational Theatre Journal* 19, no. 2 (May 1967): 124–33.

Jones, Robert Edmond, and Delbert Unruh. *Towards a New Theatre: The Lectures of Robert Edmond Jones.* New York: Limelight Editions, 1992.

Joyce, Robert Suddards. "A History of the Armbruster Scenic Studio of Columbus, Ohio." PhD diss., The Ohio State University, 1970. ProQuest Dissertations & Theses (7019326).

Kellogg, Marjorie Bradley [with sidebars by Susan Tsu and Dawn Chiang]. "Design and the Bottom Line: For Designers, It's Harder than Ever to Make Ends Meet." *American Theatre*, November 2001, 34–37.

Kidder, Frank Eugene. *The Architects' and Builders' Handbook: Data for Architects, Structural Engineers, Contractors, and Draughtsmen*. John Wiley & Sons, 1921.

Kimberly, Elizabeth Schrader. *A History of the Drama Department of Carnegie-Mellon University, Formerly Carnegie Institute of Technology, 1914–1981*. Pittsburgh: Carnegie-Mellon University, 1981.

King, Martha W. "Protecting and Representing Workers in the New Gig Economy: The Case of the Freelancers Union." In *New Labor in New York: Precarious Workers and the Future of the Labor Movement*, edited by Ruth Milkman and Edward Ott, 150–70. Ithaca, NY: Cornell University Press, 2014.

Kinnear, Mary. *In Subordination: Professional Women, 1870–1970*. Montreal: McGill-Queen's University Press, 1995.

Klein, Carole. *Aline*. New York: Warner Books, 1980.

Kook, Edward, and KOHM Group. *Porto Theatre: A New Concept in Totally Integrated Portable Theatre Design*. New York: United States Institute of Theatre Technology, 1968.

Krause, Elliott A. *The Sociology of Occupations*. Boston: Little, Brown, 1971.

Lapidus, Morris. *Architecture: A Profession and a Business*. New York: Reinhold, 1967.

Larson, Magali Sarfatti. *Behind the Postmodern Facade: Architectural Change in Late Twentieth-Century America*. Berkeley: University of California Press, 1995.

———. "In the Matter of Experts and Professionals, or How Impossible It Is to Leave Nothing Unsaid." In *The Formation of Professions: Knowledge, State, and Strategy*, edited by Michael Burrage and Rolf Torstendahl, 24–50. London: Sage, 1990.

———. *The Rise of Professionalism: A Sociological Analysis*. Berkeley: University of California Press, 1977.

Larson, Orville K. "Exhibition Catalogues: Critical Resources for Research in Theatre Art." *Educational Theatre Journal* 28, no. 3 (October 1976): 389–97.

———. *Scene Design in the American Theatre from 1915 to 1960*. Fayetteville: University of Arkansas Press, 1989.

Lawler, Mike. "Design Is Not a Private Affair." *American Theatre*, January 1, 2012. https://www.americantheatre.org/2012/01/01/design-is-not-a-private -affair/.

Lawrence, W. J. "Scenery and Scenic Artists." *Gentleman's Magazine*, June 1889, 608–14.

Lawson, Bryan. *What Designers Know*. London: Routledge, 2012.

Lawson, Edward. "He Crashed the Color Line." *Opportunity: Journal of Negro Life* 17, no. 2 (February 1939): 52–53.

Lazzarato, Maurizio. "Immaterial Labor." In *Radical Thought in Italy: A Potential Politics*, edited by Paolo Virno and Michael Hardt, 133–47. Minneapolis: University of Minnesota Press, 1996.

Leitner, Paul E. "The Scene Designs of J. Woodman Thompson." PhD diss., University of Nebraska, 1990. ProQuest Dissertations & Theses (9030135).

Lewis, Roger K. *Architect? A Candid Guide to the Profession*. Cambridge, MA: MIT Press, 1985.

Logan, Cheri. "Metaphor and Pedagogy in the Design Practicum." *International Journal of Technology and Design Education* 18, no. 1 (January 1, 2008): 1–17.

Loring, John. *Joseph Urban*. New York: Harry N. Abrams, 2010.

Lyon, Philippa. *Design Education: Learning, Teaching and Researching through Design*. Surrey, UK: Gower, 2011.

Macdonald, Stuart. *The History and Philosophy of Art Education*. Cambridge: James Clarke, 2004.

Macgowan, Kenneth. "The Myth of Urban." *Theatre Arts Magazine* 1, no. 3 (May 1917): 99–109.

———. "The New Path of the Theatre." In *American Stage Designs: An Illustrated Catalogue*. New York: Bourgeois Galleries, 1919.

———. "Robert Edmond Jones." *Theatre Arts Monthly*, November 1925, 720–30.

Madsen, Axel. *John Huston: A Biography*. Garden City, NY: Doubleday, 1978.

"The Man Who Put Consultants in Hats." *Business Strategy Review* 14, no. 3 (Autumn 2003): 63–64.

Marchand, Roland. *Advertising the American Dream: Making Way for Modernity, 1920–1940*. Berkeley: University of California Press, 2008.

Margolin, Victor. "The United States in World War II: Scientists, Engineers, Designers." *Design Issues* 29, no. 1 (Winter 2013): 14–29.

Maute, Judith. "Changing Conceptions of Lawyers' Pro Bono Responsibilities: From Chance Noblesse Oblige to Stated Expectations." *Tulane Law Review* 77, no. 1 (2002): 91–162.

McArthur, Benjamin. *Actors and American Culture, 1880–1920*. Iowa City: University of Iowa Press, 2000.

Meikle, Jeffrey. *Twentieth Century Limited: Industrial Design in America, 1925–1939*. Philadelphia: Temple University Press, 2010.

Mielziner, Jo. *Designing for the Theatre: A Memoir and a Portfolio*. New York: Atheneum, 1965.

———. "Make the Theatre Building Pay." *Theatre Arts* 30, no. 6 (June 1946): 363–66.

———. "Practical Dreams." In *The Theatre of Robert Edmond Jones*, edited by Ralph Pendleton, 20–27. Middletown, CT: Wesleyan University Press, 1958.

Mielziner, Jo, and C. Ray Smith. *The Shapes of Our Theatre*. New York: Clarkson N. Potter, 1970.

Mills, C. Wright. *White Collar: The American Middle Classes*. New York: Oxford University Press, 1951.

Moody, James L. *The Business of Theatrical Design*. New York: Allworth Press, 2002.

Moore, Thomas Gale. *The Economics of the American Theater*. Durham, NC: Duke University Press, 1968.

Morgan, George, and Pariece Nelligan. *The Creativity Hoax: Precarious Work in the Gig Economy*. London: Anthem Press, 2018.

Mullin, Michael. *Design by Motley*. Newark: University of Delaware Press, 1996.

Neilson, Brett, and Ned Rossiter. "Precarity as a Political Concept, or, Fordism as Exception." *Theory, Culture, and Society* 25, no. 7–8 (2008): 51–72.

Nouryeh, Andrea. "The Stage Door Canteen: The American Theatre Wing's Experiment in Integration (1942–1945)." In *Experiments in Democracy: Interracial and Cross-Cultural Exchange in American Theatre, 1912–1945*, edited by Jonathan Shandell and Cheryl Black, 256–73. Carbondale: Southern Illinois University Press, 2016.

Novick, Julius. *Beyond Broadway: The Quest for Permanent Theatres*. New York: Hill and Wang, 1968.

Oenslager, Donald. "Let There Be Light." *Theatre Arts* 31, no. 9 (September 1947): 46–52.

———. "Passing Scenes." *Theatre Arts* 33 (November 1949): 16–25, 93–94.

———. "Theatre Horizons of South America." *The Record* 6, no. 5 (September 1950): 12–22.

———. *The Theatre of Donald Oenslager*. Middletown, CT: Wesleyan University Press, 1978.

———. "The Theatre of Indo-China." *Theatre Arts* 25, no. 5 (May 1941): 344–52.

———. "U.S. Stage Design, Past and Present." In *Contemporary Stage Design: USA*, edited by Elisabeth B. Burdick, Peggy C. Hansen, and Brenda Zanger, 13–15. Middletown, CT: International Theatre Institute of the United States, 1974.

Osnowitz, Debra. *Freelancing Expertise: Contract Professionals in the New Economy*. Ithaca, NY: Cornell University Press, 2010.

Owen, Bobbi, and United States Institute for Theatre Technology. *Late & Great: American Designers, 1960–2010*. Syracuse, NY: United States Institute for Theatre Technology, 2010.

Parkin, Frank. *Marxism and Class Theory: A Bourgeois Critique.* New York: Columbia University Press, 1979.

Payne, B. Iden, Alexander Wyckoff, Lucy Barton, Charles Denis McCarthy, Eleanor Jewett, Mary Agnes Doyle, Theodore Viehman, et al. "Recollections and Impressions of 'T.W.'" *Educational Theatre Journal* 3, no. 4 (1951): 294–317.

Pearce, Russell. "The Lawyer and Public Service." *Journal of Gender, Social Policy, and the Law* 9, no. 1 (2001): 171–78.

Peet, John. "The New Witch-Doctors." *Economist* 306, no. 7537 (February 13, 1988): S3+.

Pendleton, Ralph. *The Theatre of Robert Edmond Jones.* Middletown, CT: Wesleyan University Press, 1958.

Perkins, Kathy A. "Black Backstage Workers, 1900–1969." *Black American Literature Forum* 16, no. 4 (Winter 1982): 160–63.

———. "Their Place in History: African-Americans behind the Scenes of American Theatre." *Theatre Design and Technology* 31, no. 3 (Summer 1995): 27–35.

Perkins, Kathy A., Sandra L. Richards, Renée Alexander Craft, and Thomas F. DeFrantz. *The Routledge Companion to African American Theatre and Performance.* Abingdon, UK: Routledge, 2018.

Peterson, Jane T. "'Not as Other Boys': Robert Edmond Jones and Designs of Desire." In *Staging Desire: Queer Readings of American Theater History*, edited by Kim Marra and Robert A. Schanke, 338–64. Ann Arbor: University of Michigan Press, 2002.

Pierce, Jerald Raymond. "Yes, Lighting Design Has a Diversity Problem." *American Theatre*, June 19, 2018. https://www.americantheatre.org/2018/06/19/yes-lighting-design-has-a-diversity-problem/.

Poggi, Jack. *Theater in America: The Impact of Economic Forces, 1870–1967.* Ithaca, NY: Cornell University Press, 1968.

Ponce de Leon, Charles L. *Self-Exposure: Human-Interest Journalism and the Emergence of Celebrity in America, 1890–1940.* Chapel Hill: University of North Carolina Press, 2002.

Pulos, Arthur J. *American Design Ethic: A History of Industrial Design to 1940.* Cambridge, MA: MIT Press, 1986.

Rein, Irving, Philip Kotler, Michael Hamlin, and Martin Stoller. *High Visibility: Transforming Your Personal and Professional Brand.* 3rd. ed. McGraw-Hill, 2006.

Remnick, David. *Life Stories: Profiles from The New Yorker.* New York: Modern Library, 2001.

Rex, Kyle. "Perry Robert Watkins (1907–1974)." *Blackpast* (blog), December 28, 2012. https://www.blackpast.org/african-american-history/watkins-perry-robert-1907-1974/.

Roach, Joseph. *It*. Ann Arbor: University of Michigan Press, 2007.

———. "Reconstructing Theatre/History." *Theatre Topics* 9, no. 1 (1999): 3–10.

Ross, Andrew. *Nice Work If You Can Get It: Life and Labor in Precarious Times*. New York: New York University Press, 2010.

Sachar, Abram Leon. *Brandeis University: A Host at Last*. Hanover, NH: University Press of New England, 1995.

Sawaya, Francesca. *Modern Women, Modern Work Domesticity, Professionalism, and American Writing, 1890–1950*. Philadelphia: University of Pennsylvania Press, 2004.

Sayler, Oliver M. "Robert Edmond Jones, Artist of the Theatre." *New Republic*, June 20, 1930.

Schanke, Robert A. *Shattered Applause: The Lives of Eva Le Gallienne*. Carbondale: Southern Illinois University Press, 2010.

Schickel, Richard. *Intimate Strangers: The Culture of Celebrity*. New York: Fromm International, 1986.

Schön, Donald. "Designing as a Reflective Conversation with the Materials of a Design Situation." *Knowledge-Based Systems* 5, no. 1 (1992): 3–14.

———. *Educating the Reflective Practitioner: Toward a New Design for Teaching and Learning in the Professions*. San Francisco: Jossey-Bass, 1987.

Schwartz, Michael. *Broadway and Corporate Capitalism: The Rise of the Professional-Managerial Class, 1900–1920*. New York: Palgrave Macmillan, 2009.

Schweitzer, Marlis. *When Broadway Was the Runway: Theater, Fashion, and American Culture*. Philadelphia: University of Pennsylvania Press, 2011.

Sedgwick, Ruth Woodbury. "Biography of a Decorator." *Scene*, March 1937, 63–66.

Shandell, Jonathan. *The American Negro Theatre and the Long Civil Rights Era*. Iowa City: University of Iowa Press, 2018.

Shanken, Andrew M. "Breaking the Taboo: Architects and Advertising in Depression and War." *Journal of the Society of Architectural Historians* 69, no. 3 (September 2010): 406–29.

Simonson, Lee. *Part of a Lifetime: Drawings and Designs, 1919–1940*. New York: Duell, Sloan and Pearce, 1943.

———. *The Stage Is Set*. 6th ed. New York: Theatre Arts Books, 1963.

Simonson, Robert. *Performance of the Century: 100 Years of Actors' Equity Association and the Rise of Professional American Theater*. Milwaukee: Applause, 2012.

Slide, Anthony. *Inside the Hollywood Fan Magazine: A History of Star Makers, Fabricators, and Gossip Mongers*. Jackson: University Press of Mississippi, 2010.

Smith, Boyd. "The University Theatre as It Was Built Stone upon Stone." *Theatre Arts Monthly* 17, no. 7 (July 1933): 521–30.

Smith, Donald K. "Origin and Development of Departments of Speech." In *History of Speech Education in America: Background Studies*, edited by Karl Richards Wallace and Speech Association of America. New York: Appleton-Century-Crofts, 1954.

Smith, Ronn. *American Set Design 2*. New York: Theatre Communications Group, 1995.

Smith, Susan Harris. *American Drama: The Bastard Art*. Cambridge: Cambridge University Press, 2006.

Standing, Guy. *The Precariat: The New Dangerous Class*. London: Bloomsbury Academic, 2011.

Starck, Lindsay. "Janet Flanner's 'High-Class Gossip' and American Nationalism between the Wars." *Journal of Modern Periodical Studies* 7, no. 1 (2016): 1–25.

Stern, Robert A. M., and Jimmy Stamp. *Pedagogy and Place: 100 Years of Architecture Education at Yale*. New Haven, CT: Yale University Press, 2016.

Stevens, Thomas Wood. "The Background: The First Plan and the Goal." *Theatre Arts Monthly* 23, no. 7 (July 1939): 491–95.

Stowell, Donald Charles, Jr. "The New Costuming in America: The Ideas and Practices of Robert Edmond Jones, Norman Bel Geddes, Lee Simonson and Aline Bernstein, 1915–1935." PhD diss., University of Texas at Austin, 1972. ProQuest Dissertations & Theses (7318499).

Stowell, Don, Jr. "Unionization of the Stage Designer, Male and Female." *Theatre Design and Technology* 38 (October 1974): 7–9, 36.

Sullivan, Lawrence. "Arthur Schnitzler's 'The Bridal Veil' at the American Laboratory Theatre." *Dance Research Journal* 25, no. 1 (1993): 13–20.

Susman, Warren. "'Personality' and the Making of Twentieth-Century Culture." In *Culture as History: The Transformation of American Society in the Twentieth Century*, 271–85. New York: Pantheon Books, 1973.

Szerlip, B. Alexandra. *The Man Who Designed the Future: Norman Bel Geddes and the Invention of Twentieth-Century America*. Brooklyn, NY: Melville House, 2017.

Taylor, Deems. "The Scenic Art of Joseph Urban: His Protean Work in the Theatre." *Architecture*, July 1934, 275–90.

Teague, Walter Dorwin. *Design This Day: The Technique of Order in the Machine Age*. New York: Harcourt, Brace, 1940.

Thomson, Ellen Mazur. *The Origins of Graphic Design in America, 1870–1920*. New Haven, CT: Yale University Press, 1997.

Traube, Shepard. *So You Want to Go into the Theatre? A "Manual."* Boston: Little, Brown, 1936.

"Two 'Baker Maps.'" *Theatre Arts Monthly* 17, no. 7 (1933): 552–54.

Unruh, Delbert. *The Designs of Jules Fisher.* Syracuse, NY: United States Institute for Theatre Technology, 2009.

Van Doren, Harold L. *Industrial Design: A Practical Guide.* New York: McGraw-Hill, 1940.

Votolato, Gregory. *American Design in the Twentieth Century: Personality and Performance.* Manchester: Manchester University Press, 1998.

Walker, Julia A. "Why Performance? Why Now? Textuality and the Rearticulation of Human Presence." *Yale Journal of Criticism* 16, no. 1 (2003): 149–75.

Wall, John. *Streamliner: Raymond Loewy and Image-Making in the Age of American Industrial Design.* Baltimore: Johns Hopkins University Press, 2018.

Waszut-Barrett, Wendy. "Historical Excerpt—'Women in Scenic Art,' Lillian Gaerstner." *Drypigment* (blog), February 6, 2017. http://drypigment.net/2017/02/06/historical-excerpt-women-in-scenic-art-part-2/.

Weber, Max. *Economy and Society.* Edited by Guenther Roth and Claus Wittich. Berkeley: University of California Press, 1978. http://archive.org/details/MaxWeberEconomyAndSociety.

Weiss, David W., ed. "Consulting in the Theatre." *Theatre Design and Technology* 6 (October 1966): 38–43.

White, Christine A. *Directors and Designers.* Bristol, UK: Intellect Books, 2009.

White, Timothy R. *Blue-Collar Broadway: The Craft and Industry of American Theater.* Philadelphia: University of Pennsylvania Press, 2014.

Wiebe, Robert H. *The Search for Order, 1877–1920.* New York: Hill and Wang, 1967.

Wilensky, Harold L. "The Professionalization of Everyone?" *American Journal of Sociology* 70, no. 2 (1964): 137–58.

Woods, Mary N. *From Craft to Profession: The Practice of Architecture in Nineteenth-Century America.* Berkeley: University of California Press, 1999.

Wright, Tom F. *The Cosmopolitan Lyceum: Lecture Culture and the Globe in Nineteenth-Century America.* Amherst: University of Massachusetts Press, 2013.

Yannacci, Christin Essin. "Landscapes of American Modernity: A Cultural History of Theatrical Design, 1912–1951." PhD diss., University of Texas at Austin, 2006. ProQuest Dissertations & Theses (3285871).

Young, Edgar B. *Lincoln Center: The Building of an Institution.* New York: New York University Press, 1980.

Zabierek, Henry C. "Interests Transcended: The Early History of Carnegie Tech." *Western Pennsylvania Historical Magazine* 53, no. 4 (October 1970): 349–65.

Zeigler, Joseph Wesley. *Regional Theatre: The Revolutionary Stage.* New York: Da Capo, 1973.

INDEX

Italicized page numbers indicate figures.

Abbott, Andrew, 11, 109, 115, 181n24
Actor-Managers, Inc., 59, 147, 149
actors, 12, 64–65, 182n30, 190n49
Actors' Equity Association (AEA), 12,
  31, 33, 38, 188n27, 189n34, 190n49
advertising, *46–47*, 48, 79, 82–83
Alexander, Philip, 60
Allied Designers, 32
Almanac (USA 829 booklet), *46–47*,
  48
Alswang, Ralph, 160, 161, 171, 221n91
amateurism, 10–11, 54, 57, 146
American Federation of Labor (AFL),
  30–31, 185n58, 190n51
American Institute of Architects
  (AIA), 80, 199nn49–50, 200n55
American Society of Theatre Consultants, 167
American Theatre Wing, 138–39, 141,
  142
Andrews v. Percival, 43–44
anti-communist pressure, 51, 192n80
applied arts fields: professionalism in,
  14–15, 28, 61, 80, 89, 187nn15–16,
  200n52; Urban and, *72*, 78–79
architects, stage (1920s), 32, 188n30
architecture: and AIA, 80,
  199nn49–50, 200n55; Beaux-Arts
  movement in, 80, 81, 100, 111, 112–15,
  209n50, 209n53, 210n57, 211n72; as
  hybrid of profession/trade, 89; as
  labor model for designers, 79–83,
  116; professionalism in, 14–15,
  28, 79–81, 89, 183n41, 187n15,
  199–200nn50–52, 201n77; self-
  promotion as distasteful in, 79–82,
  200nn55–56, 200nn58–59; as

university curricula model for scenic
  design, 100, 104, 112–14, 120, 122. *See
  also* theatre architecture
Architecture, 73
Aronson, Arnold, 7, 166, 171
Arthur, Helen, 59, 147, 149
artificial intelligence, 176
Art Institute of Chicago, 123
artist-in-residence programs, 106,
  206n26
artists, scenic designers as, 6, 66, 87,
  92, 111, 115, 118, 155, 168
artists' guilds, 25–26, 185n3
art theatres, 29–30, 146
assistants, 30, 43, 170, 175–76, 224n8

Baker, George Pierce, 99–100, *101*, 105,
  107, 119
Baker Maps, 107
Barton, Lucy, 121, 124
Bay, Howard: scenic design work by,
  48–50, *49*, 191n72; as teacher, 121,
  125, 211n77; union exam challenge
  by, 213n101; union leadership of,
  48–51, 191n73, 192n75
Beaumont Theater, 160
Beaux-Arts movement: in architecture, 80, 81, 100, 111, 112–15, 209n50,
  209n53, 210n57, 211n72; ideology of
  professionalism in, 114–15; scenic
  design instruction and, 111–16, 120,
  122, 211n72
Beggar's Holiday (1946 film), 59
Behrens, Roy R., 135
Belasco, David, 18, 95, 117
Bel Geddes, Norman: architectural
  theatre work by, 157–58, 220n79; at

241

New Stagecraft movement: beginnings of, 15, 21, 25, 183n42; characteristics of, 17, 39, 87, 102; influence on teaching, 102, 124; practitioners of, 1, 73, 107
New York Daily Mirror, 65
New Yorker, 65, 68, 71, 76, 90
New York Herald Tribune, 77
New York Times, 25–26, 63, 68, 72, 77, 88, 90–91, 94, 96, 158
New York Times Magazine, 76
New York World's Fair, 44–45, 48
Norman Bel Geddes, Inc. (Geddes & Company), 74, 76–78, 198nn42–43

Oenslager, Donald: Broadway productions by, 98, 106, 116, 204n1, 207n28; career aspect in teaching of, 98–99, 105–6, 118, 129; celebrity status of, *46*, 48, 84, 117–18; critique sessions of, 104–5, 112, 114, 206n23, 208n47; curricula in stage design by, 98–99, 101–8, 110, 206nn15–16; dual residence of, 98, 106, 116, 206n27; influences on, 112, 114–15; lectures at Yale by, 98–99, 103–4, 106, 112, 153; lectures on circuit by, 152–57, 218n62, 219n64, 219n68; as mentor, 104, 106, 206n19; in New Stagecraft movement, 39, 102, 107; portrait of, *102*; problem-solving approach of, 99, 102–3, 114–16, 206n15; on scenic designers, 86, 98–99, 115, 204n3, 210n59; studio pedagogy approach of, 111–16; as theatre architectural consultant, 157, 160, 161–63; writings by, *46*, 96, 108, 142, 154; WWII camouflage work by, 134, 135–38, *137*; at Yale University, 86, 98–99, 101–8, 110–16
off-Broadway productions, 92, 148, 154, 172–73
opera, designs for, 66–67, 70
overtime rules, union, 37, 190n48

painters. *See* scene painters
Paramount studio (Long Island), 38
Parker, W. Oren, 122
Parkin, Frank, 27, 186n14
Part of a Lifetime (Simonson), 132
Pasadena Playhouse, 123
Pattak, Cory, 169–70, 223n1
Pemberton, Brock, 90–91
Pennington, William, 3
Percival, Walter, 40, 43–44
Perkins, Kathy A., 56
personality-based journalism, 62–64, 65–66, 78, 195n10
Peterson, Jane T., 92
photographs and facial images, *63, 67, 68, 69, 72, 75–76,* 96, 197n35
Photoplay, 62–*63*, 70–71
Physioc, Joseph, 18–*20*, 184n55, 185n57, 187nn18–19, 201n76
Piscator, Erwin, 124
Polakov, Lester, 125
politics of art, Denning on, 8
Pope, Arthur, 112
Popular Mechanics, 136
Popular Science Monthly, 63
Porto Theatre, 156, 161–66, *162, 164–65,* 222n92, 222n97, 223n103
Prendergast, Shirley, 151, 171
problem plays, 19, 184–85n56
pro bono work, 144, 215n32
producers: contract and wage disputes with, 51–52, 90–91, 189n44; designers as employees of, 170; designers' creative relationships with, 18–19, 39, 95, 148, 184n55; discrimination by, 148–49, 173; gender and racial diversity of, 59; pre-union labor models of, 29; support of diverse designers by, 55, 56, 58
production-based studies of theatre design, 7
professional agency, 64–65
professionalism: of actors, 12, 64–65, 182n30; in applied arts fields, 14–15,

professionalism (*continued*)
28, 183n41, 187nn15–16; and consulting work, 144, 157–60; definition of,
10, 11–15, 26, 109, 182n29; examinations for certification and, 36–37,
101, 110, *126*–129, 213nn96–98;
exclusivity of, ix–x, 23–24 (*see
also* exclusionary practices); and
higher education, 108–10, 207n35,
207n37, 208n39, 208n41; as identity construct, 10, 12, 26, 43–44,
64–65, 81–82, 85–89, 121–22, 168;
individualism of, 26–27, 186nn7–8,
187n16; lectures and exhibits as tools
for, 152–53, 155; problem-solving
approach of, 99, 114–16, 206n15; of
scenic designers (*see* scenic design
professionalism); and service ideal,
133, 143, 213n4, 215n28, 215n32;
sociology of, 10, 12–13, 182n36
professional projects, 13, 182n36
professions/professionals, definition
of, 10–12, 181n24
profiles, celebrity, *46*, 62–65, 83–89,
201n66
publicity by USA 829 union, *46–47*, 48
public relations, 76–79, 198nn42–43,
199n47

racism in scenic design field, 23, 29,
53–54, 56–59, 150–51, 171–72, 173
Ram's Head Players (Washington, DC),
93–94
R. Bergman Studio, 1–6, *2*, *4*, 29–30,
179n13
reflective practitioners, scenic designers as, 86–87, 115–16
regional theatres, 131, 154, 172–73
Reinhardt, Max, 72, 74, 158
Reynolds, James, 68–*69*, 93–95,
203n93, 213n5
Rich, Irene, *49*
Roach, Joseph, 62
Robinson, Daniel, 117, 118

Roche, Emeline Clark: career of, 23,
54, 147–49; discrimination against,
141–42, 147–49; and Stage Door
Canteen, 22, 138–42, *139*, *141*, 148;
union activity of, 50, 56, 142, 148,
215n26
Rosenthal, Jean, 125, 145, 150, 166–67,
171, 207n33, 216n33

Salzburg Seminar lecture series, 154,
155, 219n70
Saylor, Oliver M., 90
*Scene Design in the American Theatre,
1915–1960* (Larson), 7
scene painters (scenic artists): and
mail-order scenery, 17–18, 184n50;
pre-1910, 15–21, *16*, *19*, 183n46,
184n48; reduced demand for, 37–39;
vs. scenic designers, 6, 25–26, 30, 35,
37–40, 44–50; in USA 829 union,
14, 25–26, 30, 35, 37–40, 44–45, 48,
190n59; valuation of work of, 39–40,
43–44; women as, 183n43
scenic design: anti-individualist approach to, 149; descriptions of work
of, 84–89, 201n66; education for (*see*
teaching scenic design); European
practice of, 1, 66–67, 70, 102, 111,
173, 185n3, 196n21, 200n60; international scope of, 154–55, 161–66;
post-1950s developments in, 171–76;
pre-1910 practices in, 15–21, *16*, *19*,
201n76; problem-solving approach
to, 99, 102–3, 113, 114–16, 206n15;
production-based approach to,
120–22, 211n73; scholarship on, 7–8.
See also theatre architecture
scenic designers: as artists, 6, 66,
87, 92, 111, 115, 118, 155, 168; as
craftspeople, 86, 98–99, 115, 204n3,
210n59; as distinct identity, 26,
43–44, 81–82, 85–89, 121–22, 168;
as managers, 50, 86, 88–89, 115,
136; marginalized (*see* exclusionary

David Bisaha is an assistant professor at Binghamton University, State University of New York, where he teaches theatre history, theory, and dramaturgy. His articles have been published in *Theatre Survey*, *Theatre History Studies*, and *Theatre and Performance Design* and in *The Routledge Companion to Scenography*.

Theater in the Americas

The goal of this series is to publish a wide range of scholarship on theater and performance, defining theater in its broadest terms and including subjects that encompass all of the Americas.

The series is focused on the performance and production of theater and theater artists and practitioners. The series includes studies of traditional, experimental, and ethnic forms of theater; celebrations, festivals, and rituals that perform culture; and studies of dramatic literature; and acts of civil disobedience that are performative in nature. The series includes studies of theater and performance activities of all cultural groups within the Americas, including biographies of individuals, histories of theater companies, studies of cultural traditions, and collections of plays.

Scott Magelssen, Editor, 2014-2023
Founder and Editor, Robert A. Schanke, 2000–2014

Other Books in the Theater in the Americas Series

Shadowed Cocktails:
The Plays of Philip Barry
from "Paris Bound" to
"The Philadelphia Story"
Donald R. Anderson

Adapturgy: The
Dramaturg's Art and
Theatrical Adaptation
Jane Barnette

A Gambler's
Instinct: The Story of
Broadway Producer
Cheryl Crawford
Milly S. Barranger

Unfriendly Witnesses:
Gender, Theater,
and Film in the
McCarthy Era
Milly S. Barranger

The Theatre of Sabina
Berman: "The Agony of
Ecstasy" and Other Plays
Translated by
Adam Versényi
With an Essay by
Jacqueline E. Bixler

Experiments in
Democracy: Interracial
and Cross-Cultural
Exchange in American
Theatre, 1912–1945
Edited by Cheryl Black
and Jonathan Shandell

Staging Social Justice:
Collaborating to Create
Activist Theatre
Edited by
Norma Bowles and
Daniel-Raymond Nadon

Messiah of the New
Technique: John Howard
Lawson, Communism,
and American
Theatre, 1923–1937
Jonathan L. Chambers

Composing Ourselves:
The Little Theatre
Movement and the
American Audience
Dorothy Chansky

Ghost Light: An
Introductory Handbook
for Dramaturgy
Michael Mark Chemers

The Hanlon Brothers:
From Daredevil
Acrobatics to Spectacle
Pantomime, 1833–1931
Mark Cosdon

Richard Barr: The
Playwright's Producer
David A. Crespy

Stage for Action:
U.S. Social Activist
Theatre in the 1940s
Chrystyna Dail

Women in Turmoil:
Six Plays by Mercedes
de Acosta
Edited and with
an Introduction by
Robert A. Schanke

Off Sites: Contemporary
Performance beyond
Site-Specific
Bertie Ferdman

Rediscovering
Mordecai Gorelik:
Scene Design and the
American Theatre
Anne Fletcher

Californios, Anglos,
and the Performance
of Oligarchy in
the U.S. West
Andrew Gibb

A Spectacle of Suffering:
Clara Morris on the
American Stage
Barbara Wallace
Grossman

American Political
Plays after 9/11
Edited by Allan Havis

Performing Loss:
Rebuilding Community
through Theater
and Writing
Jodi Kanter

Presidential Libraries as
Performance: Curating
American Character
from Herbert Hoover
to George W. Bush
Jodi Kanter

Unfinished Show
Business: Broadway
Musicals as
Works-in-Process
Bruce Kirle